BRITAIN AND THE WORLD
Edited by The British Scholar Society

Editors:
James Onley, University of Exeter, UK
A. G. Hopkins, University of Cambridge
Gregory Barton, University of Western Sydney, Australia
Bryan Glass, Texas State University, USA
Richard C. Allen, University of South Wales, UK
Michelle Brock, Washington and Lee University, USA

Other titles in the *Britain and the World* series include:

Britain and the World
Series Standing Order ISBN 978–0–230–24650–8   hardcover
Series Standing Order ISBN 978–0–230–24651–5   paperback
(*outside North America only*)

You can receive future titles in this series as they are published by placing a standing order. Please contact your bookseller, or write to us at the address below with your name and address, the title of the series and one of the ISBNs quoted above.

Customer Services Department, Macmillan Distribution Ltd, Houndmills, Basingstoke, Hampshire RG21 6XS, England

New Delhi: The Last Imperial City

David A. Johnson
University of North Carolina, Charlotte, USA

palgrave
macmillan

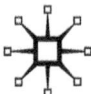

First published 2015 by
PALGRAVE MACMILLAN

Palgrave Macmillan in the UK is an imprint of Macmillan Publishers Limited, registered in England, company number 785998, of Houndsmills, Basingstoke, Hampshire, RG21 6XS.

Palgrave Macmillan in the US is a division of St Martin's Press LLC, 175 Fifth Avenue, New York, NY 10010.

Palgrave is the global academic imprint of the above companies and has companies and representatives throughout the world.

Palgrave® and Macmillan® are registered trademarks in the United States, the United Kingdom, Europe and other countries.

ISBN 978–1–137–46986–1

This book is printed on paper suitable for recycling and made from fully managed and sustained forest sources. Logging, pulping and manufacturing processes are expected to conform to the environmental regulations of the country of origin.

A catalogue record for this book is available from the British Library.

Library of Congress Cataloging-in-Publication Data
Johnson, David A., 1965–
New Delhi: the last imperial city / David A. Johnson (University of North Carolina, Charlotte, USA).
pages cm.— (Britain and the world)
Includes bibliographical references.
ISBN 978–1–137–46986–1 (hardback)
1. New Delhi (India)—History—20th century. 2. Imperialism—Social aspects—India—New Delhi—History—20th century. 3. New Delhi (India)—Colonial influence—History—20th century. 4. Politics and culture—India—New Delhi—History—20th century. 5. Public spaces—India—New Delhi—History—20th century. 6. Architecture—Political aspects—India—New Delhi—History—20th century. 7. New Delhi (India)—Social life and customs—20th century. 8. New Delhi (India)—Economic conditions—20th century. 9. India—History—British occupation, 1765–1947. 10. Social change—India—History—20th century. I. Title.
DS486.D3J64 2015
954'.56—dc23   2014049582

Typeset by MPS Limited, Chennai, India.

To my father Leland S. Johnson

Contents

List of Figures

List of Tables

Series Editors' Preface

New Delhi: The Last Imperial City is published as the sixteenth volume in The British Scholar Society's *Britain and the World* series from Palgrave Macmillan. From the sixteenth century onward, Britain's influence on the world became progressively more profound and far reaching, in time touching every continent and subject, from Europe to Australasia and archaeology to zoology. Britain's influence on the world became progressively more profound and far reaching, in time touching every continent and subject, from Europe to Australasia and archaeology to zoology. Although the histories of Britain and the world became increasingly intertwined, mainstream British history still neglects the world's influence upon domestic developments and Britain's overseas history remains largely confined to the study of the British Empire. This series takes a broader approach to British history, seeking to investigate the full extent of the world's influence on Britain and Britain's influence on the world.

David A. Johnson provides a historically rich examination of the intersection of early twentieth-century imperial culture, imperial politics, and imperial economics as reflected in the colonial built environment at New Delhi, a remarkably ambitious imperial capital built by the British between 1911 and 1931. India's changed political conditions, exacerbated by previous colonial policies such as the partition of Bengal, demanded a new approach to an India undergoing tremendous political, social, and economic transformations caused by its long interactions with Britain. British police officials could stop a demonstration with policemen armed with *lathis* (steel tipped canes), for example, but how could they prevent Indians from making cloth at home as part of an anti-colonial boycott of British goods? This powerful form of colonial resistance pressured British officials to begin thinking of new ways to assert Britain's colonial authority in India. At this critical moment and as the pre-eminent symbol of British imperial rule in India, New Delhi crucially displayed a double narrative of promised liberation and continued colonial dependence. This message, rich in ambiguity, created tension between a government intent on satisfying Indian demands for political reform with its equally important need to maintain absolute authority. Britain's last imperial capital in South Asia represented a new model of imperial hegemony based not simply on coercion but on Indian consent to further colonial rule.

Editors, *Britain and the World*:
A. G. Hopkins, University of Cambridge
Gregory Barton, University of Western Sydney, Australia
Bryan Glass, Texas State University, USA
Richard C. Allen, University of South Wales, UK
Michelle Brock, Washington and Lee University, USA

Preface

Scholars have long noted that New Delhi was a capital steeped in irony since the massive building project occurred at precisely the same time as the rise of a powerful Indian independence movement that challenged Britain's authority in India. Paradoxically, Britain's imperial power was slipping away even as it edified its power and permanence in India by erecting a new capital at Delhi, one of India's most ancient cities and a traditional seat of empire for earlier Indian empires. But this paradox exists only when we focus on New Delhi as a symbol of British colonial coercion. Any such irony begins to evaporate when we also understand New Delhi as a symbol of consent. British officials who understood, or at least sensed, a new historical thrust in India attempted to push back against the rising power and energy of the Indian independence movement by offering reform rather than simply the *lathi*. Built by Edwin Lutyens and Herbert Baker, two of Britain's most revered architects, New Delhi was the quintessential symbol of this new vision for India. As a capital of an emerging federal-like empire, promised but not yet realized in the early stages of the building project, New Delhi symbolized Britain's willingness to offer Indians a greater voice in government while never undermining its position in the region. As such, the building of New Delhi was a response not only to changing political conditions in India but also to the challenges of a new global reality where Britain faced major commercial competition from other industrial states. Though New Delhi was meant to be a capital of a distinctive British-India, its significance extended far beyond South Asia. Indeed, the building of the new capital represented a powerful attempt to re-secure India as an important pivot of empire in the larger Indian Ocean. The transfer of the capital to Delhi and its related political reforms were part of a much larger British strategy to consolidate those regions that were essential to Britain's world system.

Acknowledgements

Few authors write books in hermetic isolation freed from outside influence and relying solely on their own intellectual gifts and writing skills. This is especially true in academia because of its unique culture. Ironically, while the academy is noted for the often progressive nature of its philosophies, the foundation for how those ideas get realized is based on a medieval guild model where master craftsmen (professors) oversee apprentices (graduate students) who become fully fledged members of a particular craft only after completing their approved masterpiece (dissertation/thesis). But, of course, for many professors their graduate masterpiece continues to be a work in progress, a rough draft that still requires further research and considerable revision and peer review, often by unknown academics who are usually, but not always, more senior craftsmen in a specific field. This academic culture, rich and beautiful in a time-honoured complexity that Edmund Burke would celebrate, requires the input of massive human energy. Colleagues offer feedback as an act of collegiality and peer reviewers give it as a commitment to the discipline. Universities, libraries, archives, private and public funding institutions, and academic publishers buttress and pump life into the system. And thus by the end stages of a book length study one is left owing a tremendous debt to many individuals and entities that have shared so much of their human, institutional, and financial capital. Whatever merits are to be found in this book owe much to the guidance, support, and patience of others. Thus, I would very much like to acknowledge at this time those who helped shape and bring this study to a close. The book's shortcomings are, of course, mine alone to bear.

The rich intellectual atmosphere at the University of California, Irvine, where I did my graduate work under the guidance of Douglas Haynes, much improved the study's theoretical approach. With his incredible talent for seeing history in unique ways, Dr Haynes encouraged novel ways of seeing, understanding, and writing about British imperial history. Daniel Schroeter and Vinayak Chaturvedi gave important guidance during the early research and writing stages. Kenneth Pomeranz tremendously enriched the study's sensitivity to world history. Robert Moeller provided continued and unselfish mentoring and emotional support.

The study's initial research was conducted in New Delhi under a Fulbright India Fellowship between 2002 and 2003. I am extremely grateful to Kishori Kaul who opened her home to me, shared her family, and taught me about Indian hospitality. I also am thankful to the companionship and guidance given by Lauren Nauta, Susan Runkle, John Nemec, and Mark Elmore, all of whom knew India far better than I. The archivists and staff at the Nehru Memorial Museum, the Delhi State Archives, and the National Archives of India provided unstinting assistance and directed me to the most pertinent materials held in their collections.

Summer research trips to the United Kingdom between 2007 and 2010 added further archival material to the study. I would like to thank the archivists and staff at the British Library, the Royal Institute of British Architects, and the National Archives of Britain. It was an absolute treat to do research at these archives. Dr Kevin Greenbank of the Centre of South Asian Studies at Cambridge introduced me to excellent photos, some of which appear in this study, held in the centre's collections.

Many friends and colleagues read and gave editorial and critical advice on manuscript chapters. These include Ritika Prasad, David Gilmartin, Deepa Nair, Anne Wohlcke, John Smail, Mark Wilson, John David Smith, Aaron Shapiro, Cheryl Hicks, Gregory Mixon, Robert McEachnie, Jill Massino, Heather Perry, Steve Sabol, Peter Thorsheim, Mary Valante, Jari Eloranta, Edward Behrend-Martinez, and Sheila Phipps. Their constructive criticism greatly sharpened my prose and the clarity of my arguments. David Rabin's general editing much improved the cohesion of chapters and helped transform the manuscript into a book rather than a series of distinct arguments. Special thanks belong to John MacKenzie who read an early draft of the study, offered advice, and supported the project throughout. It is hard to imagine what British imperial history would look like without his influential and tireless dedication to the field.

I also would like to thank the editorial members of the British Scholar Society and especially Bryan Glass, series editor of *Britain and the World*, for their interest in my work. Palgrave's Jenny McCall, Holly Tyler, and Linda Auld shepherded the monograph through a very rigorous and, at least for me, an extremely complicated production process.

The study could not have been completed without the financial help of many institutions. I especially am grateful to Fulbright's Institute of International Education and its staff in India who represent the finest aspects of Fulbright's multi-cultural mission. A Bernadotte Schmitt grant from the American Historical Association helped pay for summer research in Britain. Appalachian State University and the University of North Carolina, Charlotte's internal grant systems provided further funds that were absolutely essential. A University of California Regents

Writing Fellowship allowed me to synthesize and interpret research materials.

As married academics know, book-length projects can take their toll on families. Thus, I would like to thank my partner, Dr Karen Flint, for her indefatigable support, love and patience especially when I needed it most. Lastly, I would like to thank my daughters Elysha, Madeline, Kerala, and Zia.

1
Introduction: Seeing Like a (Colonial) State

The year 1911 was a momentous one for the British Raj in India. A new viceroy with tremendous foreign policy experience, diplomatic tact, and powerful intellect was bringing his skills to bear in his first full year in turbulent India. Lord Hardinge, Viceroy of India from 1910–1916, was the perfect high official to navigate the Government of India through India's troubled waters. With his long experience as a diplomat in some of the era's most difficult foreign policy arenas, such as Egypt, the Balkans, Eastern Europe, and Russia, he had learned to seek solutions that satisfied opposing viewpoints while maintaining his country's primary requirements. His special skills were needed now more than ever in an India divided by anti-colonial agitation that threatened British security in the region. Problems had been exacerbated greatly by Lord Curzon's 1905 partition of Bengal, which communally divided the province into a Hindu west and a Muslim east. Hardinge's appointment as viceroy hinted that India's disastrous colonial status quo would soon undergo modification, perhaps as early as the end of the year when a significant event would occur. George V, the new king-emperor, planned to travel to India for an extremely rare royal tour that would culminate in a grand imperial durbar, a royal assemblage, held in the ancient city of Delhi. Two previous durbars – Victoria's in 1877 and Edward's in 1903 – had been staged in the city because it was popularly recognized as one of India's most important historical seats of empire. But George's would surpass them both in size and pageantry.[1] For the first time in the history of Britain's Indian Empire, a reigning British monarch would personally receive homage from his Indian subjects and, perhaps more importantly in the existing political climate, bestow gifts on them in return for their loyalty.[2]

A special durbar committee was set up to plan the event and to make arrangements in the Delhi District – 25 sq. miles to the north of Delhi were set aside to house the 233 camps that contained nearly 200 ruling Indian princes and chiefs, representatives of British-Indian provincial governments, 70,000 to 80,000 British and Indian troops, special guests and sightseers. Infrastructure had to be built to handle the massive influx of people, which approximately doubled Delhi's normal population of 250,000. Enough tents were raised to cover 10 sq. miles in canvas; 60 miles of new roads were built, 26.5 miles of broad gauge and 9 miles of narrow gauge railway were laid, 24 new railway stations were erected, and 50 miles of new water mains were set with 30 miles of pipeline for distribution in the camps. Markets, butchers, dairies, parks, gardens, and polo, football and review grounds were arranged. Enough electricity to light the towns of Brighton and Portsmouth was directed into the area. The actual durbar site and amphitheatre where the ceremony would take place had enough seating for 4,000 special guests, 70,000 people on a raised semi-circular mound, and space for 35,000 marshalled troops. The total cost for the durbar after the resale of tents and other reusable equipment was £660,000.

George V's imperial durbar offered the perfect opportunity to reset colonial relations in India. Throughout 1911 and with strong support from George V, Hardinge, his executive council, and Lord Crewe, Secretary of State for India, crafted a broad new policy that offered colonial reforms and administrative changes to the Raj. Using the spectacle of a grand imperial durbar and George V as their voice piece, they introduced a new direction in colonial India that would have far-reaching consequences. Held in December of that year, the durbar ceremony (Figure 1.1) came off with only a few blemishes. A controversy surrounding the king's crown,[3] his less than spectacular state entrance into Delhi,[4] and the Gaekwar of Baroda's perceived insult to the royal couple[5] were far outweighed by the king's final proclamation. At the end of a long list of boons to his Indian subjects, George V offered his greatest gift of all. He declared that it was his royal wish to transfer the imperial capital from Calcutta to Delhi and, because of this great change, to reverse Lord Curzon's 1905 partition of Bengal as recompense for that province's loss of the imperial seat.[6] According to Hardinge, the king's announcement 'came off like a bombshell ... there was a deep silence of profound surprise, followed in a few seconds by a wild burst of cheering'.[7] Due to the great secrecy surrounding the new scheme, few officials either in Britain or in India knew that the king, the Government of India, and the India Office were planning such a significant change in colonial policy in India.[8]

The grand announcement initiated a new colonial building project that would consume massive human, material and financial resources

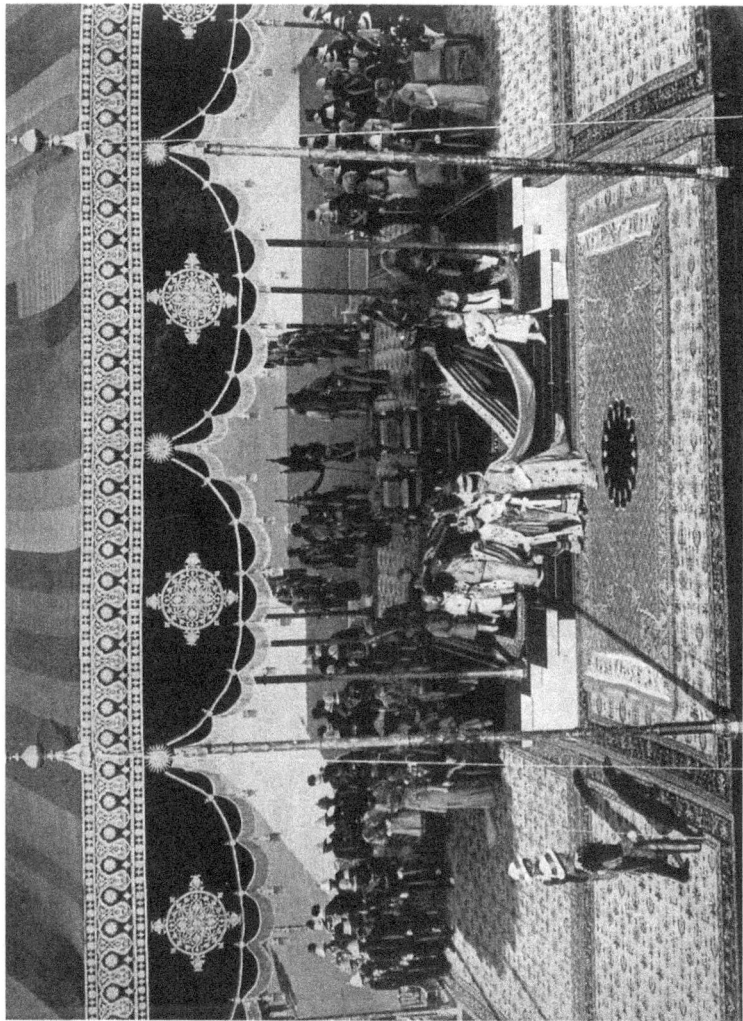

Figure 1.1 King George V (1865–1936) and Queen Mary (1867–1953) at the Delhi Durbar, India, 1911

for the next two decades. It also generated a great deal of soul-searching and subsequent heated debate amongst colonial and elected officials and interested observers concerning the meaning and purpose of empire. For the building of the new capital was far more than a shift of where the Government of India did its business; it formalized and put an official stamp of approval on a decentralizing trend in the administrative structure of the British Raj where responsibility over certain government decisions was transferred from the central government to local provinces. As a response to specific historical conditions in India in the first decade of the twentieth century, the transfer of the capital from Calcutta to Delhi was designed to be 'a bold stroke of statesmanship.'[9]

New Delhi as a symbol of coercion and consent

The transfer of the capital and its related reforms represented the intersection of early twentieth-century imperial culture, imperial politics, and imperial economics as reflected in the colonial built environment at New Delhi, a remarkably ambitious imperial capital built by the British between 1911 and 1931. Hardinge, the man most responsible for transferring the capital, initiated a building project that came to represent a multifaceted vision of the late colonial state in South Asia where colonial reforms that were intended to give Indians greater political freedom simultaneously bound them more closely to the British Empire. As Indian resistance to British rule became greater in the twentieth century, older colonial methods of domination and control became increasingly less effective in dealing with Indian nationalists. British police officials could stop a demonstration with policemen armed with *lathis* (steel tipped canes), for example, but how could they stop Indians from making cloth at home as part of an anti-colonial boycott of British goods? This powerful form of colonial resistance pressured British officials to begin thinking of new ways to assert Britain's colonial authority in India. India's changed political conditions, exacerbated by previous colonial policies like Curzon's partition of Bengal, demanded a new approach to an India which was undergoing tremendous political, social and economic transformations caused by its long interactions with Britain. The new capital symbolized Britain's attempt to resolve the contradictory goals of giving Indians greater political power while at the same time strengthening Britain's paramount power in India. As an important pivot of empire that constituted a significant percentage of Britain's worldwide direct investment, India's security had become essential to the economic health of Britain's imperial world system, a fact not lost on those very Indian agitators who called for boycotts of British manufactured goods.

The transfer and building of a new capital at Delhi was an important response to the global challenges of a new geopolitical reality in which Britain was just one among many powerful industrial states, and not the best positioned one in regard to its supply of natural resources as the famous historian, John Robert Seeley, had noted in the early 1880s.[10] Seeley claimed that states blessed with abundant natural resources such as the United States and Russia were destined to outpace Britain in the next century unless Britain changed its view of the empire and of itself. What was needed was a genuine and broad appreciation by the British people for the importance of empire, what it had done for Britain, and how it was central to Britain's status as a world power. Britain needed a new imperial worldview, a 'Greater Britain' as he called it, based on communities of religion, race and economic interests shared by Britain, Canada, Australia, New Zealand and South Africa. This new political, social and economic order, which combined the human and natural resources of Britain and its great dominions, would save Britain from slow decline in the face of foreign competition by more populated and resource-rich states. The role of India in this Greater Britain was always an uncomfortable fit for Seeley because it did not share with Britain a sizeable community of race or religion, but officials like Hardinge, Edwin Montagu, Undersecretary of State for India, and especially Fleetwood Wilson, Finance Minister to the Government of India, saw economic and political opportunities to better unify Britain and India.

The new capital's grand neo-classical architecture and its rigid geo-metric town plan with multiple traffic circles and intersecting avenues has encouraged scholars to see the city as an expression of Britain's attempt to control India by reimposing its coercive authority in the first decades of the twentieth century. Anthony King, for example, rigor-ously detailed New Delhi's layout and the architectural styles employed by its two primary architects – Edwin Lutyens and Herbert Baker, two of the most gifted and celebrated architects of the era – who physically rendered the colonial social order and its world through the colonial built-environment.[11] The power structure of colonialism and its culture determined the spatial and symbolic relationship of objects within the capital and of the capital itself to the existing Indian city of old Delhi, or Shahjahanabad as it was officially known.[12] Robert Grant Irving also focused on Baker and Lutyens, arguing that the design of their city reflected Britain's unification of an extremely diverse South Asian conti-nent through the Raj's material superiority.[13] Metcalf's intellectual history of British architecture in India, on the other hand, convincingly showed that New Delhi represented the culmination of a long history of experimentation in colonial architecture that ended with the building of New Delhi as a symbol of Britain's power and permanence in India.[14] Stephen Legg's historical geography of the Delhi District showed how the physical built environment and its policing could be read as a colonial discourse that both represented and created relationships of power within and between new and old Delhi's colonial landscapes.[15] The studies above, in short, focus on New Delhi as a site of imperial coercion.

Yet there is a deep and important disconnect between what one *sees* in the built environment and what one *reads* in the archives. While this study certainly accepts the assertion that New Delhi was used to symbolize Britain's power over India, it sees this as only half the story. Using Antonio Gramsci's Marxist interpretation of hegemony, it argues that the new capital also was meant to encourage Indian consent to Britain's colonial domination. Much as Gramsci argued that capitalist states use powerful forms of manipulation to encourage subjects to consent to their coercion, the Government of India offered political reforms to win Indian consent to continued British colonial rule.[16] At this critical moment and as the pre-eminent symbol of British rule in India, New Delhi crucially displayed a double narrative of promised liberation and continued colonial dependence. Britain's last imperial capital in South Asia was certainly a site of traditional imperial authority, but it was also a symbol of Britain's willingness to address, and thus hopefully control, the political demands of its Indian subjects. As this study shows, the language of the most important colonial officials who crafted New Delhi's new vision of empire reflected a willingness to engage educated Indians through political reforms. Even George V, as F. A. Eustis and Z. H. Zaidi long ago argued, desired a greater effort on the part of colonial officials to conciliate Indians.[17] Metonymically and allegorically, the new capital may have projected imperial power and permanence, but it also symbolized the underlying strands that connected British political reform with the reinforcement and reaffirmation of continued British rule. If the new capital was meant to symbolize a new direction in British-India, it also was intended to show the absolute inseparability of the two peoples and their nations. This message, rich in ambiguity, created tension between a government intent on satisfying Indian demands for political reform with its equally important need to maintain its absolute authority.

Thus, in many important ways, New Delhi and its builders reflected the 'high modernism' that James C. Scott describes in *Seeing Like a State*.

Though grounded in the Enlightenment's celebration and elevation of natural law as the shaper of human destinies, Scott suggests that high modernism was more of a faith than a science. It was never the hand-maiden of any one government or culture but, 'as a faith', according to Scott, 'it was shared by many across a wide spectrum of political ideologies'.[18]

Like other high modernist cities, such as Brasilia, the building of New Delhi was a lesson in the state's simplification of extremely complex socio-economic conditions in the Delhi District as well as what can only be called a gross vulgarization of the area's history. The government's massive acquisition of lands in the district for the new capital was one example of this simplification. The building project gave the local government freedom to transfer privately owned Indian lands into government controlled public lands, simplifying the tax revenue system in the process. What had been a rather confused jumble of property tenures and tenants exhibiting a richly textured social organization became a much more simplified system with the Government of India serving as the largest landowner in the Delhi District.

Historically, the Delhi District's rich past, which could be traced as far back as the ancient *Mahabharata*, became recodified as a mere backdrop to British imperial rule. The architectural remnants of past Hindu and Muslim empires, which were scattered throughout the selected building site, were incorporated into the new capital's town plan as sites of interest or as vista points. The neighbouring Indian city of old Delhi became a simple foil, a site of unplanned disorder against which the new capital could be favourably compared. The planners' tremendous focus and concern with Delhi's history represented a marked divergence from other high modernists such as Le Corbusier who tended to negate any history perceived as representing inferior forms of social, political, and economic order.

In contrast, New Delhi's town planners and architects embraced those aspects of Indian history, both human and architectural, that could be reshaped to reinforce their new vision for British-India. Still, as a high modernist city, the new capital served to remake Indian society in ways that were more measurable, easier to predict, and easier to manipulate. As a symbol of political devolution,[19] New Delhi encouraged Indians, who were being rewarded with political reforms, to remake themselves as productive rather than counterproductive members of Britain's Indian empire.

The building of New Delhi exemplified the colonial state's use of the built environment to project a high modernist vision of itself to its subjects, both Indian and British. At the heart of this vision was a mathematical sense of universal truth, which town planners and architects championed in their designs. Hardinge and his architectural board, made up of Edwin Lutyens and Herbert Baker, sought to capture what Scott calls *techne*, the settled knowledge of 'self-evident first principles'.[20] These were truths that exist outside humanity 'regardless of what human beings do and say'.[21] A circle, for example, would always be 360 degrees, whether the builder was an ancient Greek or a modern engineer. With its love of natural order, the Enlightenment became intertwined with the western classical tradition in a neo-classicism that equated a uniformly laid out city with a strong state. Intellectually and artistically shaped by this long western building tradition, Baker and Lutyens found it impossible in their architectural designs to escape from this neo-classical western tradition with its strong sense of geometric *techne*. In a famous letter to *The Times*, Baker even quoted Christopher Wren's famous dictum that good architecture must have the 'attributes of eternal'.[22] Indian architecture's predilection for curves, ornamentation, and pointed arches could never satisfy these men because they believed it lacked the universal truth and settled knowledge of the western classical tradition. Of the two, the far more intellectual and politically savvy Baker gave Indian architecture a long and studied look, but in the end he largely failed to find a solution that would combine both great building traditions in a truly meaningful way.[23] For his part, Lutyens made his views clear when he described the process by which Indian builders designed and erected structures, 'Set square stones and build childwise ... Before you erect, carve every stone differently and independently, with lace patterns and terrifying shapes. On the top, build over trabeated pendentives an onion.'[24] Ironically, the whimsical Lutyens, who stubbornly resisted Hardinge's repeated pressure to give the government structures an 'oriental motif', designed a Government House that seamlessly unified Indian and British architecture in such a way that he created a unique style of architecture that represented a new British-India.[25] If Calcutta was the enclave for British commerce and British residences, a symbol of Britain's foreign presence in India, then Lutyens' magnificent and novel dome atop his neo-classical structure symbolized a new British-India where Britain not only belonged but also was essential to India's political and material development.

Much like Scotts' Le Corbusier, who 'was expressing no more, and no less, than an aesthetic ideology – a strong taste for classic lines', Lutyens and Baker were seeking to connect the universal truth of classicism and the science of the Enlightenment to the spirit of British rule.[26] The often impassioned and lofty rhetoric used by designers and proponents of the new capital connected British rule to these universal truths, which they believed Britain was handing down to India. Hardinge and his allies were absolutely confident in the British Empire's ability, if not destiny, to be a force of progress that used the values of the Enlightenment to help modernize and develop India's political life, its material culture, and its economy.

Baker and Lutyens' unification of architecture with the Enlightenment was incredibly important to an empire that considered itself an enlightened despot. Yes, Britain had conquered India by the sword, but as officials commonly noted, it was a different kind of empire because its rule was based on reason rather than autocratic will. The underlying principle behind the permanent settlement of land in India, for example, was the notion that private property was a necessary precondition of human self-improvement much as Adam Smith and other Enlightenment economists had argued.[27] Britain's political economy, which had spurred India's material development, was based on what the British believed were the natural economic laws of the free market. Similarly, Britain's Indian subjects were bound by a unified rule of law and judicial system that made no distinction between the prince and the peasant. The sword of the autocratic had been beaten into the pen of the civil servant and district judge who oversaw the administration of the rule of law and justice. Hardinge, his town planners, his architects, and the government bureaucracy he created to oversee the building project captured in stone and bronze the meaning of what they believed was Britain's gift to India: the rule of law, good government, and now political reforms that would lead India toward greater responsible government.[28] Thus, the capital was not simply a symbol of colonial coercion, a powerful emblem of British dominance, but a city that modelled a British paternalism that rewarded Indians for good behaviour. This was later evidenced by the placement of placards on Herbert Baker's Secretariats that read, 'Liberty does not descend to a people ... It is a blessing that must be learned before it can be enjoyed.'[29]

As such, the new capital symbolized Britain's absolute authority over India's political evolution. For while political reform concomitantly encouraged greater Indian consent to British rule, it also reaffirmed the existing colonial order and colonial power structure. What resolved this seeming contradiction was the very nature of liberal reform in India. As Barry Hindess argues, before colonial subjects could be given greater liberty, they needed to undergo 'extended periods of discipline' because, as British officials believed, they lacked the 'capacities required for autonomous conduct' due to their long history of autocratic rule.[30]

New Delhi and its related politics of devolution served as what Uday Mehta calls a 'liberal strategy of exclusion' where Britons and Indians alike were reminded of who was privileged and who was not, who was politically advanced and who was politically backwards in the context of liberal forms of government.[31] The differences in Britain and India's political history could 'be redressed only through the instrument of political intervention and in the register of future time'.[32] As Thomas Metcalf has argued, British colonial assumptions about India derived from this 'creation of difference'.[33] It was clear that Britain and India shared a deep past with each other, as Sanskrit scholars such as William Jones had shown, but the two cultures had diverged markedly over time. To many contemporary observers, India's cultural and political evolution had been arrested by a faulty ethos or by invasion. Britain, in contrast, had continued to advance along stadial lines that inexorably led to a superior material, political and economic order. If the very notion of imperialism posed significant problems for the British who prided themselves on their own progressive history and its driving force, the pursuit of liberty, India's supposed historical, political, and cultural inferiority justified its domination by Britain. Any guilt about the colonial project could be alleviated if British imperialism brought material and social benefits to India that outweighed the costs of domination. Certainly, giving Indians a greater voice in provincial government meant opening the doors to the passage of legislation that potentially weakened the empire, but political reform benefitted the British by encouraging Indian consent to British rule, by drawing off support for the Indian nationalist movement while fracturing its unity, and by shifting the focus of the Indian independence movement from the Raj's political centre, now at Delhi, to the provinces of British-India. Most colonial officials who strongly supported Indian national aspirations remained staunch supporters of empire. They never doubted that it was Britain's role to lead India *by the hand* toward responsible forms of government because Indians simply lacked the history and political culture to do it on their own. Thus, liberal reform took on an authoritative nature in India's colonial context, leading to an ironic condition where Indian independence became possible only through continued British domination.

New Delhi: a British imperial story set in India

Other than Donald Ferrell's 1969 PhD dissertation, Stephen Legg has provided the most substantial book-length analysis of New Delhi's connection to the liberal imperial project.[34] The current study diverges considerably from Legg's analysis, however, in its breadth, its approach, and in the questions it asks. Where this study devotes itself entirely to examining New Delhi as a building project driven by the antipodes of coercion and consent, Legg's analysis, though wonderfully rich, is only partially concerned with the illiberalism of the liberal imperial project. More importantly, whereas Legg grounds his study solidly in Foucauldian post-structuralism, this study uses a Marxist interpretation to understand why New Delhi was so important to Britain's global empire. A discursive analysis is incredibly helpful if one wants to *read* New Delhi's colonial built environment as a cultural or intellectual narrative, but the questions that can be asked become limited to *how* the city performed empire or *what* its impact was on the local community. In contrast, using the historical-material model of hegemony to approach a study of New Delhi provides greater historical texture and allows one to ask a broader range of questions. Not only can we ask *how* and *what* but *why*. Why was the transfer and building of a new capital so important at this precise historical point in Britain's Indian Empire? Why was the project so essential to Britain's global empire and economic world system? Why did the city, if it was so important to the health of the empire, fail in its original purpose to keep India within the British Empire? And perhaps of greatest importance to the historiography of British-India, why did the British spend such time, such care, and so many resources on a new capital for an Indian Empire that seemed to be unravelling?

These questions are answered by focusing on New Delhi as a site of hegemony where new colonial reforms, which expanded Indian involvement in colonial government, intersected older forms of colonial domination. By approaching the building of New Delhi from this perspective, the study raises important questions about the historical models we use to understand the imperial project in India. While considerable and often exceptional historical work has been done on the history of British-India in general, much of it has been done by historians specialized in South Asian rather than British history. The problem here is two-fold. South Asian historiography, because of its often subaltern orientation, leaves little room for analyses of the liberal imperial project and subsequent attempts at conciliation because it is so focused on the coercive aspects of British imperial rule. Second, these studies often encourage us to lose sight of the forest for the trees. We learn a great deal about the disruptive impact that British rule had on local Indian communities, but we learn little about the relationship of India to Britain's *world* system as well as the larger concerns and debates that shaped the general thrust of colonial policy. This is not to say that Lord Hardinge and his town planners and architects crafted a new vision of empire that was any less oppressive than Ranajit Guha's description of colonial rule as a 'dominance without hegemony'.[35] In fact, their vision was likely more insidious in that it encouraged Indians, by offering political reforms, to discipline themselves as more loyal colonial subjects. This reading of New Delhi suggests the development of a far more powerful type of colonial ideology wherein colonial subjects willingly consented to their colonial dependence. But this historical process is difficult to examine and understand in the absence of British historical models.

Thus, this study examines the building of New Delhi as a British imperial story set in India. It does so by using Peter J. Cain and Antony G. Hopkins' 'gentlemanly capitalist' thesis to better understand the criticism generated by the transfer of the imperial capital from Calcutta, a city built for and by maritime commerce, to Delhi, a city rich in Indian imperial history but lacking significant commercial and financial importance.[36] In particular Cain and Hopkins are used to understand why the major criticism of the policy emerged within the business community in Calcutta and amongst certain Parliament members who were tied either to the old colonial system or to commercial and financial communities in Calcutta and London. Much of their concern had to do with the manner in which the building of a new capital transformed the business of British rule. Cain and Hopkins argue that London-based financiers, who were heavily engaged in imperial investments, drove both imperial expansion and the reasons for having an empire in the first place.[37] Because England's aristocracy saw finance capitalism as a respectable way to spend one's time and money, many members of London's financial community were either drawn from England's landed elites or shared similar public school educations and other cultural affinities. Thus, London's masters of finance were deeply intertwined with a powerful *rentier* class, which had served as local and national political figures at least since the revolutionary settlement after 1688.

The study also draws inspiration from John Darwin's conclusions that in the early twentieth century Britain's primary colonial concern was consolidating those regions that were essential to the British world system. The proponents of the transfer of the capital and its related political reforms were the kind of officials who, as Darwin argues, 'equated empire with the exercise of global power and treated their formal empire of dependent territories as components of a world system strategically dependent on Britain, economically complementary to Britain and culturally under its influence'.[38] As such, colonial officials accepted, 'sometimes grudgingly', that 'building up the Commonwealth as a system of worldwide influence required some deference to the anti-colonial opinions of its non-white members'.[39] This deference, always partial and given with certain safeguards, led to a central contradiction that plagued the British empire in this era of rapid colonial development and subsequent political disruption. In the House of Common's East India Budget debate of 1913, Noel Buxton wonderfully captured this basic paradox when he claimed, 'the great test of the future ... is the reconciliation of democracy and imperialism'.[40] Hardinge and others were trying to resolve that issue in India with the decision to transfer the capital, to end unpopular colonial policies such as partition, and to include greater numbers of Indians in the colonial administration. Yet Buxton's declaration remained as unfulfilled in 1947, when India received full independence, as it did in 1913, suggesting that empire systemically lacked the capacity to reform itself. Perhaps Gandhi's greatest inspiration, if I may, was his realization that empire, no matter how reformed-minded its officials may want to be, must always maintain a monopoly over the state's most coercive powers, and that this alone erodes any possibility of true democratic advancement.

The 'old dispensation' and the men who changed it

The transformation from a post-rebellion colonial vision to a new colonial vision for the twentieth century is at the centre of the history of the building of New Delhi. Thomas Metcalf long ago argued that Britain turned to a more conservative approach to governing India after the Sepoy uprising in 1857 when anti-British sentiment boiled over in northern India.[41] Blaming the event on reforms in land tenure as well as misconceived interventions into the social, political, cultural, and even religious life of India, a generation of post-rebellion colonial officials moved away from the liberal project in India. Even after half a century, many British military and administrative officials still carried memories and fears tied to this transformative moment. These memories continued to shape the assumptions of old-India hands who saw the subcontinent and its peoples through mutiny-tinted lenses.[42]

Scholars have looked at a variety of causes for the Indian unrest that exploded in 1857. Indeed, Thomas Metcalf believes that no other event in Indian history has 'provoked more impassioned literature'.[43] The morale of the East India Company's vaunted Army of Bengal, which underpinned British rule in India, began to deteriorate when British recruiters started to seek fresh troops from new ethno-religious groups such as Sikhs, Pathans, and Gurkhas.[44] Subsequently, traditional Sepoy families increasingly found it more difficult to place their sons in the service of the company. Adding to these grievances, Sepoy pay was not keeping pace with India's rising cost of living, and they had lost extra pay for foreign duty with the annexation of large parts of north-west India.[45] Furthermore, British officers and the company in general had become increasingly contemptuous of their Indian soldiers and their socio-religious beliefs. E. I. Brodkin points to the General Service Enlistment Act, which required Sepoys to serve abroad, as a major culprit of Sepoy anger with company rule.[46] Many Sepoys were outraged by the act since military campaigns or service that took them across the Bay of Bengal or the Arabian Sea represented a loss of caste.

Sepoys were not the only Indians to reject British rule in northern India. A large swathe of non-Sepoys from across Oudh and Rohilkund joined them. This uprising of non-military castes, according to S. B. Chaudhuri and Thomas Metcalf, was caused by the East India Company's reforms in land tenure.[47] Metcalf, in particular, argues that these reforms represented a 'wholesale agrarian revolution' aimed at promoting the interests of poor farmers, but in reality they simply empowered moneylenders who seized control of lands when these farmers could not meet their debts.[48] For Metcalf, the rebellion can be explained by Oudh's traditional land-owning class's desire to take back what British land reform had taken away. Building on Metcalf, Brodkin claims that these disempowered traditional landowners were 'instrumental in originating and maintaining the state of rebellion'.[49] Similarly, Ira Klein sees the rise of Indian antagonism to British rule stemming from colonial attempts to reform India through indirect means. Here, the invisible hand of economic modernization, officials believed, would transform Indian society by promoting the individual over traditional socio-religious organizations, namely caste allegiances.[50] This attempt to socially transform India led to perhaps the most famous reason for the uprising, the introduction of the new Enfield rifle, which used heavily greased cartridges.[51] From this perspective the uprising reflects a religious element where Sepoys rose up to fight for their various religions in response to over-zealous Christian missionaries and evangelical government policies.

The events of 1857 had long-lasting effects both on British colonial policies in India and on British views of Indians in general. The most obvious change was that company rule ended and crown rule began with a cabinet member serving as Secretary of State for India. A new viceroy in council led a much more centralized Government of India where colonial policy was dictated from the centre and used the supposed natural leaders of Indian society, the princes and landed elites, as liaisons between the colonial government and the people. Caution in the pace of reform became the watchword, thus ending years of liberal experimentation in India.[52] Indeed, reform became a dangerous word on the subcontinent.[53]

Perhaps the greatest impact of 1857 was the broadening and quickening of British suspicions of Indians as alien and unpredictable, even capable of rising up against those who sought to improve their lives.[54] Brodkin argues that the often faulty labelling of Indians as loyal or rebels determined later behavioural patterns amongst Indians themselves. In reality, as Brodkin suggests, 'the vast majority of the Indian population ... cannot be designated accurately as either rebel or loyal' since many Indian leaders, including the Mughal Emperor, pragmatically responded to dangerous local conditions caused by either the absence of British authority or the direct presence of rebellious Indians.[55] Similarly, Hugh Tinker's assessment of the rebellion problematizes whether or not the uprising was a 'prelude to the nationalist movement' since so many Indians continued to support the British.[56] Tinker reverses the equation of rebel and loyal by asking the question, 'Can one equate support for the rebels with patriotism and support for the British with disloyalty?'[57] Dan Randall has studied how mutiny narratives became foundational in Britain's imperial mythology. Using a series of sermons concerning a national day of fasting in England on 7 October 1857, Randall argues that a 'misapprehended Mutiny became firmly fixed in the British public imagination by highly public sermons that consolidate[d] existing patterns of thought and emotion'.[58] Thus the sermons became a way to ritually communicate an event that most people had not witnessed first-hand. This ritualization was an important part of what Ranajit Guha has called 'the prose of counter-insurgency'.[59] With marked xenophobia, 'the sermons work[ed] to demonize Indian culture and Indian colonial subjects'.[60]

Yet India's rapid economic development at the turn of the century and the subsequent social and political transformations that encouraged Indian national aspirations began to erode this post-mutiny model of government. A new breed of pragmatic colonial official who realized that Indian national ambitions could no longer be ignored began to move into positions of power. Powerful officials like Lord Hardinge, Fleetwood Wilson, and Edwin Montagu – who were at the heart of the Government of India and the India Office – began to formulate a new vision of empire to meet India's changing political landscape.

Wilson was a highly effective Government of India finance minister from 1908 to 1913, the senior-ranking member of the Viceroy's Council, and even became interim Viceroy of India for a short period during Hardinge's convalescence after an assassination attempt.[61] In some ways, he shared the same colonial hubris of many colonial officials who believed in the power of the British Empire, if properly employed, to improve the lives of colonial subjects. On his visits throughout upper India he always made sure to pay homage at the various mutiny sites.[62] And like many other Englishmen, he too used India as a way to prove his manhood and his mettle, especially through such rites as the hunting expedition. Upon leaving England, Wilson claimed, 'I made up my mind to shoot at least one of every kind of the dangerous wildbeast [sic] family in India', a boast he more than lived up to.[63]

Yet Wilson was a different kind of imperialist as well. Raised in Italy until the age of eighteen, he never went to British public school or to Cambridge or Oxford and thus missed much of the indoctrination that helped shape the imperial attitudes and predilections of many of his peers.[64] His lack of a traditional English boyhood and his limited economic means also meant that he never quite fit in with his fellow high-ranking colonial administrators.[65] Most importantly, as the son of British ex-patriots living in Florence, he came of age during Italy's *Risorgimento*. This transformative experience influenced the way he saw India, its peoples, and their national aspirations. For him, the post-rebellion view of India and its peoples was precisely the cause of Britain's recent problems in South Asia. His friendship with Gopal Gokhale, who he called the 'Gladstone of debate' in India's Legislative Assembly, showed his desire to work with Indian moderates who he believed would stay loyal if Britain paid attention to their national ambitions.[66] Wilson even invited Gokhale to stay at his Simla residence, Peterhof, for a week. Gokhale said to Wilson afterwards, 'When I go to England I am invited to stay with distinguished men of the political, academic, and literary world, but yours is the first Englishman's roof in India under which I have been invited to sleep.'[67]

When describing Indian members at their first session of the reformed legislative council, Wilson wrote, 'They ... devour with avidity any remarks illustrative of the House of Commons methods, for a Parliament is their ideal, a Parliament they mean ... to get, and a Parliament in the end they will possess.'[68] Just as he had witnessed as a boy in Italy, the forces of nationalism meant that India, one way or another, was going to have self-government. The question was whether India would choose to remain or to leave the British Empire. Would Britain follow the lead of the old Indian guard and make the mistakes of the Austrian Empire, which he considered the quintessential model of autocratic brutality, or would it listen to the will of the Indian people?[69] For this very reason, Wilson believed that British conciliation with Indian nationalists would have to occur in the near future before moderates like Gokhale were turned away forever.

Montagu was a talented undersecretary of state who dominated the annual East India Revenue debates while he held that position. Even J. D. Rees, member for Nottingham East in the commons and a vocal critic of New Delhi and its related reforms, applauded Montagu's ability to satisfy members of his own party while beating back the attacks of the opposition, leaving him in sole 'possession of the house'.[70] Montagu was a strong supporter of Indian political advancement and travelled to India twice to study the problem, once as Undersecretary of State for India and again as Secretary of State for India. As undersecretary he even claimed in the House of Commons that race no longer applied in India and that Britain need not fear the proponents of Indian agitation against British rule. Indeed, he suggested that these men had a reason to be upset with a status quo that denied them from more fully participating in the colonial government. His most significant piece of legislation in this regard was the 1917 Montagu-Chelmsford Agreement, which outlined further political devolution. The agreement became the road map for a new Indian constitution passed as the Government of India Act of 1919. The Act divided up government responsibilities – known as reserved and transferred subjects – between Indian provincial governments and the Government of India.[71]

Charles Hardinge, Viceroy of India from 1910–1916, was the most significant proponent of the transfer and building of a new imperial capital at Delhi.[72] He came from a family whose members had served in high military and diplomatic offices, but his own immediate family had limited means.[73] Still, his father earned enough as Undersecretary of State at the War Office to educate his five sons, of which Hardinge was the second, at some of the best schools in England. Hardinge began his education at Cheam, a fashionable and expensive school that channelled students into the top public schools in England. He entered Harrow at fourteen and Trinity College, Cambridge when he was eighteen. It was at Cambridge that he first met Curzon who was on break from Oxford. Their lives and careers would intersect, often in antagonism, for the next half century.[74] Hardinge took his degree in January 1880 and joined the Foreign Office in May of the same year. He would stay in the diplomatic service for nearly 43 years, holding the highest positions offered by the service and in the process becoming one of the most decorated officers outside the royal family in British history.[75]

His appointment as viceroy of India was one of two crowning career achievements, the other being his appointment as ambassador to France. Lord Knollys first asked Hardinge in January 1909 during a visit to Windsor if he would accept an appointment as Viceroy of India.[76] Hardinge immediately said that he 'would do so without hesitation since it was [his] highest ambition to go to India as Viceroy'.[77] However, King Edward, who relied on Hardinge to be his eyes and ears in the Foreign Office and who had grown extremely fond of Hardinge, was strongly against the appointment.[78] Thus, one of Hardinge's most important allies became his greatest obstacle for the nomination. The death of Edward in May 1910, however, changed the entire picture. A little over a month later, while Hardinge and his wife were waiting for the arrival of Edward's funeral procession, Lord Morley, Secretary of State for India, again asked Hardinge if he would accept the appointment, which he did on 10 June 1910. Lord and Lady Hardinge and their daughter, Diamond, arrived in India on 18 November of that year.

Hardinge was party to some of the most important foreign policy decisions made by the British government in the late nineteenth and early twentieth century.[79] Yet the man and his tremendous career have been largely overlooked and under-examined. Some have suggested that his viceroyalty, though promising, was marred by deep personal loss.[80] His wife, Winifred Selina Hardinge died in London on 11 July 1914 while on leave from India and was followed almost six months later by their son, Edward, who died of wounds suffered on the front.[81] This suggestion of failure due to personal loss seems less than cogent. His most important decisions as viceroy – the reversal of Curzon's partition of Bengal and the transfer of the capital from Calcutta to Delhi – were made before the deaths of his wife and son. It should also be added that he ended his Indian career by achieving extremely important initiatives after their deaths. He oversaw the culmination of his wife's dream to build the Lady Hardinge Medical College, which was the first of its kind in India to train female Indian doctors. He also pressured the Home Government to end the practice of Indian indentured labour in the colonies and even went so far as to publicly state in Madras, a major indentured labour recruiting area, that his government was in 'deep and burning' sympathy with Indian demands for better treatment in South Africa.[82] Hardinge also pressured the British government to abolish the excise duty on Indian cotton goods, which had been imposed to protect Lancashire's textile industry, because it 'exposed the British

Government to the accusation that India was being governed in the interests of Lancashire rather than India'.[83]

Hardinge's support of progressive causes, however, should not belie his deeply held loyalty to the king and his love for the empire. He was a pragmatic imperialist who practised a kind of 'old diplomacy' learned from Lord Dufferin who he worked under as private secretary in Istanbul and Cairo.[84] He considered this time the 'most profitable and most happy years' of his career.[85] At the centre of this diplomatic strategy was an emphasis on finding balances of power to achieve security in the British Empire even if its realization meant conciliation. Under Dufferin, Hardinge learned that Britain's position in the world had been strongest when its diplomacy had been an 'iron fist in a velvet glove'.[86] His Indian viceroyalty, which often seemed to send mixed messages, must be seen in this light. For example, his correspondence at the time and his memoires abound with astonishing examples of his Anglo-centric chauvinism. After describing Sir Pertab Singh, the Maharajah of Idar, as a man who 'did not know what fear meant', Hardinge concluded that 'he was truly a white man among Indians'.[87] The right kind of Indian, for Hardinge, was as loyal as a faithful pet. When he visited a hospital in Bombay for wounded Indian soldiers, he met a mortally wounded young man. Describing the encounter in his memoires, he wrote, 'as I stood by his bedside I placed my hand on his forehead, and I shall never forget the smile of happiness that lighted up his face, and I remained with him till he died, smiling'.[88] Hardinge concluded after this moving moment, 'The simple Indian has a most attractive and lovable nature.'[89] In true Kipling-esque fashion, which divided the world into the orient and the occident, Hardinge claimed, 'The working of the Hindu mind is really beyond anybody's comprehension.'[90] Yet as a diplomat Hardinge was willing to set aside these assumptions of Indians and to cede specific points to those across the table from him as long as they did not undermine Britain's security on the subcontinent. As he proudly claimed in his memoires near the end of his viceroyalty, 'It was a source of satisfaction to me that I was able to hand over my charge to my successor with the knowledge that India ... was absolutely quiet and loyal ... the situation was infinitely better than when I arrived in India.'[91]

Hardinge was also a man of intellect and art. Throughout his diplomatic career, he showed great capacity for finding elegant solutions to difficult problems. He had little regard for clumsy diplomatic manoeuvres. This trait was on display with the decision to build a new capital at Delhi. What Hardinge understood better than any previous viceroy was that sustainable British rule in India meant including more Indians in the governing process and that security in India was essential to the health of the larger empire. He did not create the notion of political devolution in India, but he certainly understood its importance in maintaining Britain's rule in India. Much later, as an old man looking back on his Indian viceroyalty, he wrote:

> It is interesting now to look back on the fact, now that Dominion Status had been declared by Lord Irwin as the ultimate goal of political development in India, that I endeavoured to impress upon the Imperial Legislative Council [a body in India that consisted of appointed and popularly elected officials, many of whom were Indians] that the self-governing institutions existing in the Dominions had been achieved not by a sudden stroke of statesmanship but by a process of steady and patient evolution.[92]

The political process that he began in 1911 was reaching its fulfilment under Lord Irwin's and Lord Willingdon's Governments of India in the early to mid 1930s. Hardinge's vision fused a stadial narrative based on material and political development in the colonial world with India's profoundly important place in Britain's world system. The building of New Delhi and the subsequent debates it engendered not only in India but also in the halls of Parliament provides a window into the contradictions and limitations inherent in this new direction in imperial government.

2
The Transfer of Britain's Imperial Capital: 'A Bold Stroke of Statesmanship'

The building of a new capital in India was the key to Britain's new imperial vision. It served not only as an important symbol of a new direction in British India but as the mechanism by which the Government of India extricated itself from previous colonial blunders that had energized anti-colonial resistance to British rule. This is clearly seen in the original debates concerning the transfer of the capital from Calcutta to Delhi and the related reunification of Bengal in 1911. The building of a new capital helped conceal the Government of India's previous inability to master Bengal's anti-colonial movement while at the same time safely relocating ultimate authority within the British colonial administration. As such, the decision to build a new capital reflected tension between the need to silence Indian agitation through the vehicle of political reform and the requirement that Britain maintain its position of paramount power in India.

Historians of New Delhi often have focused on the great architects – Edwin Lutyens and Herbert Baker – and the meaning, style, and architectural genealogies of the buildings they designed. This chapter shifts the focus from architects and architecture to a discussion of India's political culture that helped link and shape the relationship between the transfer of the capital and the reunification of Bengal, which had been partitioned by Lord Curzon in 1905. With remarkably subtle legerdemain, Lord Hardinge's government rescinded partition but claimed that Bengal's reunification was simply an ancillary component of the larger colonial policy regarding the transfer of the capital. Somewhat fanciful, perhaps, but certainly an elegant idea, New Delhi would serve as the answer to India's growing anti-colonialism while resecuring the subcontinent as an important pivot of Britain's world system.[1]

Britain's 'Bengal problem'

Hardinge's Government of India, with the full support of the Secretary of State for India, Lord Crewe, used the transfer to halt India's seeming decline into chaos caused by Curzon's partition of Bengal.[2] Publicly, Curzon argued that partition was necessary to help alleviate the administrative problems caused by the province's large population, nearly 80 million people by the turn of the century, and its great diversity. Bengal consisted of a vast array of different groups with different needs and aspirations – from Nagaland's hunter-gatherers to the Gangetic plain's *zamindars* (landowners) and *ryots* (peasants), to Calcutta's labourers, small shop owners, bankers, and western educated elites.[3] Yet government correspondence at the time also shows that Curzon's aggressive colonial policy toward Bengal stemmed from his fear of the rising political power of western educated Bengalis who called for a greater voice in government. Partition, he hoped, would break this emerging political bloc. H. H. Riseley, Home Secretary to the Government of India at the time and a man with extensive knowledge of Bengal's different castes and tribes, claimed, 'Bengal united is a power; Bengal divided would pull in different ways'.[4] Partition divided Bengal's Hindu majority between East and West Bengal, simultaneously weakening Hindu political power while strengthening that of Bengali Muslims in the new Eastern province.[5] Hardinge later admitted the true spirit of Curzon's policy in a note to Crewe during their deliberations to transfer the capital. While the stated goal of partition was to give administrative 'relief to the over-burdened province of Bengal', Hardinge pointed out, 'the desire to aim a blow at the Bengalis overcame other considerations in giving effect to that laudable object'.[6]

Partition was met with anger by many Bengali Hindus who rightly saw it 'as an act of flagrant injustice without justification' and a direct threat to their political aspirations.[7] The policy seemed explicitly autocratic because it was made behind the closed doors of the Viceroy's executive council with little input from Indian leaders. Of course, Curzon's own personality, which could be pompous and overbearing, simply added to the assumption that he was governing India as a despot.[8] Bengalis with nationalist aspirations began to make public denunciations of the new policy, especially in Calcutta, which became a hotbed of Indian nationalist agitation.[9] As Hardinge cuttingly wrote of Curzon and his partition, 'It did not require much foresight on the part of anybody with any insight ... to realize that the Bengalis would never tamely submit to a position of inferiority in their own province, due to an artificial manipulation of the populations inhabiting Bengal and the adjacent divisions.'[10] Using his own biased assumptions of the Bengali character, Hardinge argued, 'the Bengalis are born agitators, and ... they will never cease to agitate until they have obtained modification of the partition'.[11] For Hardinge, Crewe, and many others, partition had created the exact opposite of what its original goal had been. Rather than breaking the political will of Bengali nationalists, partition had energized it by giving nationalists a serious grievance to organize around and to agitate against.[12]

Fleetwood Wilson, one of India's most enigmatic Finance Ministers, described the severity of this anti-colonial agitation, some of which was quite violent, in a daily diary that he kept while serving in India.[13] What surprised him the most was the way in which the 'poison of sedition had eaten into a section of the Indian community' that had once been relatively loyal to the British.[14] As Wilson recognized, many of the perpetrators were young, western-educated men from respectable families. In December 1907, a bomb was placed under the train carrying Sir Andrew (Lovat) Fraser, the Lt Governor of Bengal. In the same month, the District Magistrate of Dacca was shot with a revolver. Incidents continued into 1908 with the shooting of Mr Hickenbotham of the Church Missionary Society in March. In April there was an attempt to assassinate the mayor of Chandernagore, and a bomb meant for the Presidency Magistrate at Calcutta was thrown instead into a carriage carrying a Mr and Mrs Kennedy. In May the Maniktala bomb conspiracy was discovered.[15] In June a bomb was thrown into a railway carriage at Kankinara. In September a young man was convicted of sending a bomb by post to the Magistrate of Nadia. In November another assassination attempt was made on Fraser, the Native Sub-Inspector of Police was shot in Calcutta, and the primary witness against a secret anti-colonial association, the *Anushilan Samiti*, was murdered and decapitated near Dacca. A series of *dacoities* (armed banditry) also occurred in 1908. In June a *dacoity* ended with the killing of two people near Nawabganj. Another *dacoity* was committed at Serampore, and more occurred in October near Malda and Faridpore. In response to this agitation, John L. Jenkins, Home Member for the Government of India and the man most responsible for security in India, introduced a bill to control explosives and explosive devices in June 1908. He also introduced a criminal law amendment bill. These measures, however, were largely ineffective in combatting a far more challenging form of anti-colonial agitation, nationalist boycotts of goods made in Britain. No amount of criminal legislation could force Indians to buy something they refused to purchase. While bombs maimed or killed individuals, boycotts struck at the empire's life's blood, commerce and its associated ventures such as shipping, insurance, and investment capital.[16]

Hardinge's decision to transfer the capital and to reverse partition exemplifies John Darwin's conclusion that in the early twentieth century Britain's primary colonial concern was consolidating those regions that were essential to the British world system. Clearly, Calcutta's commercial community, as a long-standing and powerful bridgehead, felt itself threatened by any colonial policy that reduced its influence over the government's financial and commercial decisions. Yet Bengal's anti-colonial agitation, which had reached a fevered pitch by 1910, was beginning to damage the economic health of Britain's world empire. According to Sir George Paish, a contemporary liberal economist, India accounted for almost 11 per cent of Britain's worldwide direct investments, which was near £4,000,000,000 in 1913.[17] Public investment in India and Ceylon at around the same time was close to £365,400,000, a total that did not include investments made through private channels.[18] Additionally, Britain held 49 out of 72 million sterling (around 70 per cent) of India's import trade with fully half of this total coming from Lancashire cotton piece goods.[19] It was this exact imported good that Indian nationalists had quite wisely decided to boycott, giving their anti-colonial agitation a powerful economic sting.[20]

Boycotts were made worse by the rise of foreign competition in the global market place. As Wilson claimed in his annual presentation of the Indian budget, 'Modern methods of production have extended throughout the world; not only Western countries like the United States and Germany, but the far east and Japan have enormously increased their productive power, and external markets for their goods have become a vital necessity to the stability and progress of their trade.'[21] Since the late 1880s, British exports to India had fallen from 91 to 70.5 per cent. Britain clearly maintained a large advantage over its foreign competitors, but the downward trend was unmistakable. At the same time, on the Indian export side, Britain had 'ceased to be the chief external market for Indian products'.[22] Britain consumed around 32 out of 123 million (over 26 per cent) of India's exports. Wilson concluded, 'it is clear that the development of India in the future must be dependent on, and primarily affected by, the policy pursued by the British Empire as a whole and particularly by the United Kingdom'.[23] Regaining stability in Bengal was not simply an Indian matter; the health of Britain's world economic system required it.

Hardinge's 'bold stroke of statesmanship': the transfer of capital and the end of partition

In 1910, Lord Hardinge came to India determined to resolve Britain's problems in Bengal while at the same time solidifying British power in India. His solution was to reverse simultaneously Curzon's partition of Bengal and to transfer the imperial capital to Delhi. The two interlinked policies were arguably the defining moments of his viceroyalty. They were also the most controversial.[24] Both consumed tremendous portions of his government's finances, time, and energy. Still, he had no definite plan for reversing partition when he first arrived in India in late 1910 and was not sure if the policy actually could be reversed even though it had been 'a festering political sore and the cause of all the anarchical agitation in Bengal'.[25] This initial misgiving soon evaporated as the Indian Office began sending Hardinge strong signals to resolve Bengal's deteriorating political situation even if it meant reversing partition. In January 1911, just a month after Hardinge's arrival, Crewe issued a proposal to modify partition in order to 'satisfy that section of the Indian political community who regarded the partition as a mistake'.[26] Crewe's proposal raised Bengal from a lieutenant governorship to a full governorship with a new capital at Dacca. Commissionerships directly responsible to the viceroy would then be created for the Bengali-speaking divisions of Burdwan, Rajshahi, Dacca, Chittagong, and the Presidency. Calcutta would remain the imperial capital as an independent enclave directly under the control of the viceroy.[27]

After careful study, Hardinge rejected Crewe's proposal because it did not alter what he considered one of the most pressing problems in India's colonial administration: the overly close association between the Government of India and Bengal. For Hardinge, Calcutta's politics, its agitation, and its intractably self-focused European community had far too much influence over the general direction of all-India British policy. As he stated in a note to his council, 'The opinion of Calcutta, European and Indian, is unsatisfactory and less reasonable than anywhere else in India, and it is a pity that the Government of India should be more subject to its influence than to that of the more sane opinion of other parts of India.'[28] This was no idle concern. Calcutta's European community's incensed response to the 1883 Ilbert Bill, which permitted senior Indian magistrates to supervise cases involving British subjects, showed just how inflexible this population could be when it felt itself threatened.[29] Likewise, India's Legislative Assembly, now expanded under the Morley-Minto Reforms of 1909, was located in Calcutta, the centre of much of the anti-colonial intrigue.[30] Hardinge believed this allowed Bengalis to unduly influence the activities of the assembly.[31]

Hardinge also was deeply troubled that the call to end partition had become 'a traditional demand based on racial reasons, like Home Rule for Ireland'.[32] As he claimed:

> [Bengali agitation was] deeper and more persistent than the most pessimistic ever imagined possible; and unless a remedy be found, there is little hope that it will disappear for many years to come. It is now becoming a traditional grievance based on racial feeling, like Home Rule for Ireland, and as long as it exists we must be prepared for trouble in the two provinces.[33]

Wilson agreed in a reply to Hardinge. 'Many of the features of the agitation,' Wilson claimed, 'reminded me greatly of the earlier phases of the Home Rule movement (in Ireland) ... the unyielding, *non-possumus* attitude adopted by England towards the political-racial aspirations of the Irish people contributed largely to the terrible trouble England has had to face in regard to Ireland.'[34] Wilson saw the 'Celtic and the Bengali-Hindu races' as being extremely similar: 'they are both highly imaginative, very sensitive, passionately devoted to their land and to their religion and easily moved to nurse a sense of injury, real or imagined'.[35] For Hardinge and Wilson, little was needed to recreate in India the same problems that had plagued Britain in Ireland. In a report sent to Crewe, Hardinge claimed, 'all the *dacoities*, outrages and assassinations which have taken place in recent years ... are set down by Bengali politicians directly to the partition, and ... there appears to be no immediate prospect of the cessation of the deeds of violence'.[36] Crewe's proposal was a good start, but it was too moderate. Anti-partition agitation in Bengal was so deeply rooted that only bold policies would mitigate the unrest.

Hardinge also realized that his government needed to make a powerful statement about partition because the impending royal visit raised Indian nationalists' expectations that the king would use his durbar to make a major colonial policy announcement to 'remove this injustice'.[37] Lord Crewe admitted as much in the House of Lords in February 1912 as he defended the Government of India's new policies:

> I am convinced that there would have been a feeling all over India of bitter disappointment if it had turned out that the Durbar was merely an occasion for spectacle and pageantry, however unexampled and however magnificent, that no serious import was to be

attached to the unique event of the King-Emperor's visit, and that
the whole occasion was simply one of show and of parade.[38]

For months the Indian press in Calcutta had been calling for the king
to reunite the two Bengals, and nationalists had written two memorials to the king as well. The first called on him to reverse partition. The
second called on him to end the killing of cows, an issue that many
(Hindu) nationalists had coalesced around for several decades. The king
would be incapable of accepting the memorial on cow killing since
Indian Muslims and Europeans residing in India ate beef, and reversing
partition would be seen as a sign that agitation worked. A rejection of
both memorials might promote further agitation by Bengali Hindus.
Disconcerting to Hardinge and his council, some members of the Indian
press even had begun to assert that the king had no sovereign powers,
and that 'his visit ... [would] be profitless and a source of disappoint-
ment to all'.[39] What the Government of India needed was a new, grand
policy that would silence agitation in Bengal once and for all.

John Jenkins, who had become a close confidante of the viceroy,
provided Hardinge with the germ that would grow into Hardinge's bold
new colonial policy for dealing with India's anti-colonial agitation. In a
memorandum that contained an ambitious vision, Jenkins argued that
political stability could be achieved by following an incredibly elegant
three-pronged approach. First, the imperial capital should be transferred
from the heated political climate of Calcutta to Delhi, a historical
seat of Indian empires. This daring move, he claimed, would represent
'a bold stroke of statesmanship which would give universal satisfaction
and mark a new era in the history of India'.[40] Second, Jenkins proposed
that the transfer be closely associated with the reversal of partition.
And third, the announcement of these profound colonial changes
should flow from the mouth of the king himself. This would remove
the major cause of Bengal's unrest, partition, while the change of capital
'would be magical since, in the imagination of the masses of the people,
Delhi and Empire have been associated from time immemorial'.[41] The
scheme's power and beauty derived from its royal nature and from its
element of obfuscation. The transfer of the capital was so magisterial,
so far-reaching, so unexpected, and so grand that the reunification of
Bengal seemed secondary by comparison.

Jenkins' proposal was precisely the courageous solution that Hardinge
desired. It went far beyond Crewe's original proposal, and it resolved
major issues that Hardinge felt were adding to Bengal's instability.
First and most important, the reunification of East and West Bengal

as a presidency satisfied those who were doing most of the agitating, Bengali Hindus. Additionally, raising Bengal from a lieutenant governorship to a full presidency with a governor in council would ensure that the most visible communities in Bengal would be represented and that under-represented communities, such as the lowest castes or communal minorities, would be protected.[42] The scheme also provided convenient administrative units in north-east India. Assam was removed from Bengal and turned into a Chief Commissionership that served as a kind of north-east frontier. Assam's administrative elevation to Chief Commissionership also increased the ability of colonial authorities to police such activities as the trafficking of opium and other goods such as tea and jute. The regions of Bihar and Orissa, which were part of West Bengal, were separated from the new Bengal presidency and united under a new lieutenant governorship located at Patna. As Hardinge argued, the people of these two regions had long sought independence from a province in which they had no common 'language or sentiment'.[43]

The scheme's impact on Muslims in East Bengal, who for the most part had been loyal and content since partition, required some self-delusion. Hardinge and Jenkins argued that Bengali Muslims would not be harmed by the loss of East Bengal and its reunification with the western province. The new and more powerful governor would protect their rights and remain in close contact with Muslim sentiment. Besides, as Hardinge painstakingly made clear to his council, the political position of Muslims in East Bengal was never a determining factor in Curzon's original decision to partition Bengal. Their political 'gain was incidental and an afterthought', he argued.[44] Thus, Curzon's primary objective of breaking Bengali Hindu power had not been met while one of the main arguments against its reversal, namely angering Muslims in East Bengal, was theoretically null and void. Hence, any attempt to appease Muslim sentiment, such as returning the imperial capital to its traditional Muslim seat, could be read only as another example of the benevolence of British rule in India.

Most importantly, the transfer of the capital from Calcutta to Delhi created the appropriate political conditions to reverse Curzon's resented partition without looking as if the British were surrendering to nationalist clamour and agitation. Indeed, the transfer was the 'keystone of the whole scheme', as Hardinge pointed out, for the magnitude of the decision to transfer the capital would conceal the main purpose of Bengal's reunification – the silencing of agitation.[45] Lastly, the transfer satisfied one of Hardinge's major concerns about Calcutta's undue influence on all-India policy; it removed the Government of India from the political influence of Bengal's Indian and European communities.[46]

Hardinge forwarded the proposed scheme to his council for consideration and response on 20 June 1911. He urged council members to keep the plans secret, stating 'it would be better if the question were not even discussed except in council, as walls have ears'.[47] Jenkins agreed, claiming, 'any premature disclosure would rob the announcement of it by His Majesty of much of its due effect'.[48] Secrecy was also important for another reason. If the Secretary of State for India did not endorse the ambitious scheme or if it was not ultimately carried out due to political pressure at home, its early disclosure to the public might stimulate further agitation. Secrecy also sidestepped Parliament, which surely would reduce aspects of the scheme and thus rob it of its full force.

For the most part, Hardinge's executive council positively responded to the scheme. Their major concerns had to do with how best to work within Bengal's complex communal politics, the impact the scheme would have on the Muslim community in East Bengal, and the potential for an angry response from Calcutta's European community and its commercial leaders. Only two members of the executive council, Sir Robert W. Carlyle, member for Public Works, and Sir Harcourt Butler, member for Education, showed great scepticism.[49]

Not surprisingly, John Jenkins was fully behind a proposal of which he was a principal drafter.[50] From his standpoint, it was sound colonial policy to remove what he called the 'partition ulcer' without exposing the government to the accusation that they were yielding to agitation.[51] He was particularly adamant about paying close attention to the political importance of religious communes in the selection of what districts should make up the new Bengal and its neighbouring provinces and commissionerships. Thus, even as Jenkins pushed for policies that would mollify a certain powerful section of Indian public opinion by ending partition, he continued to reflect Britain's long use of ethnic and religious differences to gain colonial advantage. It was a practice that Curzon had employed in the decision to divide Bengal originally. Jenkins noted that a reunified Bengal would have a Muslim majority of about two million if only the five Bengali speaking divisions were included in the new province. If the divisions of Chota Nagpur (Hazaribagh and Manbhum) were included with the previous five, the population numbers would be almost equal. As the Government of India thought about how best to modify the partition of Bengal to satisfy Indian opinion, it never strayed far from political calculations that balanced India's emerging electorate.

Likewise, Syed Ali Imam, Law Member to the Government of India and the only Indian on Hardinge's executive council, took up the question of communal politics in his response to the proposed scheme.[52] For Imam it was essential that Muslims remained in the majority in Bengal after restructuring the political boundaries of the province. Administrative divisions or districts that had large Hindu majorities, according to Imam, should not be included in a unified Bengal (Table 2.1). Hence, Assam should be its own commissionership since its Hindu population was twice as large as its Muslim population. For this same reason, the districts of Cooch Behar, Sikkim, and Hill Tipperah should be included with Assam. Similarly, the districts of Manbhum and Hazaribagh, which also had large Hindu majorities, should be included in the proposed Bihar-Orissa lieutenant governorship. Neither Manbhum nor Hazaribagh had a Bengali-speaking majority. The people of Manbhum spoke Rarhi Boli in the east and Hindi in the west. The people in Hazaribagh spoke Hindi. Thus, along ethnic and sentimental lines, according to Imam, neither of these districts belonged with Bengal.[53] For him, those opponents of partition who demanded that these districts be included in Bengal did so out of a desire for the rich coal fields located there and not because of any affinity of 'race and language'.[54] Himself a Bihari, Imam hoped that these resource rich districts would fall under the administration of the proposed province of Bihar-Orissa.[55]

Imam recommended that a restructured Bengal should consist of only the Bengali-speaking divisions of Rajshahi, Dacca, Chittagong, Burdwan, and the Presidency (Table 2.2). This type of structure would place all the Bengali-speaking peoples under one administration while still giving Muslims a majority of more than two million. To include other districts in Bengal would place Muslims at a numerical disadvantage, something that could not be tolerated since they were already losing political advantages because of the loss of East Bengal.

Table 2.1   Communal populations in north-east India[56]

Region	Hindu	Muslim
Assam	3,429,099	1,581,317
Cooch Behar	397,946	168,236
Sikkim	38,306	21
Hill Tipperah	119,192	45,323
Manbhum	1,132,619	62,799
Hazaribagh	954,105	119,656
Total	6,071,267	1,977,532

Table 2.2 Communal populations of Bengali-speaking divisions[57]

Division	Hindu	Muslim
Rajshahi	3,061,876	5,283,182
Dacca	3,524,287	7,209,562
Chittagong	1,251,423	3,333,326
Burdwan	6,855,164	1,084,820
Presidency	4,502,490	4,405,537
Total	19,195,240	21,316,427

Imam was particularly concerned with safeguarding the rights of Muslims who had been loyal since the partition and felt that the Muslims of East Bengal would not be reconciled by numerical equality with Hindus even if it meant giving them a full governorship and returning the capital to Delhi. Their loss of real political power in East Bengal outweighed their sentimental ties to Delhi as the traditional Muslim seat of empire.[58]

The greatest sceptic of the scheme, Robert Carlyle, also voiced concerns about how Muslims would receive the announcement to reunify Bengal. It was of the utmost importance that Bengali Muslims were not led to believe that their political development and power were being sacrificed for Bengali Hindus, particularly if this sacrifice was due to Hindu agitation. For Carlyle, rescinding partition was a thorny issue for the British since it meant favouring Hindus who had agitated while punishing Muslims who had remained loyal. Muslims required some form of assurance. After all, they would lose the political advantages they had gained in East Bengal if partition was rescinded. To 'defraud' Muslims in particular of their political rights was to exhibit 'bad faith', argued Carlyle.[59] Hence, no settlement would be satisfactory or conclusive if it did not conciliate Muslim sentiment.[60] Carlyle was sceptical that returning the capital to its traditional Mughal seat would ameliorate Muslim anger over losing East Bengal. Drawing on what he saw as deep-seated communal antagonisms, Britain needed to protect Muslims from Hindu domination if partition was reversed.[61] Hence, he believed that the settlement might work if Muslims were given separate Muslim electorates in every administrative body.[62] In addition, East Bengal should have a Chief Commissioner, subordinate to the proposed Governor in Council at Calcutta, but independent in its local administration. Only in this way, according to Carlyle, could the British guarantee that Muslim interests would be safeguarded. Harcourt Butler, another sceptic, agreed with Carlyle about creating a Chief Commissioner for East Bengal.

He argued that the building of a new Government House at Dacca, the capital of East Bengal, had represented a positive transformation in British-Muslim relations, but the elimination of East Bengal as a distinct province would reverse this positive development. Butler claimed that he would only support Hardinge's scheme if a 'semi-independent Commissioner' with his own budget were appointed to East Bengal and if a separate High Court and university were created there.

Sir William H. Clark was more concerned about how Calcutta's European community would respond to the scheme. He agreed that the separation of the Government of India from Bengal would have immense political advantages, but the benefits would come at great cost. As Commerce and Industry Secretary, Clark argued that the transfer to Delhi would harm the relationship between government and Calcutta's commercial community. In Calcutta the Government of India remained in close contact with many of India's largest and most influential commercial firms and banks, but the relationship would break down with the government's isolation at Delhi.[63] The transfer also would lessen interactions between the government and some of India's most important industries such as tea and jute. Increasing the tours of the Commerce and Industry member could ease the problems of the government's commercial isolation, but this seemed unpromising to Clark since on tour he was the one who was being 'entertained' and not the one doing the 'entertaining'.[64] Furthermore, touring took the member away from Calcutta's clubs where much business was discussed through ordinary social intercourse.[65] Clark presaged the hostility that would arise among the European community in Calcutta due to the change in capital: 'the difficulties [of moving the capital] ... will be urged by that section of the European community who will object very strongly to the change ... and I feel Calcutta will object vigorously'.[66] Yet Clark generally supported the proposal. He noted that the transfer would ease the jealousy that other commercial centres, most notably Bombay, had for Calcutta. He also believed that the Railway Department would greatly benefit from the transfer since Delhi was the most important rail hub in northern India.[67]

Harcourt Butler also was deeply concerned about Calcutta's response to the transfer. After all, Calcutta was the only 'European city' in India. 'All our associations are with Calcutta, our institutions have grown up there, the High Court, the Museum, the Victoria Memorial, &c., will be stranded, [and] the *Statesman* will become a purely local paper', Butler argued.[68] He believed that Bengal's agitation had reached its final phase and would be over in several years; therefore, the Government of India would be foolish to base long-term colonial policies on ending anti-partition agitation. Still, Butler claimed that he would support the scheme if the Governorship of the proposed Bengal province were open to members of the Indian Civil Service. Initially, Hardinge had wanted governors appointed from England to avoid the scandal of nominating someone with political, business, and social allegiances in Calcutta or Bengal. But Butler argued that the situation in Bengal was so complicated that it required a Governor with intimate knowledge of the country. He also believed that opening the position to internal recruitment would improve the morale of the Indian Civil Service.

While most executive council members agreed that the scheme remain secret, Robert Carlyle was concerned about the subsequent lack of public debate. He believed that representatives from the European, Hindu and Muslim communities should be consulted about a settlement of such magnitude. If the scheme was as good as Hardinge and Jenkins suggested, then it should be able to bear discussion in a public forum. Not doing so might create 'well-founded' discontent among the communities who were not consulted about the transfer. Playing devil's advocate, Carlyle questioned what would happen if the settlement announced by the king at his durbar met with bitter controversy. 'We cannot risk a leap in the dark', Carlyle claimed.[69] By not consulting the different communities that would be affected by the settlement, the Government of India could be placed in an embarrassing situation in which a royal boon meant to benefit loyal subjects became a bane hated by all. Far worse, the lack of public debate, especially in Parliament, raised constitutional questions for Carlyle. 'It might be justifiable at a critical moment to adopt so unconstitutional a procedure to cut short agitation against some unpopular measure of vital importance,' argued Carlyle, 'but it is surely setting a bad precedence to take such action in any case where it can be avoided.'[70] This was a claim later raised in Parliament by opponents of the scheme. According to R. E. Frykenberg, opposition leaders, who had been informed of the announcement only the night before the durbar, stood up in the House of Commons and Lords to decry the absence of debate.[71] As Lord Lansdowne stated in the Lords shortly after the king's durbar announcement, '[the announced changes raise] such grave issues that no consideration ... would justify us in hurriedly passing a judgment upon them or in doing anything which might hereafter be regarded as depriving us of our right of freely criticizing what is suggested'.[72] In the end, such accusations about the Government of India's unconstitutional actions were aired in Parliament but never pursued. As Hardinge and Crewe knew perfectly well, Parliament would find it extremely difficult to revoke the king's announcement to transfer the capital without embarrassing the most important symbol of the empire, the king-emperor himself. As a symbol of colonial strength and as a sign of Britain's single-mindedness in the face of recent anti-colonial agitation in Bengal, Parliament had to follow the king's will, *fait accompli*, to show imperial stability and unity.

Fleetwood Wilson, who had deep sympathies for Indian nationalism, was a strong supporter of the scheme because he saw it as a way to mend British and Indian relations.[73] In his reply to Hardinge, Wilson claimed, 'Your Excellency was pleased, on a recent occasion, to allow me to indicate the view I hold, so it is hardly necessary for me to say that I have read your minute with the most lively satisfaction; that I am in general agreement with it; and that the change Your Excellency suggests will have my unswerving support.'[74] Wilson had arrived in India with little knowledge of the colony he was supposed to financially manage, but he quickly became obsessed with how best to work with the Indian independence movement. As he claimed, the question was 'ever present all day and every day and, alas, many nights'.[75] Upon receiving the new scheme from Hardinge, Wilson claimed that he too had decided as early as 1909 that a modification of partition was imperative. The problems in Bengal would never improve, he believed, as long as the Government of India remained associated with Calcutta. The violent events there forced the Government of India to pass policies that were perhaps justifiably harsh but solidified British and Indian animosities. Furthermore, the problems in Bengal inordinately took up the government's energies and distracted it from the needs and concerns of other Indian provinces such as Madras and Bombay. Repeating the general sentiment of Hardinge and Jenkins, Wilson argued that the pacification of Bengal had to be 'based on some other re-adjustment of so much greater importance as to overshadow the actual partition re-arrangement'.[76] The transfer of the capital did just that.

In the end, Hardinge and his supporters were able to bring the scheme's major detractors, Carlyle and Butler, in line with the project with very few changes. By August 1911 the final draft of the report was completed. Butler, who still held to his belief that agitation in Bengal was weakening, set aside his personal views and agreed to sign the report in order to maintain a show of unanimity.[77] East Bengal did not receive its own Chief Commissioner, as Butler and Carlyle desired, but Dacca was announced as the second official capital of Bengal. The new Governor of Bengal would be able to stay in touch with Muslim sentiment in east Bengal by residing in Dacca for a portion of the year. Butler's demand that the governorship be open to members of the Indian Civil Service was granted as well. Hardinge and Jenkins' arguments for supreme secrecy outweighed Carlyle's warnings that the lack of parliamentary debate on such a momentous decision would cause a constitutional crisis. To let the Indian and British public know that the Government of India had made an attempt to find a solution to the problems in Bengal and had failed would not only stimulate further agitation against partition but also engender a lack of confidence in the current government. Muslim sentiment continued to be a concern, but Hardinge and his council believed that the administrative safeguards and territorial restructuring included in the proposal protected Muslim political interests.

After hearing his council's objections, Hardinge sent the proposal to Crewe on 19 July 1911. In a detailed letter that accompanied the scheme, Hardinge informed Crewe that while there were potential costs and objections to following the scheme, 'it was the best and only certain means of securing peace and reconciliation in Bengal'.[78] Hardinge also urged secrecy in the letter. Indeed, he was so concerned about concealing his government's intentions that he made his own copies of all his correspondence and the members of his council wrote their own notes.[79] On 7 August, Crewe replied that Hardinge 'had his entire support and full authority to proceed' and that secrecy was indeed paramount.[80] In the end, perhaps a dozen people in India and roughly an equal number in Britain knew of the scheme. Crewe also asked Hardinge to draw up an official dispatch to be published as a state paper on the date of the durbar. By doing so, the scheme became a stated fact rather than a proposal to be discussed and modified. Crewe then contacted the king to inform him about the proposed scheme and the important role the king would play in announcing it. The king accepted the scheme 'with great keenness' and agreed that secrecy was essential since it would amplify the majesty of the announcement.[81] The king kept the secret so well that the queen was just as surprised as everyone else by his announcement at the durbar.[82] The members of Asquith's cabinet, especially John Morley, were 'deeply impressed and favourable, being struck with the adroitness with which the creation of new grievances was avoided while removing old ones'.[83] Asquith, in particular, liked the 'bigness of the idea' and thought the scheme's advantages far outweighed its costs.[84] On 3 November, Crewe informed Hardinge that the India Council in London liked the idea and the Cabinet accepted it as well.[85]

The transfer of the capital as colonial legerdemain

The transfer of the capital from Calcutta to Delhi remained the central feature of the resettlement of Bengal since it concealed Britain's inability to adequately deal with anti-colonial agitation in the province. The transfer was seen as the primary colonial policy from which stemmed Bengal's subsequent administrative and territorial reorganizations. In the process, Bengali agitation, which had played such a significant role in the new policy, officially disappeared. This is clearly seen by an examination of two original drafts of the scheme: one meant for the eyes of Lord Crewe alone and the other for the *Gazette of India, Extraordinary*, an official journal of the Government of India which publicized government activities. Both documents, titled *Draft A* and *Draft B*, were penultimate reports of the settlement, but the first, a private report, concerned information that was elided in the latter, a public document. These elisions tellingly point to the central role that Bengali agitation played in bringing about the transfer of the capital to Delhi and the resettlement of Bengal.

Large sections of *Draft A* were removed from *Draft B*. Of the 31 paragraphs in *Draft A*, 15 were either edited or deleted for *Draft B* to hide or diminish the importance of anti-colonial agitation in shaping British colonial policies. Anything showing British weakness in Crewe's draft had been cut from the report meant for the public eye. For example, an entire paragraph from *Draft A* concerning the memorial to rescind partition was elided in *Draft B*. To include the paragraph would have suggested that the memorial had actually influenced the decision to reverse partition.

Similarly, Hardinge's government further masked imperial weakness by turning to imperial symbolism. The crowning of King George V as Emperor of India at an imperial durbar offered a unique opportunity to rescind partition, to reaffirm British imperial rule in India, to move the government of British-India from troubled Calcutta to Delhi, and to show Britain's desire to bring modern forms of government to India. As Bernard Cohn has shown, the durbar was a perfect example of coercion and consent. Its highly ritualized placement of objects and people cemented the emperor's authority, but it did so through a system of exchange.[86] During a durbar, the emperor bestowed gifts on subjects who then gave him their loyalty. In the process, the imperial bond between emperor and subject was strengthened.[87] Realizing the durbar's tremendous value as an imperial tool, the British adopted the ceremony as their own. By 1911, durbars had become an important element in expressing Britain's imperial authority as well as its benevolence. A common practice was to give concessions as a form of gift-giving. For example, George V released almost 12,000 prisoners during his durbar.[88] The transfer of the capital and the reunification of Bengal were seen as forms of concession as well. By reunifying Bengal and by raising the colonial status of Bihar and Orissa to a lieutenant governorship and Assam to a chief commissionership, the king worked within a traditional durbar discourse of imperial gift-giving. His concessions reaffirmed the legitimacy of British rule by relocating colonial authority in the emperor as the ultimate gift-giver who ruled India through a Governor General in council. The symbolism of the king as the fount of all great gifts can be seen in the very words of George V who announced at the end of his durbar:

> We are pleased to announce to Our people that on the advice of Our Ministers, tendered after consultation with Our Governor-General in Council, We have decided upon the transfer of the seat of the Government of India from Calcutta to the ancient capital of Delhi, and simultaneously, and *as a consequence of that transfer*, the creation at as early a date as possible of a Governorship for the Presidency of Bengal ... It is Our earnest desire that these changes may conduce to the better administration of India, and the greater prosperity and happiness of our beloved people.[89]

In addition, the traditional symbolism surrounding the king's most important concessions obscured the Bengali agitation that led to the Government of India's decision to end partition. Thus, agitating Bengalis became loyal colonial subjects who deserved to have their province reunified.

Ultimately, the transfer of the imperial capital offered a way to reaffirm British rule in India by regrounding the empire in a new imperial vision that was both modern in its offer of political reforms and yet ancient in its setting at Delhi. The new capital would be built amidst the architectural remains of past empires, which allowed the British to rewrite themselves into India's deepest past. Delhi's central place in Indian history was repeated again and again in early reports about the transfer. Hardinge claimed in August 1911, 'Delhi is still a name to conjure with. It is intimately associated in the minds of the Hindus with sacred legends which go back even beyond the dawn of history ... and among the masses of the people it is still viewed as the seat of the former empire.'[90] In his response to the Government of India's proposal, Lord Crewe returned to Delhi's historical significance, 'To the races of India, for whom the legends and records of the past are charged with so intense a meaning, this resumption by the paramount power of the seat of venerable empire should at once enforce the continuity and promise the permanency of British sovereign rule over the length and breadth of the country.'[91] While showing the importance of Delhi to the Indian imperial past, Crewe also pointed to the direct connection between history and politics in India and the benefits the British Empire could derive from their linkage. 'From the historical standpoint,' claimed Crewe, '...not only do the ancient walls of Delhi enshrine an Imperial tradition comparable with that of Constantinople, or with that of Rome itself, but the near neighbourhoods of the existing city formed the theatre for some most notable scenes in the old-time drama of Hindu history, celebrated in the vast treasure house of national epic verse.'[92] Muslims also would receive with 'unbounded gratification' the return of Delhi, the capital of the Mughals, to its rightful place as the imperial seat of India.[93] Hardinge agreed, 'Throughout India, as far south as the Mahomedan conquest extended, every walled town has its "Delhi Gate", and among the masses of the people it is still revered as the seat of the former Empire.'[94] By building on this history, Britain positioned itself as the rightful heir to India while simultaneously deauthorizing past Indian empires as dead and decayed.

Yet the new capital was much more than a symbol of the imperial past and imperial coercion. It also represented a new direction in British-India. For Hardinge and his allies, the new capital allowed the British to claim that their imperial role in India had not diminished but had simply evolved to suit new social and political conditions caused by India's rapid economic development. The political turmoil that followed Curzon's recent partition had more than shown the folly of colonial policies based primarily on coercion. New and more nuanced methods that encouraged Indian consent to colonial rule were needed. For a consummate diplomat like Hardinge, the chief goal was to create and nurture conditions that ensured Britain's paramount position in the region. For him and for other like-minded officials, Britain needed to take on a greater paternal and pedagogical role that guided India toward responsible government. As John Darwin has suggested, 'So long as constitutional change made no difference to [the fundamentals of British imperial paramountcy], British policy makers were able to regard it as an inconvenient, sometimes distasteful, necessity, but not of over-riding importance.'[95] For Indians, the message was clear: India could have responsible government someday but only under the watchful eye of Britain and only when Britain deemed India ready for it. The transfer of the capital, then, can be understood as part of a larger, progressive plan to create a federated governmental structure in India that devolved responsible government on Indians at the provincial level. The intimate connection between the transfer of the capital and political devolution was taken up in paragraph three of the official state paper that informed Parliament and the public about the Government of India's new colonial policy. This connection and the parliamentary debates it engendered are addressed in the following chapter.

3

New Delhi's New Vision for a New Raj: An 'Altar of Humanity'

George V's durbar proclamation generated great enthusiasm at first, but within weeks open criticism of the plan began to appear in Parliament as the political and economic consequences of the decision became apparent. The viciousness and duration of the criticism suggests that there was much more at stake than simply the transfer of the capital. Indeed, the expansiveness of the policy, which included not only the transfer of the capital but also a broad array of administrative changes throughout India, triggered broad arguments in Parliament about the meaning and purpose of empire. The breadth of issues argued in Parliament as well as the heated, often insulting, tone of the debates arose from the way in which the transfer of the capital and its related administrative changes began to modify traditional forms of dominance and privilege.[1] Examining the people who were most upset by the transfer as well as what in the new colonial policy made them the angriest, helps us to understand the full meaning of the new capital.

Two members of Hardinge's executive council, William Clark and Harcourt Butler, had warned of the possibility of an angry backlash, but few were prepared for the level of animosity and the depths to which Calcutta's two main European presses, the *Statesman* and the *Englishman*, would descend in decrying the transfer. The European community in Calcutta was 'simply rabid, and no words were too bad for me', Hardinge later claimed in his memoires.[2] Immediately after the durbar, the *Statesman* ran a leader declaring H. M. G., 'Hardinge Must Go.'[3] Hardinge was even likened to Siraj-ud-daulah, the supposed perpetrator of the famed Black Hole of Calcutta and the quintessential example of Indian depravity in the British colonial imagination.[4] One story claimed the new capital's foundation stones, which the king and queen laid with great ceremony after the durbar, were said to be grave markers. Another story claimed that lightning had struck the British flag, a supremely dark omen, just as Hardinge was officially leaving Calcutta for the summer capital at Simla.[5] The *Statesman* and the *Englishman's* attacks on Hardinge were so vicious that Crewe, in the Lords, called the papers' attitudes and stories seditious. When the papers protested the suggestion, Crewe replied that 'the press laws in force in India applied to the English press equally with the Indian press'.[6] These stories were so pervasive that Hardinge claimed he heard them again when he visited India twenty years later for the inauguration of New Delhi. Additionally, powerful men in Parliament kept Calcutta's anger alive in London political circles. As Hardinge related, 'The agitation raised in Calcutta to set aside the king's announcement was violent and with the support of Lansdowne, Curzon and Minto in the House of Lords was kept up during the whole of my stay in India. No effort was spared to put a spoke in my wheel.'[7]

One of the most hotly contested aspects of the transfer and building of the new capital at Delhi was the policy's connection to political reform. This connection was made explicit in paragraph three of the official report to transfer the capital. At length it read:

> It is certain that, in the course of time, the just demands of Indians for a larger share in the Government of the country will have to be satisfied, and the question will be how this devolution of power can be conceded without impairing the supreme authority of the Governor General in Council. The only possible solution of the difficulty would be gradually giving the provinces a larger measure of self-government until at last India would consist of a number of administrations, autonomous in all provincial affairs, with the government of India above them all and possessing power to interfere in cases of misgovernment, but ordinarily restricting their functions to matters of imperial concern.[8]

The paragraph laid out a road map for continued British rule in the twentieth century based on a new hegemonic vision where Indians were given greater authority within India's imperial system. At the same time, the viceroy in council's 'supreme authority' over the life of India assured British paramountcy. The turn to political reform in India was a practical response to Indian anti-colonialism, but the policy created tremendous debate. The arguments that arose around paragraph three represented fractures in the colonial regime caused by India's rapid economic development and the subsequent social and cultural transformations that followed at the turn of the century. India's economic development, which simultaneously expanded the size of India's educated middle classes while encouraging Indian national aspirations, led a growing number of Indians to call for a greater voice in the colonial government. These changes placed tremendous pressure on a colonial system shaped by the horrific events of the 1857 Indian uprising. At the same time and largely stemming from the same transformations, increasing numbers of colonial officials began to question the colonial government's hyper-centralization and other policies that caused anti-colonial sentiment in India. Hence, the post-rebellion vision of empire began to be challenged from both official and non-official sides. The transfer of the capital was at the heart of this debate since it offered a newer, more pragmatic vision of empire that attempted to address India's new economic, social, and political dynamics.

Debates in Parliament made it clear that paragraph three's reforms were not mere window dressing. Combined with the Indian Councils Act of 1909, which expanded the number of elected Indians on legislative and municipal councils, the paragraph articulated a new colonial formula that brought increasing numbers of Indians into the political process both as legislators in popularly elected provincial councils and as government civil servants. The policy was not exactly new. The Government of India had long used Indians and Anglo-Indians in its clerical establishment, and it had transferred some less essential administrative responsibilities to provincial governments. But Hardinge's new policy was the first full embrace of devolution as the defining colonial policy of the British Raj. As such, it profoundly changed the general tenor of empire in India. The new capital symbolized a fresh start for Britain and India and encouraged Indians to work with, rather than against, the British Raj because cooperation with colonial rule brought potential benefits and the promise of greater responsible government.

Yet old colonial habits, especially ones drawn from and influenced by such appalling events as 1857 and supported by men of great influence, can be slow to change. The ambiguity of this new vision of coercion and consent set in motion forces that simultaneously pushed and pulled at the very soul of the Raj. Curzon and his allies in the Commons and Lords, most of whom saw themselves as old India hands with special insight into the needs and habits of the Indian peoples, believed that centralization rather than devolution secured British rule in India. They positioned themselves against not only Hardinge's government and the India Office but also parliamentarians such as John Morley and Antony MacDonnell, both of whom were sensitive to Indian demands for a greater voice in government. Devolution, for Curzon and others, was seen as retreat in the face of Indian anti-colonialism and a clear sign of Britain's weakened imperial vitality. Thus, not surprisingly, discussions in Parliament often became antagonistic and excessively personal due to the high stakes.

Yet, in the end, both sides wanted the same thing when stripped of their over-heated rhetoric, namely, to secure British rule in India. They simply had different approaches for achieving that end. While the colonial government of Queen Victoria had created direct British rule in India, the colonial government of George V was giving it a morality and a purpose – to prepare India for greater responsible government. The new capital's new vision was meant to strengthen British rule not merely by force but by the consent of the colonized. The political reforms surrounding the transfer of the capital were part of a larger attempt to consolidate those imperial territories that were essential to the maintenance of British global power.[9] The shift toward engaging Indians who demanded more political power and New Delhi's connection to this new thrust in colonial government needs to be seen in this light.[10]

Parliament and the New Delhi scheme

Parliament's responses to the transfer of the capital and its related political reforms were sharply divided. Some members applauded the king's proclamation, which seemed to offer, much like Queen Victoria's 1858 proclamation, a new direction in British-Indian relations. John Morley, one of the last great Gladstonian liberals in Parliament and one of the few members who had been part of the original deliberations to transfer the capital, proudly announced the king's durbar proclamation to the Lords a day after the king's speech in Delhi. At the first full reading of the bill in February 1912, he cautioned those who predicted that the cost to build the new capital would be exorbitantly high and the capital itself would prove unbeneficial to British rule. Morley claimed he was just as concerned as everyone else about India's finances and had himself, as Secretary of State for India, dealt with India's financial complexities, but he continued, 'I can only say that many predictions about India in the past have failed to come to pass.'[11] Pointing to similar warnings of disaster concerning his own council reforms in 1909, which he co-sponsored with Lord Minto, Morley claimed that '[it] was a project which was regarded by a great many people as dangerous, a hazard in the extreme, as opening the door to all kinds of mischief',[12] but the reforms had 'turned out extremely well'.[13]

Likewise, Antony MacDonnell, another member of the Lords, was a powerful voice of support for the transfer and particularly the reversal of the partition of Bengal. He had served in high office throughout India, helping to pass the progressive Bengal Tenancy Act of 1885, which secured protection for tenant farmers. He also had been one of the loudest critics within India of Curzon's partition of Bengal, which he believed reflected a partisanship that 'conferred political dominance on the Mahomedans in East Bengal'.[14] MacDonnell pointed to why the policy had exacerbated communal antagonism, which he believed was 'one of the most fundamental and serious difficulties we have to contend with in India'.[15] Giving Muslims predominance 'in a country which was essentially a Hindu country, in which the great landholders are nearly all Hindus, was calculated to produce throughout the whole of Eastern Bengal that particular difficulty which Indian governments are most desirous to avoid', argued MacDonnell.[16] Not surprisingly, the result was an aggrieved Bengali Hindu population that believed partition was purposely passed to weaken them as a political bloc. Fear and anger amongst members of this community had led to 'the bitterest feelings of animosity and revenge, and these feelings found expression in the outrages and assassinations which have taken place'.[17] MacDonnell continued:

> It is my firm belief that that state of things would have increased and grown worse as the effects of the policy of partition became more fully realized; and therefore, ... no more happy event has ever occurred in our Indian history than His gracious Majesty's declaration in Durbar, by which the current of thought of an entire people has been changed from discontent to loyalty.[18]

In his support for Hardinge's new policy, MacDonnell referenced Queen Victoria's 1858 proclamation to India, 'In their prosperity will be our strength, in their contentment our security, and in their gratitude our best reward.'[19] According to him, the partition of Bengal had been a breach of the queen's promise but Hardinge's new policy would close the gap, 'Happy Bengal, fortunate England, now that the breach has been restored from the throne.'[20] During the second reading of the bill in the Lords in June 1912, MacDonnell once again applauded the Government of India's new policy, which helped mend the divisive consequences of partition, claiming, 'if we pursue the policy that we are now pursuing – a policy which has for its object the equal treatment of all classes in India – we shall be able to carry through to its legitimate conclusion the policy which was declared by his majesty at Delhi'.[21] For MacDonnell, the king's visit had restarted dialogue between British colonial officials and Indians with national aspirations. 'There cannot be any doubt', claimed MacDonnell, 'that a pronouncement of a far-reaching and unique character was expected from his Majesty's presence in India. I will go so far as to say that the great durbar at Delhi would have missed its object if some pronouncement, far beyond the common, ... had not been made by his majesty.'[22]

Lord Reay, who had served as Governor of Bombay and Under-Secretary of State for India, called the new policy and the pageantry of its announcement 'an unprecedented event in the brilliant annals of India, I think that my noble friend the Secretary of State for India and the Viceroy and their advisors are sincerely to be congratulated on a policy which was so well conceived and so admirably carried out, and which I think will have effects of lasting value for the benefit of India'.[23] George Harris, who also had been Governor of the Bombay Presidency, agreed, calling the transfer and the king's announcement 'a stroke of genius'.[24] Lord Ampthill, who had been Governor of Madras, also praised the new policy and its announcement, 'I confess that I admire the courage of those who made themselves responsible for this new policy, for it was a courageous act ... In my view this scheme appeals to the imagination and ... it is a great act of imperial statesmanship.'[25] These men applauded the Government of India's scheme and saw it as a new, progressive, and beneficial direction in British-India.

However, the transfer of the capital and its related political reforms horrified other Members of Parliament who saw the policy as a dangerously radical change in the fundamental structure of the British Raj.[26] Lords Minto, Midleton, Cromer, Lansdowne, and Curzon carried out a full-throated assault against the transfer in the House of Lords throughout 1912. Their animosity toward the Government of India's new policy was mirrored, though often less elegantly, in the House of Commons. Here, the debate broke down along Unionist and Home Rule political divisions. Indeed, both sides drew comparisons between Ireland and India in their arguments for or against the transfer and its political reforms. Unionists such as George Wyndham (member for Dover), John David Rees (member for Nottingham East), William MacCaw (member for West Down), and Lawrence John Ronaldshay (member for Hornsey) repeatedly attacked the Government of India's new policies. They were joined at times by the liberal Joseph King (member for North Somerset), who was a persistent critic not necessarily of the transfer but of the make-up of the town planning committee.[27]

For many critics, the king's proclamation was a gross violation of Britain's constitution.[28] Throughout 1912, considerable parliamentary debate, especially in the House of Lords, dealt with this question. Opponents of the new policy claimed that the king, with reckless encouragement from Lord Hardinge and the India Office, had over-stepped his constitutional limitations by introducing such drastic changes in colonial policy before they had been discussed in Parliament. The logical conclusion to be made about why the Government of India chose such secrecy was simple, according to Lansdowne, 'It is that when a new departure in policy is likely to meet with an inconvenient reception you may rush the public into it and dispense with all the usual and time honoured ... processes which have always been resorted to in India and elsewhere when some great new departure takes place.'[29] He continued to chastise the party opposite, especially Lord Morley, for the secrecy surrounding the new scheme:

> What an argument for Liberal ministers to use! They are supposed to welcome the free breeze of public discussion. The noble viscount (Morley) himself has introduced popular representation in India. All this to be ignored whenever it suits the convenience of his Majesty's Government to do this, and they resort to what I can only describe as something very like a *coup d'état*, because if they had not done so they might have found it difficult to get their proposals through.[30]

Curzon, especially, used his substantial skills as a debater to under-mine the transfer, at times drawing on his experience as viceroy and at times personally attacking the competence of Hardinge, Crewe, and Montagu. No aspect of the new colonial policy was spared his caus-tic, often vicious, examination. For Curzon, only the supposed gross inexperience of Hardinge's government and Crewe's India Office could account for such a dangerously abrupt change in colonial government. Hardinge, Montagu, and Crewe were admittedly men of great intel-ligence, but their lack of Indian experience made them incapable of formulating sound policy for the country in their care. Taking umbrage at not being asked for his own advice on transferring the capital and suggesting that those responsible for the new policy were naïve about Indian issues, Curzon argued, '...I think it should be known that this step [the transfer and its reversal of partition] was taken on the initiative of a viceroy ... who had only been in India a few months, of a Secretary of State who had not enjoyed his great position for a longer period, and without any reference to those officers who had been responsible for the Government of India for a period of nearly a quarter of a century.'[31] Decrying Hardinge's reversal of partition as a foolishly dangerous act, Curzon argued, 'this is the moment ... when the benefits of partition have been conclusively vindicated, when everything is going well in the new province, that a new viceroy appears on the scene and in a few weeks is enabled to inform the world that all of us have been entirely wrong'.[32] Picking up on the real reason for transferring the capital, a desire to reverse partition and thus win over Indian public opinion, Curzon claimed:

> They desire to escape the somewhat heated atmosphere of Bengal and to say good-bye to the Bengali friends for whom they have just done so much. I have some sympathy with that feeling, but do not let us be hypocritical about it. If that is the reason why you are leaving Calcutta, do not attempt to assign other reasons which are of greatly inferior importance.[33]

Curzon also attacked the general tone and nature of Hardinge's government, which he believed was strong on sentiment but weak on substance. Cuttingly, Curzon claimed,

> I dare say your lordships will remember that ... the writer of the despatch in India [Hardinge], with all the enthusiasm of a happy parent contemplating his first born offspring ... told us that this policy would excite a wave of enthusiasm throughout India, that the Mahomedan would receive it with unbound gratification, and that unprecedented satisfaction would be the attitude of the bulk of the people. I have never seen a despatch of the Government of India ... which exhibited so fine a frenzy.[34]

Though he denied it in the Lords, Curzon was particularly maddened by the fact that the transfer reversed his signature colonial policy in India, the partition of Bengal. George V's durbar proclamation wounded Curzon to the core. The near simultaneous publication of Sir Andrew (Lovat) Fraser's *India under Curzon and After* only added to the insult.[35] In the book, Fraser, who had been Lt Governor of Bengal under Curzon, argued that partition was the defining moment of Curzon's viceroyalty and that it would have a lasting impact on India.[36] Curzon became so apoplectic at times that his criticism bordered on the outrageous. In one of the first debates in the Lords concerning the transfer and its administrative changes, he told the story of a recently decorated Indian soldier who threatened to hang himself by the ribbon of a medal recently given by George V. The soldier's reason for doing so was because he was so distraught by Britain's announcement to transfer the capital and to reverse partition.[37] Curzon told the story, which he claimed came from an unimpeachable source, to highlight Britain's loss of credibility in reversing a colonial policy that the government had promised to uphold. Ending partition, for Curzon, was bad colonial policy. It sent a message to Indians and the world that Britain had lost its colonial vigour and could be influenced by anti-colonial agitation. 'The Secretary of State speaks of the removal to Delhi as proof of the unalterable determination to maintain British rule in India...' but, countered Curzon, '...how the shifting of the capital from the English city with which it has been associated for 150 years to the dead capital of Mahomedan Kings can indicate a fixed determination to maintain your rule in India, I cannot tell.'[38] The story later was proven to be utterly without merit and Curzon faced several minutes of condemnation in the House of Lords from Lords Crewe, Morley, and Ampthill, all of whom criticized Curzon for bringing up such an offensive story that later was proven to be untrue. Still, as an argumentative style, the use of the story showed how far Curzon was willing to go in his attacks on the transfer of the capital and its related political reforms.

Building on Curzon's arguments and even more importantly justifying his own signature policy, the Indian Councils Act of 1909, Lord Minto argued that the situation in India during his tenure as viceroy from 1905 to 1911 had improved. Minto claimed that when he left India 'agitation against partition was stone dead' and thus Hardinge's new policy was unnecessary.[39] Like Curzon, he complained that these important changes in colonial policy were done 'without consultation with a single soul in India outside the Viceroy's Council, and without the advice of a single public man in this country, no matter how specially qualified he might be to give it'.[40] Minto was careful not to critique Curzon's partition policy but he did allude to the fact that his Indian Councils Act helped to ease tensions in India. After describing the 'dangerously electric' political climate in which he entered office, Minto claimed, 'but before I sailed ... great administrative reforms had been introduced and many of the just claims of India had been recognized. Much already had been done to restore public confidence in the justice of British rule, and a dangerous smouldering discontent was everywhere giving way to a more friendly feeling.'[41] Minto also pointed to what many critics of the transfer believed – Hardinge and his government had been duped by a handful of Bengali agitators who fed falsehoods to supporters in England for publication in the British press. These agitators purported to speak for all Indians, according to Minto, but they actually represented a minority opinion. As he claimed:

> Bengal is full of advanced political thought and of political rami-fications which the greatest Indian expert would find difficulty in unravelling. I can find only one explanation for what has been done. A sop has been given to a certain faction in Bengal as a recompense for the removal of the capital from Delhi.[42]

If Hardinge had had more Indian experience, he would have readily recognized the truth of the situation and thus avoided the radical direction he had chosen.

MacDonnell challenged Minto on this point, claiming that he had been informed through high channels that 'the removal to Delhi has been widely taken by the native public as a wiping out of the evil memo-ries of the Indian mutiny and the establishment of the British Raj upon a fresher basis'.[43] Raising an eyebrow at Minto's claim that a faction of Bengalis were conspiring with certain British elements that supported Indian independence, MacDonnell asked, 'Will we lose anything by being relieved of touch with that native opinion which has been described to you by ... Lord Minto – that element which he regards with suspicion as apt to enter into these proceedings and correspondence of which he did not always approve?'[44]

Like MacDonnell, Morley was deeply disappointed in Minto for not supporting the transfer, and he saw Minto's support of Curzon as a betrayal of their earlier work on Indian council reform. 'For five years he and I were good comrades in a rather stormy voyage', Morley declared in reference to the debates surrounding the passage of the Indian Councils Act.[45] Upon examining Minto and Curzon's claim that expe-rienced Indian hands had not been asked about their opinions on the transfer of the capital and the reversal of partition, Morley argued, 'what would have been gained by asking their opinion upon a point which depended, *not upon old history*, not upon old arguments threshed out, but upon the present actual situation?'[46] Here, Morley was highlighting the current political fractures within the British colonial administration as well as within Parliament between those who believed their long experiences in India gave them special insight into India's soul and those who believed that India had been changed forever by its rapid development. The India of the old Indian hands was gone and thus their post-mutiny approach was not only antediluvian but damaging to

Indian progress as well. For Morley, a new way of thinking about India was required, and Hardinge's transfer of the capital and his reversal of partition were positive steps in India's political evolution. He especially applauded Hardinge for having the courage to do something that he simply could not do during his tenure as Secretary of State, reversing Curzon's partition of Bengal. According to Morley, while he had wanted to reverse partition as early as December 1906 and was strongly encouraged by many of his closest friends and political colleagues to do so, he could not touch this sensitive subject for fear of damaging his own attempt to pass council reforms.[47]

Similar debates about the transfer of the capital and its related reforms occurred in the House of Commons as well. During the 1912 and 1913 East India Budget debates, Montagu encouraged his fellow members to see India as a 'progressive country' that was inexorably and rapidly moving toward a new national reality.[48] In this emerging world, there was no room for the old methods of colonial rule. For those who wanted to bring back the old days of partition, Montagu claimed, 'the *maxim divide et impera* – one of the most dangerous maxims – has no place in our textbook of statesmanship'.[49] He warned his fellow members in Parliament, 'you cannot now, even if you would, embark on a policy of reaction. The mighty mass in India is moving in response to our own stimulus, and to try and force it back into condition of sleeps, which would now be an unwilling sleep, and could only be achieved, if it could be achieved, by repression, would be a calamity-producing blunder.'[50] Curzon's partition, which had stirred rather than diminished Bengal's anti-colonialism, had more than shown the folly of repressive colonial policies aimed at tamping down Indian nationalism. Slapping back criticism emanating from old India hands, Montagu warned, '...India is never the same today as it was yesterday, and will never be the same tomorrow as it is today, the man who relies on out-of-date knowledge ... is a man whose advice must not be accepted without question.'[51] Pointing squarely at what he saw as the end of the post-rebellion conservative colonial system, he chastised those men of the old guard 'who regret the good old days when they were sent out to govern the people, who were content to be governed, and lament the fact that they have now to co-operate with the people and the Government of India. With all respect and all recognition for their services in the past, we do not want these men in India.'[52]

Montagu's warning was a direct rebuttal of Curzon and his allies' claims that those who supported colonial reform did not understand the needs of India. No one could argue that Curzon and other experienced India hands were unknowledgeable about India. The problem was that this knowledge had grown stale and did not account for India's great social and economic transformations, which could only be add-ressed through deeper British and Indian interactions made possible by political reform. These reforms might have unintended consequences, but, according to Montagu, '...if we are to do our duty by the enormous responsibilities which we have undertaken we must move forward, however cautiously, accepting the consequences of our own acts and inspirations, and keeping ourselves informed as intimately as we possi-bly can of the modern and changing aspects of the problem with which we have to deal.'[53]

Fleetwood Wilson, writing from India as Finance Minister to the Government of India, agreed with Montagu and Morley's views that colonial rule without the consent of the governed no longer worked in India. 'The old dispensation answered well enough in the past,' claimed Wilson, '...but it [was] unsuited to present day conditions.'[54] A little over a year after his arrival in India in 1908, Wilson held a large dinner party at the Bengal Club in Calcutta for all members of the newly reformed and enlarged legislative council, which now included expanded numbers of elected Indian officials because of the Indian Councils Act. When Wilson approached more experienced colonial officers about the idea, they 'threw the coldest of cold water on the proposal', telling him that 'Indians would resent it – Mahomedans would object to dine with Hindoos and *vice versa* – high caste and low caste would decline to meet – Europeans would keep away – I did not know India – this sort of thing would not do – and so forth.'[55] Wilson ignored the concerns of these experienced officers and threw the party anyway. The result, according to Wilson, was a well-attended party that 'was warm and appreciative' and 'proved that you have only to get Indians and Indians and English and Indians to rub shoulders unof-ficially to obtain a very happy result'.[56] What Wilson also learned from the experience was that the old India hands no longer understood the social and political dynamics of India. Though new to India and the issues it faced, he believed he had a better sense of the way forward than experienced officials. The problem with these men, for Wilson, was their insularity. They were products of both an India that no longer existed and an out-dated colonial view that had been shaped by the events of 1857. As he claimed, the 'early impressions they received [of India] appear to dominate their views'.[57] As a result, Wilson explained, 'I have already learnt that as a general rule the most unreliable opinion is that of men who have passed most of their lives in India. They seem unable to appreciate to their full extent the vital, incessant, and very rapid changes which are taking place in India.'[58] The worst of these men knew much about India but little of the world. As Wilson claimed, 'It is the wider knowledge of the world rather than the restricted knowledge of India which I have so often found lacking in those who have to guide the destinies of this country.'[59]

Old India hands did not take the criticism lying down. J. D. Rees, in particular, was angered by members of Parliament who had little or no Indian experience but still passed judgments both on issues facing India and on men who had spent their best years in India.[60] Rees ended his response to Montagu's 1912 presentation of the East India Revenue Accounts in the House of Commons by angrily declaring, 'it is better to be sunbaked in India than to be hide-bound with arrogance in England'.[61] The following year Rees again turned his anger on Montagu who had travelled to India to get a sense of the major issues facing the colonial government. Rees complained, 'I do think that he [Montagu] should have followed the precedent set by another Gentleman, Mr. Curzon, and that he should have become an Orientalist before taking office.'[62] The transfer of the capital and its related changes exemplified, for critics like Rees, the present government's hubris, inadequacy, and the need to hold the line against colonial reform.

A new vision for a new kind of raj: paragraph three of the official dispatch to transfer the capital

Both supporters of the new policy and those that criticized it pointed to the language of the official dispatch announcing the transfer of the capital and its related administrative changes. In particular, paragraph three, which called for the devolution of political power to a greater number of Indians, was used as evidence that Hardinge's government had forever changed British rule in India. John L. Jenkins, Home Secretary to the Government of India, crafted the language found in the paragraph during the original transfer deliberations in the second half of 1911. For him, the day was coming when India would be a federation of autonomous provinces with Indians making decisions at the provincial level but with the British still holding the reigns of ultimate power at the centre with the viceroy in council.[63] The stability of this type of colonial structure required that the capital not be associated closely with any one province. Thus, Jenkins welcomed the decision to transfer the capital to Delhi because, as the new heart and soul of British-India, it would help 'facilitate the development of the government along sound and safe lines'.[64]

Curzon and his allies, however, were concerned by paragraph three's political implications, which transformed both the structure of colonial government and the relationship between the provinces of British-India and the viceroy in council. Coupled with the earlier Indian Councils Act, the new policy not only encouraged Indians to have a greater voice in government, it outlined how they would realize it through a federal form of colonial government. For Curzon, the paragraph 'was a very compromising, a very unnecessary, and a very unwise declaration'.[65] Hardinge's new policy represented 'a scheme or a sketch of the future Government of India wholly different from that which has hitherto prevailed', argued Curzon.[66] This new direction in imperial rule, now much more than a proposal but the stated wish of the king-emperor, was a major shift in what had been a hyper-centralized post-mutiny government. While the British-dominated centre, now at Delhi, would continue to control all-India political subjects such as the military, the police, and foreign policy, the provinces of British-India would eventually gain control over purely provincial matters. Lansdowne, too, immediately realized the nature of these reforms. 'It is intimated', he pointed out in the Lords, 'that what the Government of India have in their mind is an ultimate arrangement under which there would be a number of autonomous governments with a Viceroy directing the whole system from some central point, where he would be cut off equally from all those autonomous Governments.'[67] For Lansdowne, this kind of devolution as outlined in the dispatch might prove to be good or bad, but he poignantly argued, 'it certainly is not a policy into which we ought to be rushed in the manner in which we are being rushed into these other changes'.[68] Connecting events in India to Ireland, Lansdowne claimed, 'If His Majesty's Government really carry out their craze for devolution to the extent that they are meditating – if they contemplate the introduction in India of some federal system of the kind which apparently they have in view for parts of the empire nearer home – they raise a vast question of policy which ought surely to be fully discussed and examined before we are committed.'[69]

Curzon also connected paragraph three's call for devolution in India to similar calls for Irish Home rule. He admitted that some devolution of political powers had taken place in the past and that more would necessarily occur in the future, but the policy proclaimed by the Government of India via the king was on a different scale altogether. With well-known hyperbole, Curzon pointed directly at Asquith's liberal government and claimed that this sort of 'Home Rule all around abandon[ed] that uniformity in the main principles of government, in the guiding tenets of your administration, ... I venture to say the result can only be to lead through disruption to disaster'.[70] Worse, for Curzon, these liberal tendencies to move colonies toward responsible government were weakening rather than strengthening Britain's position in India. Curzon claimed during the first reading of the bill in the House of Lords:

> My fear about this establishment of the capital at Delhi is that your central government, instead of becoming stronger, will become weaker. My view is that you will become disassociated from the life and administration of India, and that gradually, as the Provinces follow the line you have laid down and demand increasing Home Rule, your viceroy in Delhi will become a sort of puppet as the Moguls were towards the end of their regime, and India will break up into separate fragments, as it did in the expiring days of Aurungzeb and his successors.[71]

Curzon, who saw himself as a student of Indian history and as viceroy had taken keen interest in preserving Indian architecture and monuments, could not help but connect the present British Raj to the end days of the Mughal Empire. The splintering of the latter had been forced by *nawabs* (provincial governors) who had grown more powerful than their Mughal emperor. Thus, for Curzon, devolution's weakening of central authority was a sign that Britain, much like the previous Mughal Empire, had reached the end days of its own imperial rule in India. 'It is not by divided governments that the Indian empire has been built,' Curzon explained, 'but by the existence of a strong central authority, controlling and supervising all, which you have persuaded in times past the best of your statesmen and administrators to take up, and which have taken up to the advantage of India and the credit of our country'.[72] Even after Crewe's avowal that devolution would strengthen British rule, Curzon argued, 'When trouble comes ... it will not be by separate provinces acting on their own account that India will be saved, but by a strong central government exercising supervision and control over all.'[73] For Curzon and his allies, any strengthening of the provinces at the expense of the centre was seen as a dangerous path.

   Curzon and his allies' critiques concerning the transfer's related policy of devolution forced Crewe to address in more detail the meaning of paragraph three. Crewe explained during the first reading of the bill in the Lords that the Government of India did not intend to institute a federal system of government immediately. Instead, Hardinge's reason for writing paragraph three 'was to draw attention to the general trend and tendency of the form of Government in India',[74] which was, namely, 'the devolution of power to be conceded ... without impairing the supreme authority of the Governor-General in Council'.[75] During the second reading of the bill in June 1912, Curzon reminded his audience about Crewe's earlier clarification but lamented that recent pronouncements made by Montagu proved otherwise. Curzon quoted from a speech given by Montagu at Cambridge, just days after Crewe's above explanation:

> We have endeavoured to look ahead to coordinate our changes in Bengal with the general lines of our future policy in India, which is stated now for the first time in the Government of India's Despatch that has been published as a Parliamentary Paper ... We cannot drift on for ever without stating a policy. The [Indian] moderates look to us to say what lines our future policy is to take. We have put off answering them for too long. At last, and not too soon, a Viceroy has had the courage to state the trend of British policy in India and the lines on which we propose to advance.[76]

For Curzon, 'Nothing ... could have been more direct, more explicit, more unmistakable than the interpretation put by the Under-Secretary of State upon that passage in the Despatch.'[77] Claiming that Montagu's speech was no 'accidental platform aberration', Curzon pointed to a later statement made by Montagu in the House of Commons in April 1912. When asked in the Commons about paragraph three, Montagu stated:

> The Viceroy showed that there was some definite aim and object to which, in the opinion of the Government of India, all these changes might be correlated; that we were there (in India) not merely to administer but to develop India on a plan which had been thought out by those who had been advising the Secretary of State. That is as I understand the meaning of paragraph three, and as such I regard it as one of the most important parts of that historic Despatch.[78]

The problem, argued Curzon, was that although Crewe and Montagu placed different stress on the importance of paragraph three, public opinion in India had settled on the latter's interpretation. Curzon evidenced this by quoting the views of the *Bengali*, a newspaper that held some of India's most advanced nationalist views, 'It was the prospect of autonomous self-government in all provincial affairs which largely reconciled the Bengalis to the deposition of Calcutta.'[79] Curzon also related a speech given by the moderate nationalist leader Gopal Gokhale, who argued:

> [Indians] had to work for attaining in practice that equality with Englishmen which was already theirs in theory, and under pledges solemnly given; and in that connection they could now take their stand on the memorable announcement of policy made at Delhi ... a policy to which the word, not only of the Government of India or the Secretary of State, but in a way that of the king-emperor himself, now stood committed. That policy was the policy of autonomy for the different provinces. Whatever attempts might now be made to explain away the passages in the Despatch which bear on the point ... the passages were there, and they in India were entitled to take their stand on them, and ask for the realization of the policy contained in them.[80]

During the East India Budget Debate of 1912 in the Commons, George Wyndham also raised the question of paragraph three's potential to rouse Indian demands for greater autonomy. Wyndham asked the Government of India to refrain from 'announcing a policy in terms which are capable of misinterpretation in India, and which may be felt to mean more there ... than the Government means looking into the far future, and more than it is within their power or their intention to perform in the near future'.[81] Likewise, Lord Ronaldshay urged the government to be more simple and clear in its policy language for India, for 'it is very unfortunate that language of an ambiguous kind would be used by spokesmen of the Government when they are making declarations of policy which excite hopes in India which clearly cannot be fulfilled'.[82]

In the Lords, Crewe responded to the above warnings about a public Indian outcry or a radicalization of Indian national sentiment caused by paragraph three. 'I have heard nothing', claimed Crewe, 'from a very close study both of the European and the native press, or from any other source at my disposal, which makes me think that any change of opinion adverse to this project of ours has taken place since his majesty left India in January.'[83] Additionally, Crewe argued that if one were to examine the various allusions to devolution made by viceroys and Secretaries of State, 'we should often find ... the expression of hopes that, as education spread and as the sense of responsibility grew, more influence and more actual power should be placed in the hands of local Governments and of local bodies than it is possible to place at present'.[84] Crewe pointed to Curzon, the most vocal critic of the transfer and its devolution, as emblematic of this trend. On at least two different occasions, once during a budget speech in 1904 and again during a dinner given by the United Service Club at Simla in 1905, Curzon had called for devolution in matters of provincial revenue and expenditure. Describing Curzon's policy whereby local governments were given more permanent control over their revenues and expenditures, Crewe quoted Curzon as saying, 'this we succeeded in doing in the case of Madras, Bengal, the United Provinces, and Assam, and have thereby laid the foundation of national autonomy which I hope will steadily develop and enable the local governments in the future to undertake enterprises from which they are now debarred'.[85] Curzon later explained to his United Service Club listeners that in matters of finance he had settled in favour of local governments, because 'there cannot be much autonomy where there are not financial resources'.[86] When Curzon's government was accused of over-centralization, Curzon claimed during his 1904 budget speech that 'if the occasion has anywhere arisen where it was possible to develop or depute powers it was taken. This new settlement constituted a most important step ... and will, I hope, be the forerunner of others in the future.'[87] Thus, for Crewe, Curzon's rejection of devolution was purely political theatre and a direct contradiction of policies that he himself had pursued at times while viceroy.

According to Crewe, paragraph three's call for intelligent political reforms also created political conditions that encouraged Indians to consent more readily to British colonial rule. Again, using Curzon's own dinner speech, Crewe quoted Curzon's remarks that India needed 'a strong Government of India holding the reins, but it ought to ride the local governments "on the snaffle and not on the curb" ... I would do all in my power to consult their feelings, to enhance their dignity, and to stimulate their sense of responsibility and power.'[88] For Crewe, these words, made only several years earlier by Curzon, was precisely the foundation upon which the Government of India should build its rule in the twentieth century. 'If you say that your duty is to stimulate the sense, not merely of responsibility, but of power in the minds of a local Government, the local Governments will undoubtedly think that what you desire to do is to enlarge within the limits which you have stated the actual measure of those powers.'[89] In this regard, the political devolution called for in paragraph three of the dispatch was not novel; it had been the trend in British rule for some time.

Still, Crewe was not ready to advise that India was ready to become a dominion along the same lines as Canada for example. After being repeatedly pushed by opponents to take a stand on the interpretation of paragraph three, Crewe finally admitted, 'I do not believe that the experiment ... of attempting to confer a measure of real self-government, with practical freedom from Parliamentary control, ... is one which could be tried.'[90] Still, he felt it was Britain's duty 'to encourage in every reasonable and possible way the desire of the inhabitants of India to take a further part in the management of their own affairs'.[91] For Crewe, this elevation of Indians to positions of influence was a personal matter, 'I therefore will never have it said of me that I am indifferent to, or could be unmindful of the ambitions of Indians with the capacity and distinction to serve their country in the fullest degree and to the best advantage.'[92] Curzon had attempted to colour the official dispatch to transfer the capital as a sign of the Government's unwillingness to maintain strong imperial rule in India, but Crewe described a vision of empire where well-deserving colonial subjects should be given greater political responsibility. Yet this political empowerment for Indians was always within a British imperial framework where British power was paramount.

Whereas Crewe and even Hardinge showed later signs of softening on paragraph three, Montagu experienced no misgivings about the new vision it formulated. During the East India Budget Debate in 1912, Montagu argued that the spread of English education in India had stirred Indian national aspirations. 'I would express once again my belief that there is a growing spirit of nationality in India, the direct product and construction of British rule', he claimed.[93] Educated Indians across India might speak different languages, but 'they come together to discuss the affairs of the nation which is growing under British rule in the language of the British people'.[94] This emergence of Indian national identity could not be turned back, as Curzon had attempted to do with his disastrous partition policy, but there was no reason why the British government could not incorporate this energy into the imperial system with intelligent political reforms. As Montagu argued:

There is an old doctrine that we govern India by the sword. I do not want now to dispute the fundamental truth, but I want to assert ... that it is because we also govern India by the consent of those who know, and by the cheerful and willing acquiescence of those who do not realize all that it means, that his Majesty's welcome was so wide and so real as it was last year.[95]

While it was unclear what type of society would emerge in India due to devolution, Montagu claimed that it would reflect what he believed was the internal spirit and driving force behind both cultures:

> Nobody can possibly foretell what will be the eventual characteristic of the population we shall form in India; the India which must be a heritage, not only of its Asiatic population alone, but also of that small handful of Europeans who have unified it, giving it its trend, brought to it its traditions and its ideals, and which must be reckoned in its destinies. There is a trite quotation ... that the 'east is east and west is west' ... But, as a great Bengali writer [Rabindranath Tagore] has laid it down, the east and west must meet at the 'altar of humanity'.[96]

This meeting between east and west would be made more amicable by pursuing political reforms that encouraged greater political interaction between Indians and the British. Only in this way, claimed Montagu, could this meeting of both cultures be made 'not with clash or discord, but in harmony and amity'.[97] When comparing the geniuses of the two nations, he claimed, '...the forces are not mutually destructive, they are mutually complimentary. Each has learnt much and has much to learn from the religion, the art, and the philosophy of the other.'[98] The strengths of both could be melded into a new British-India where 'the ascetism of the Oriental, the simplicity of his code of life, and the modesty of his bodily needs, are meeting the restless spirit of progress in material things, the love of realism, the craving for the concrete, and the striving towards advancement which come from the west'.[99] The building of a new capital based on the combined ideals of Britain and India would realize Tagore's 'altar of humanity'.

The foundation of political reform: education, opportunity, consent

The problem for Hardinge's Government of India and the India Office in London was to offer Indians political reform while never losing the ultimate authority of the viceroy in council. This meant locating and working with the right kind of Indian during this grand devolution experiment. Reminiscent of Thomas Babington Macaulay's famous 'Minute on Indian Education' in 1835, Montagu believed that the process of devolution would be greatly aided by a focus on educational reforms. Just as Macaulay had claimed that 'we must ... do our best to form a ... class of persons, Indian in blood and colour, but English in taste, in opinions, in morals, and in intellect',[100] Montagu argued that a greater focus on education in India would create a class of Indian willing to work with rather than against the British. It was an idea shared by Morley and Wilson as well. They argued that this class's desire for greater responsibility in the government of their own country was the inevitable and logical outcome of Britain's introduction into India of western education. Morley provided what he believed were the reasons for this new atmosphere in India. After describing the tremendous influence on himself of Milton, Burke, Macaulay, Mill, and Spencer, Morley eloquently asked:

> Who can be surprised that educated Indians who read these high masters and teachers of ours are intoxicated with the ideas of freedom, nationality, self-government, that breathes the breath of life in those inspiring and illuminating pages? Who of us that had the privilege in the days of our youth, at college or at home, of turning over those golden chapters, and seeing that lustrous firmament dawn over youthful imaginations, – who of us can forget, shall I call it the intoxication and rapture, with which we strove to make friends with truth, knowledge, beauty, freedom? Then why should we be surprised that young Indians feel the same movement of mind when they are made free [by] our own immortals?[101]

Wilson could not have agreed more about the transformational power of education and its importance to the hegemonic vision that the transfer of the capital championed. What is wanted in India is light, he claimed, 'more light, always light, and it is education alone which will give us that light'.[102] Sounding much like Montagu, the primary lesson that Wilson had learned during his time in India was 'trust and confidence in the Indian people ... Let the appeal be made to trust and confidence – and there is nothing that educated Indians will not do, there is no sacrifice they will not make for the maintenance of British rule'.[103] Education was moving India toward a better future, for Wilson, 'Only let there be more mutual trust, more mutual confidence, more mutual good-will, for these are the bonds with which the fabric of every great empire is strengthened.'[104]

Montagu described the importance of educational reforms in India during the East India budget debate in 1912, 'if the educational ideal which we have in mind is realized, we will have laid the foundation of a national system of education by a network of really valuable schools, colleges, and universities, so that facilities will be opened to Indians to qualify themselves in their own country for the highest positions in every walk in life'.[105] Yet this was only the first step in a successful process of devolution. As Montagu argued, 'the problem before us when we have educated Indians is to give them the fullest opportunity in the government of their own country to exercise the advantages which they have acquired by training and education'.[106] Because of these advances it was necessary, according to Montagu, to 'distinguish and segregate legitimate aspirations for advancement from sedition'.[107]

Wilson agreed with Montagu's stance on the connection between education and opportunity. Yes, there were sporadic anti-colonial outbursts, for Wilson, but it could be dealt with through colonial reforms that encouraged cooperation rather than intrigue. Wilson defined India's unrest as either impulsive unrest or resultant unrest. Impulsive unrest represented a sudden impulse to change one's conditions; it was a spontaneous and sporadic desire for something different. In contrast, resultant unrest, which he believed characterized much Indian anti-colonialism, stemmed from 'prolonged and often misdirected thought, tending to dwell upon and develop a sense of injury'.[108] The West, according to Wilson, had offered Indians 'a new view of life', but with this 'rapid and wholesale increase in intercommunication, the spread of knowledge born of western education, and the self-reliance created by more accurate knowledge of western conditions, there has radiated from the educated Indians a sense of undue subordination to an alien race'.[109] After giving an important sector of Indian society western ideals, it was 'idle to suppose that a mild despotism [could] remain acceptable to the India of the twentieth century', Wilson argued.[110] Thus, it was important not to be carried away by 'sporadic outbursts' as indicative of the entire nation.[111] India had its loyal moderates like Gokhale and its disloyal extremists who assassinated government officials. The method for dealing with both was to 'do nothing to drive the former into the arms of the latter'.[112] There was nothing to fear if the Government of India responded to Indian demands with intelligent reforms that ameliorated their sense of injury. What made reform even more important was that, according to Wilson, many educated Indians still looked to Britain for answers. As evidence he pointed to the words of Sir Krishna Gupta, who had served in high positions in the Government of India, 'While there is a growing consciousness in India of the inevitable drawbacks of alien rule, there is also widespread conviction that national salvation can be attained under the fostering care and guidance of Britain.'[113] For Wilson, what the 'best minds among the Indians' hope for is not independence from Britain but self-government 'so that she may take her place in the empire not as a mere dependency but on terms of equality and coordination'.[114]

Reaching out to the right kind of Indian was a perfect example of how the Government of India would achieve a new hegemony in India. Educated Indians would be given opportunities for employment in high office in the civil service and thus rewarded for their loyalty and administrative skills. After chastising those in the commons who held to a post-mutiny vision of empire where Indians and Britons remained aloof, Montagu argued, '[We do not] want to listen for one moment to those men who tell us that they do not like the educated Indian, and that the educated Indian does not like us.'[115] For those critics who saw in devolution the end of empire, Montagu chided, 'the old era of hard and fast division between government and the governed on racial lines has long ago disappeared. The watchword of the future is co-operation. We are pledged to advance, and we mean to advance, but it must be steadily and prudently.'[116] 'The progressive section of the Indian community' simply needed to be patient; political reform and greater involvement in the colonial government eventually would come to them.[117]

This new vision for India would not be easy to realize but it was absolutely essential to create a stable and prosperous India, one that remained in the British Empire even as it gained greater responsible government. As Montagu argued, 'after all, what did we go to India for? If the people of India have not made any progress under British rule, if the problems of the government are still today what they were a hundred years ago, or in the days of Lord Clive, then I think we have failed in our justification.'[118] Much as MacDonnell had argued about the importance of winning back Indian confidence in British rule, which had been damaged by hard line policies such as partition, Montagu claimed that the government's focus on education would help rebuild trust. Montagu encouraged his parliamentary colleagues not to fear educated Indians but to attempt to win over their opinion, 'Our part, difficult and worthy, is to bring the educated Indian on to our side, and to go on helping him in order that he may help us, or to ask him to help us in order that we may go on helping him.'[119]

For Montagu, increasing India's prosperity and its material advancement by building new schools, universities, and even hospitals was simply the first step. It needed to be followed by a new kind of colonial government based on cooperation that gave an Indian 'increasing opportunity in the country which is his own, and increasing assistance in the development of his capacity for local government and administration'.[120] What this meant was that Britain needed to be better prepared to address the current and future demands of their Indian civil servants.[121] By 1913, Montagu had determined three interconnected areas that were problematic: government salaries that did not keep pace with the rising cost of living in India; the growing complexity of a colonial bureaucracy that led to over-work; and persistent attacks made by parliamentary members on the Indian Civil Service. The service was over-worked and under-paid in comparison to the private sector. Both problems led to diminished work performance that opened the service to parliamentary criticism. With administrative complexity came increased reporting by civil service officers. 'I have heard of an officer', claimed Montagu, 'who said that when he joined the service a small number of rules was sufficient to guide him when he went into camp; now he has to pack a portmanteau with codes and regulations'.[122] This avalanche of regulations, rules and guidelines overburdened the colonial official and it constrained the initiative of civil servants who put their energy into writing reports.[123] Rules were important in that they created transparency for parliamentary oversight. But over-regulation had created a systemic problem that was apparent in all levels of the Indian government, from the district officer at the bottom to the Secretary of State at the top, where each level of the colonial administration was writing reports for the next higher level of government. For Montagu, there was a simple solution to this burdensome overload of paperwork: devolution. 'We must seek to find indigenous voluntary agencies to conduct a large amount of our detailed work', argued Montagu.[124] This would ease the administrative burden placed on British officers and give Indians greater responsibility in the colonial government. Yet Montagu saw devolution as much more than simply expanding the Indian clerical establishment. Though Indians had served in the Indian Civil Service as clerks for generations, devolution would open the doors to positions of greater influence in the colonial administration. Though Montagu did not believe that Indians and Europeans would approach government responsibilities in the same way, he nonetheless claimed, 'Even if there be some loss of efficiency, even if a district board be worse run, a municipal body be less capable, we ought to find the indigenous agency in India which will alone ensure our progress being real and complete.'[125] This structural transformation in how the Raj used its human resources was a necessary next step in Britain's Indian Empire. As Montagu declared, 'All these things are a matter of degree, and, as times goes on and you take steps in India to bring the government more and more face to face with the people, every step you take in India in that direction ought to lesson control here.'[126]

Wilson had made similar claims in 1910. He wrote in his Indian diary, 'the human equation is a factor which cannot be ignored, and it is but human to prefer reasonably good government administered by one's own race rather than extreme efficiency at the hands of an alien race'.[127] Wilson added, '... whilst the English race is absolutely the first in the creation of a colony, it inclines to ignore that the child has grown up ... Undoubtedly British India is not yet ripe for self-government, but if all goes well it very soon will be, and if British India is to continue, prudent statesmanship will plough the self-government furrow and put the seed into it.'[128] At the end of his tenure in 1913 as Finance Secretary to the Indian government, Wilson claimed that India's atmosphere had improved 'from dark and sullen to hopeful' because of the Indian Councils Act and Hardinge's promises of further devolution.[129] His perception that British-Indian relations had improved in the last several years as well as his friendship with such educated Indian moderates as Gokhale caused him to go farther than even Montagu dared. Wilson called for Indian self-government, a term few British officials, even those who believed in reform, would use to describe the general trend and purpose of British rule. Most officials, including Crewe, Hardinge, and Montagu, used the term 'responsible government' because 'self-government' was likely to be read by Indians as independence. The ambiguity of the term responsible government, on the other hand, gave the British greater latitude in the introduction of political reform and the speed by which it was introduced. Even Wilson counselled patience. At a farewell dinner given to him by Indians in Simla in June 1913, he warned:

> Do not condemn our English honesty and veracity if you find that we move very slowly forward towards the goal of your hopes. Do not mistake that slowness for want of faith ... We do wish to be absolutely honourable in our conduct towards India. That is part of our conception of an English gentleman. But you will always find us politically hesitating and almost over cautious. We test one step ... before we take another ... That is our nature ... do not be surprised at all this caution, but expect it from us and never look for anything else, or you will be disappointed.[130]

The words were aimed at moderates like his friend Gokhale who were willing to work within constitutional means to bring about change. Self-government would come more quickly, more fully, and with more stability by working with the British through the constitutional process.

If Indians pushed too rapidly for reform, if self-government was forced rather than freely given, then chaos and revolution would ensue. His words also were meant for fellow British officials who he hoped would continue enacting and supporting political reform in India. He ended his dinner speech with the line, 'Let East and West combine to allow naught to overcloud that promising sky.'[131] Wilson's warning was clear; the advances recently made to reduce tension between the colonial government and Indian elites could be easily reversed by undue British hesitation. After witnessing repeated attacks on the New Delhi scheme, Wilson warned, 'The real danger which confronts us lies in a policy of alternate repression and concession, a refusal to grant reforms ungrudgingly and in time, and a failure to fully recognize the inevitable effect of our own introduction into India of western education and western ideals.'[132]

Much as John Darwin has warned, it would be a great mistake to see these reformers as galloping defeatists who could not wait for the end of empire.[133] Indeed, Hardinge, Crewe, Montagu, Wilson and their allies were staunch supporters of empire and saw their policy of devolution as the only way to secure British rule in an India whose development was rapidly creating a class of Indian who desired more say in their own governance. The only way forward in these political and social conditions was to encourage greater Indian involvement in the work of the colonial government by offering policies that empowered the right class of Indian.[134] Thus, the cause of Britain's so-called Indian problem, the introduction of western education, was also its answer. This was a dramatically different vision from the one that had dominated India since the end of the Indian uprising in 1857, but the intended results were the same, namely, to secure British rule in India. For Curzon and his allies, this security best arose from a strong, centralized British colonial government. For Hardinge and his supporters, however, this view had led to the recent colonial agitation and outrages that had paralysed the administration of Bengal. The genius of New Delhi as a colonial strategy was that in its hegemonic symbolism it represented the visions of both Curzon's old guard and Hardinge's reformers. Though the Government of India had yet to design its new capital and, indeed, still had not determined a suitable building site in the Delhi area, the city eventually built would be both a symbol of colonial coercion and colonial consent.

4
Colonial Finance and the Building of New Delhi: The High Cost of Reform

The transfer of the capital and its related administrative changes introduced not only a new colonial ideology but also a new financial model for how the Government of India did its business. As such, the purpose and meaning of empire was transformed in ways that were even more controversial perhaps than the proposed political reforms that were associated with the building of the new capital. Some of the most heated debates about Hardinge's new colonial vision had to do with its cost, which included not just the building of a new capital and other administrative changes but also the potential ramifications the transfer would have on Indian commerce and the financial health of the British Empire. Some critics feared that the Government of India's effort to realize Hardinge's new vision for India would negatively impact Indian and London financial markets. There was only so much investment capital available, and now a large amount of it would be shifted toward a building project and related colonial reforms that many in Parliament and the financial world found questionably beneficial. The consequences were clear to men deeply involved in or representing the interests of finance capitalists. Moneys that should have gone into revenue-making investment opportunities such as railroads would now go to non-revenue yielding government expansion. Hence, many people in Parliament and in the commercial world saw the transfer as an extravagant waste of money that drained precious capital from proven revenue-making ventures in India. If they were sceptical of the colonial ideology grounding the Government of India's new stress on devolution and its political reforms, they were absolutely threatened by the government's strategy for raising the necessary capital to build New Delhi.

After repeated calls from Members of Parliament to provide an estimate for the transfer and building of a new capital at Delhi, the

Government of India announced that the cost would be no greater than £4,000,000.[1] As many people immediately recognized, the number was overly optimistic and misleading since it did not include the entire cost of the transfer and its related policies.[2] Lord Ronaldshay, in the Commons, estimated the cost to be £10,000,000 to build the new capital and as high as £50,000,000 when the transfer's related administrative changes and reforms were included. In the Lords, Curzon found the £4,000,000 estimate laughable and suggested that the real cost for just the new capital was more likely to be £8,000,000 to £12,000,000. Likewise, Lord Midleton was unconvinced about the Government of India's proposed estimate and called for a more realistic and detailed statement of the overall cost of the broad new proposals. He did not want to go back necessarily on the king's durbar proclamation but to resist the immediate transfer of the government to Delhi until the cost of the plan could be better studied. Caught off guard by the secrecy surrounding the king's proclamation, Midleton called for delay in the hope of influencing the transfer after the fact, 'I cannot help asking the noble Marquess [Crewe] whether he has gone too far to make it impossible for him, not to change his policy, but to stop this, as it seems to us, gratuitous destruction of the existing system before it has been fully realized what the cost will be.'[3] The royal and very public nature of the announcement to transfer the capital created a difficult political climate, as Hardinge and Crewe knew it would, for opponents in Parliament to criticize the proposal. Still, Midleton claimed, 'I am certain that it is not only more loyal on our part but more far seeing to endeavour to secure that his majesty's proclamation is carried out economically, rather than allow the change to Delhi to lie like a millstone round the neck of the other services.'[4] Midleton asked that the Government of India show greater patience and not rush into the transfer of the capital until it had 'a real scheme for making good this great change – a scheme the presentation of which ought ... to have preceded the proclamation rather than follow it'.[5] Here, Midleton was speaking for all critics who were angered that such an expansive and expensive colonial policy was never publicly debated in Parliament.

The Government of India, as opponents of the transfer well knew, had no real sense of what the cost would be to transfer the capital and to make its prescribed administrative changes. Curzon pointed to the Government of India's budget debate in Calcutta in March 1912 as evidence. Fleetwood Wilson, India's Finance Minister, had admitted that the government was 'not yet in possession of any estimates of the cost', even seven months after the transfer had been approved.[6]

Curzon lamented that the lack of details about the transfer's finances was 'unprecedented in the financial history of this country or of India, or … any civilized country'.[7] Based on his past experience as Viceroy of India, Curzon provided a much more thorough list of what Hardinge's government would need to spend to achieve all its goals as described in their official dispatch to transfer the capital. The building of new government structures to house the viceroy and the various departments of India were only part of the cost to build a new capital. Other significant costs included land acquisition and compensation, the building of a new cantonment to protect the capital, the building of temporary housing while the new capital was being erected, the building of a country retreat near Delhi for the viceroy, and the shifting of railway lines and canals. After learning that the official town planning committee sent to India to select a building site had determined that the European civil lines were inadequate for the future capital's needs, Curzon added that all the moneys previously invested in lighting, roads, railways, water supply, and structures for the recent durbar ceremonies would be lost since all these improvements occurred in an area far to the north of where the capital was going to be built. The estimate also did not account for the administrative changes that would take place across India. The Government of India planned to build a new university at Dacca, which Curzon argued was a salve to placate eastern Bengali Muslims who had lost their own province due to the transfer policy's reversal of partition. The new government buildings at Dacca, which had been the capital of East Bengal during partition, would never be used and the government buildings at Calcutta would become vacant.[8] Additionally, the newly created province of Bihar and Orissa would receive a new capital costing between £333,000 and £500,000 to build, a summer station for the Lt Governor costing tens of thousands more, a board of revenue costing £13,000 per annum, an executive council costing £13,300, and the potential building of a new university at Patna to balance the university at Dacca. Bihar and Orissa and the Central Provinces would require new buildings to house their high courts and legislative councils as well. Lastly, the government's Commerce and Industry Department would need to have its staff increased to assuage fears about the removal of the capital from Calcutta, which in the past had kept the government in close communication with India's commercial interests. In total, Curzon listed eighteen additional expenditures that were connected to the transfer of the capital but had not been accounted for in the £4,000,000 estimate. The consequences were clear, argued Curzon, much of the capital invested in the transfer and its related changes to the bureaucratic machinery of the Government of India would be wasted on increasing the size and complexity of the British Raj with little added benefit to the nation's gross national product. The real loser in this reckless experiment, according to Curzon, was the Indian taxpayer who was having a 'millstone' hung round his neck 'which will weigh him down for many years to come'.[9]

Crewe defended the Government of India's vague estimate for the transfer and its ancillary costs as strategic: 'I must point out that to decide at this stage what you are prepared to spend either upon your governmental buildings, upon your municipal buildings, or your Government House would be ... unwise.'[10] A government could choose to spend moderately or exorbitantly, for Crewe, and be proven to be correct on both accounts. For Crewe, 'It surely requires the fullest consideration and the nicest balancing of advantages and disadvantages, after you have been able to get the best plans and the ideas of the best minds at your disposal, as to whether you are prepared to go into a scale of what might be called extravagant expenditure in order to get a building which, besides being serviceable, would also be of the nature of a great national monument.'[11] Thus, the estimate of £4,000,000, as Crewe explained, was simply a working figure. The Government of India was in no way limited to that number. Ultimately, expenditures for any given year would depend on the economic health of India.

The transfer's financial impact on Indian commerce

Curzon and his allies remained unconvinced by Crewe's defence of the estimate and continued their attacks in both the Commons and the Lords throughout 1912 and 1913. In particular, they focused their criticism on two related areas: what would the building of a new imperial capital do to Indian finances and how would it damage India's commercial interests? As they did so, they drew comparisons between Calcutta, the commercial centre of Britain's Indian Empire, and Delhi, a city rich in imperial history but relatively isolated from India's most important port cities and their business communities. The two cities represented entirely different historical trajectories for Curzon. Delhi's rapid decline from greatness in Mughal India was matched only by Calcutta's equally rapid rise as one of the great imperial cities of the world.[12] Compared to Calcutta's business community and its importance to Britain's maritime commercial empire, Delhi had become a mere industrial and railway town that produced and moved manufactured and agricultural goods from India's hinterlands to its ports.[13] Summing up what he believed to be Delhi's greatest flaw while at the same time disparaging industrial capital, Curzon declared, 'Delhi cannot be a great commercial city – it can only be a manufacturing city or a distributing centre on a small scale – for the trade of India must rest on the sea.'[14] For Curzon, a great imperial city was one that engaged in trade rather than manufacturing.[15]

Throughout 1912, when the topic of New Delhi came up in both the Lords and the Commons, Parliament members showed concern that the transfer would isolate the colonial government from what they believed gave British-India its life's blood – commerce. 'When you have built your new capital,' Curzon asked in the Lords, 'will it be a source of influence and of strength to your government? Will it enable them better to understand the heart of India, and to grasp its problems?'[16] No, warned Curzon, it would become both a 'territorial' and a 'political enclave', 'aloof from public opinion', 'shut off from the main currents of public life', and 'immersed in a sort of bureaucratic self-satisfaction'.[17] Calcutta, in contrast, brought the government into contact with the 'surge and movement of life ... you heard the opinions of every variety and form – opinions of merchants, bankers, traders, businessmen of every sort'.[18] It was from Calcutta that Britain had forged an empire in South Asia.[19] For Curzon, the city had 'always seemed ... to be a worthy capital and expression of British rule in India, it is English built, English commerce has made it the second city in the Empire ... English statesmen, administrators, and generals have built up to its present commanding height the fabric of British rule in India'.[20] This great *entrepôt* of commerce and trade, claimed Curzon, 'brightened our minds, it widened our outlook, it brought us into the main stream of national existence'.[21]

In response to Hardinge's argument that winning back Indian popular opinion was an important calculation in the transfer of the capital and its related political reforms, Curzon made it clear that a far more imperative body of public opinion mattered more, Calcutta's business community and the Chamber of Commerce that represented it.[22] When discussing the motives of the Calcutta business community, which had loudly decried the transfer, Curzon declared that:

> They object to it ... because they regard this policy as involving a cruel waste of public money, because they distrust the financial methods by which the money is going to be raised, and because they regard with dismay the effect that will be exercised both upon the Government of India and upon commerce, in their opinion, by the removal of the capital of India to Delhi.[23]

Similarly, Lansdowne reminded the Lords that the opinion of the Calcutta Chamber of Commerce should not be ignored since it represented a significant sector of the Indian commercial community. Rising in support of Curzon, he focused on the importance of Calcutta and commerce, claiming, 'Calcutta seems to me to possess all the attributes calculated to make the city a worthy capital. It has a very large population. It is a great emporium of trade. It has a large, varied, and representative community, native and European.'[24] Most importantly, for Lansdowne, 'the commercial element [was] strongly represented'.[25] He pointed to a recent publication by the Calcutta Chamber of Commerce concerning the transfer to Delhi of the Department of Industry and Commerce:

> For nine months of the year the Department will be completely cut off from the commercial centres of India. What merchants want is ready and convenient access to the responsible financial, commercial, and railway officers of the Government, the officers who are in authority and with whom the decision in important cases rests.[26]

The shift to Delhi would place the department nearly 1,000 miles from Calcutta and Bombay, the two largest commercial centres in India. Lord Minto succinctly summed up the concern of his fellow antagonists in the Lords by simply declaring, 'the interests of Calcutta cannot with justice be ignored'.[27] For these men, Calcutta represented the essence of empire with its large flows of maritime commerce, shipping, and merchants.

The debate about commerce continued in the Commons into 1913 with Mr William MacCaw (member for Down West) who reflected many of the original concerns aired by Sir William H. Clark, member for Commerce and Industry for the Government of India.[28] MacCaw's scathing criticism in the Commons proved Clark was more than correct in warning Hardinge that commercial interests in Calcutta and their allies in Parliament would resist any move that distanced government officers from Calcutta's business community. Indian commerce was suffering, according to MacCaw, because the Government of India had ignored the concerns and interests of the Calcutta Chamber of Commerce. He claimed, 'the Bengal Chamber of Commerce represents the whole of the trade, not only of Calcutta but also of the adjoining districts in Bengal and Assam, and it is composed of men who have most extensive commercial and financial interests at stake in the country'.[29] Picking up on criticisms so often heard the previous year, MacCaw claimed that 'one of the chief arguments to my mind against the change is, and always has been, that it would place the Government of India completely out of touch with that body of non-official opinion with which it ought to be in constant and regular contact'.[30] MacCaw already disapproved of the Government of India's annual migration between Calcutta and Simla because it reduced the amount of time government officials resided in Calcutta to roughly four months out of the year. This placed a strain on the system, but at least the short period in Calcutta 'enabled the officials and the merchants, lawyers, and other non-official men to meet together and exchange ideas for the mutual benefit of themselves and the country generally'.[31] The transfer of the capital meant that this short period would be done away with entirely, and government would simply migrate from Simla to Delhi, 'where for all practical purposes, they are just as much isolated from the general community as if they remained in Simla all the year round'.[32]

MacCaw reminded his audience that Curzon's government had created a Minister of Commerce to help cement the bond between government and the commercial community. John Hewett, an experienced Indian Civil servant, had filled the position admirably precisely because he was intimately acquainted with India's commercial community, according to MacCaw. Yet even if the Government of India selected an officer as talented as Hewett, he would be unable to build productive relationships with members of the commercial community because of his isolation at Simla and Delhi. The Government of India had responded earlier to these concerns by devising a scheme whereby the Minister of Commerce and Industry would tour India annually to hold meetings with government officials and members of the various business communities throughout the country. MacCaw, however, simply scoffed at these 'flying visits', saying that they 'were inadequate for the proper discussion of grave commercial questions, neither will they allow the minster to acquire the necessary information to enable him to perform his duties in a really effi-cient manner'.[33] He ended his criticism with a plea to the Government of India to end its new Indian policy, which he believed 'injured' rather than 'fostered' Indian commerce.[34] Hardinge and Crewe proceeded at their own risk if they ignored the commercial opinion of Calcutta, which he believed, much like Curzon, was the most important opinion in India.

In response to Curzon and others' criticism concerning government becoming isolated from Calcutta's commercial opinion, Crewe and his allies argued that that was precisely one of the great benefits of transfer-ring the capital from Calcutta to Delhi. As Crewe claimed in the Lords:

> The commercial community of Calcutta is a most admirable soci-ety, but, like other prosperous and highly considered societies, it is

perhaps fallen into the way of looking at matters only from its own point of view, and even has been sometimes tempted to forget that another point of view can exist ... When you talk of Calcutta opinion in India, nobody means the opinion of the Government; they mean the opinion of the mercantile community and the Chamber of Commerce.[35]

Antony MacDonnell was even more pointed in his support for transferring the capital away from Calcutta's commercial influence. In no uncertain terms, he countered Curzon and his allies by claiming, 'In Calcutta you lose all native opinion except that of Bengal. By leaving it, you will bring yourself into touch with the thought of the more virile native society in India, and you will get out of the enervating influences of the coast fringe.'[36] Calcutta's commercial community, he continued, was a self-interested body that pursued its own narrow interests over the economic health of the entire country. 'The European merchants and professional men of Calcutta are engaged in making money', he claimed, 'and they regard the questions, when they pay any attention to them, that come up before the Government of India from the standpoint of private interest or the interests of their class.'[37] Crewe and MacDonnell argued that the overpowering presence of Calcutta's business community damaged the government's ability to meet the needs of the rest of the country.

Building a new capital at Delhi would help ensure that imperial policy in India was potentially less influenced by Calcutta, but there was a major cost, for many critics, in separating imperial politics from commercial opinion. If commerce was removed from the new capital, then what precisely did this say about the purpose of British rule in India and who was this rule meant to benefit?[38] This important question got to the heart of the criticism of the transfer. The king's announcement at his imperial durbar to transfer the capital from Calcutta to Delhi did not simply move government from one location to another; it introduced a new way of envisioning the role of British rule in India and who would be best served by that rule, colonial subjects or business interests.

The building of New Delhi and the opium revenue

If critics in Parliament were upset by the capital in Delhi becoming isolated from commercial opinion in Calcutta, they were even more agitated by the question of how the Government of India planned to finance the building project and its related reforms. During his presentation of the 1912 East Indian Budget, Montagu told the Commons that New Delhi would be built using two sources of capital: (1) annual surplus revenues when available and (2) loans when necessary. The Government of India's Finance Department, under the leadership of Fleetwood Wilson, had systematically created extremely large revenue surpluses since 1909. These surpluses would be used to finance the building of the new capital as long as they existed. Herein lay one of the more astonishing aspects of the early financing of the New Delhi building project. Much of this surplus came from opium revenues.

The connection between opium revenues and the building of the new capital did not go unnoticed in London during the 1912 East India Budget Debate. After listening to several members hotly denounce the evils of the opium and alcohol trade in India, George Wyndham, rising as a member of the opposition, drew the house's attention to the Liberal government's plan to partially finance the building project through opium budget surpluses. Wyndham sardonically let the Common's know, 'I understood the right hon. Gentleman [Montagu] to say that the cost of building some of the public offices in Delhi ... would come out of what I considered to be a temporary source of revenue.'[39] While Wyndham feigned shock at the connection between opium revenue surpluses and the building project, his real concern was that these surpluses were wildly unpredictable, and thus government should in no way use them to finance a long-term building project.

Other members of the Commons, such as J. D. Rees and Lord Ronaldshay, focused their criticism on what they considered a misguided zeal for reform on the part of some Liberal members in the Commons. Both used the importance of the opium revenue to the building of the new capital as a way to push back against those reformers who used what they considered mere sentiment rather than sound economic reasoning in their colonial policies. As a man of the world who had spent considerable time in India and continued to be involved in a multitude of financial ventures in India and Central Africa, Rees argued that 'the British nation is based on trade, and you must take effective steps to see that British merchants are not placed at a disadvantage by treaties made for humanitarian or other reasons, and that they have the perfect justice done to them'.[40] Rees chastised certain speakers for not tempering 'their zeal with a little sense of humour'.[41] Specially pointing out John Herbert Roberts (member for Denbighshire West), Rees quipped, 'Yet, so wanting are hon. Gentlemen in an elementary sense of humour that year by year they suggest this country, which is not the most temperate country in the world, should actually teach the most temperate population that ever existed to abstain from the use of liquor and drugs.'[42] Ronaldshay joined Rees in his condemnation of the anti-opium wing of Parliament, 'Let us remember, when we are patting ourselves on our backs over our virtues, and congratulating ourselves on the acquisition of merit – let us remember that we are acquiring our merit entirely at other people's expense.'[43] Those people, according to Ronaldshay, were not just the opium plantation owners and merchants who profited from the trade but also the general Indian public which indirectly benefited when government used budget surpluses rather than new taxes to fund its needs.

The transitory nature of the opium surplus was precisely the reason for its remarkable growth in the Indian budget. For the last several years Wilson had purposely underestimated government revenues earned from the opium trade. He did so for two reasons. First, the opium market had become highly volatile. In the ten years prior to 1907, the cost of a chest of opium had remained relatively flat at 1,400 rupees per chest. However, costs began to wildly fluctuate after 1907 when Britain and China agreed to reduce the production of opium.[44] In October 1911, for example, the cost had risen to 6,000 rupees per chest at the beginning of the year, but then declined to 1,800 rupees by the end.[45] It again rose to 5,500 rupees in May 1912. Because of these large fluctuations, Wilson was forced to dramatically underestimate the revenues from opium to ensure positive budget balances. At the same time, amidst these fluctuations, the general trend of the cost per chest of opium continued to rise as supplies shrank, leading to higher demands and subsequently higher prices. Second, Wilson underestimated the opium revenue because he purposely wanted to create large surpluses that could be drawn on for ad-hoc government needs. This allowed the government to avoid raising taxes in an already antagonistic political climate in India. In many ways, this was an example of simple budget manipulation to create revenue surpluses, but it also reflected the colonial government's attempt to win back Indian good will, which had been diminished by such autocratic policies as the partition of Bengal or by such insults as the earlier Ilbert Bill controversy.[46]

By the time of Wilson's departure in 1913, India had some of the strongest positive balances it had ever seen.[47] The large imbalances between projected and real opium revenues left the government with enormous revenue surpluses at the end of the fiscal year. Though Wilson, for example, had estimated a general surplus of £819,200 for the 1911–12 budget year, in reality it had reached £4,848,300. In that year, the opium revenue surplus, which amounted to £2,069,100, accounted for 43 per cent of the entire budget surplus (see Table 4.1).

Table 4.1 Opium revenue budget surplus[48]

Budget year	Exceeds estimate by (%)
1905–1906	23
1906–1907	10
1907–1908	29
1908–1909	24
1909–1910	25
1910–1911	75
1911–1912	79

In raw numbers this meant that since 1905 the Government of India had received £20,250,000 in real revenue against the £11,200,000 budget estimate.[49] Real revenue had exceeded the estimate by 55 per cent on average.

Supporters of the transfer and building of the new capital considered Wilson's budgets sound financial policy and boons to the Indian public; critics saw them as accounting sleight-of-hand. The latter were extremely sceptical of Wilson's activities as finance minister, not only because of his open sympathy toward moderate nationalists like Gokhale, but also because of his budget surpluses and the way he was creating them.[50] In three long-winded diatribes – once in February and twice in June 1912 – Curzon fumed against the Government of India's plan to use Wilson's budget surpluses for building the new capital.[51] Curzon disparagingly referred to them as 'fancy surpluses' because they were, in essence, artificially created by Wilson's underestimation of revenues. Curzon and his parliamentary allies argued that, first, these surplus revenues would be insufficient to build the capital and that second, the unpredictability of surpluses created 'obscurity and mystery in the matter' of making annual budgets and tracing expenditures.[52] Curzon claimed:

> The practice is when you ask the consent of the taxpayers of a country to the provision of large sums of money, to give them complete estimates of the manner in which the money is going to be spent, [but] ... this is the most gigantic leap in the dark that the financiers of India or of this country have ever taken.[53]

The government's financial plan for the building of the new capital not only changed the economics of colonial building projects in India, it transformed one of the most important economic reasons for imperial rule in India. For Curzon and others, the time-tested approach to finding capital for a large colonial building project was to seek it from investors. In this way, much more exact and predictable amounts of capital could be raised.[54] More importantly, as Peter Cain and Antony Hopkins have shown, colonial governments operating in close association with financiers often advertised loans as securities that offered guaranteed returns to subscribers. Benefitting both government and financial interests, these secured loans gave the colonial government revenue yielding infrastructure like railways and canal colonies while wealthy individuals and financial institutions were given investment opportunities to safely store and grow capital. The problem with using surplus revenues was that they precluded investment opportunities and thus generated no additional wealth for individual 'gentlemanly capitalists' or for larger financial institutions.[55]

Lord Midleton agreed with Curzon's criticism of the Government of India's artificial surpluses and warned '… what I do wish the noble Marquess (Crewe) to remember is that this financial question is having a most damaging effect on the credit of India in the stock market'.[56] He then compared India's creditworthiness to the London County Council, one of the largest borrowers in England. While Government of India stock had declined steadily since Wilson's appointment as finance minister to the Government of India, London County Council stock had risen. Five years earlier the reverse had been true, according to Midleton. 'There must be some reason for that fall', he queried.[57] He felt no need to answer his own question; the markets had answered for him. Wilson's budget manipulations, he believed, had damaged the creditworthiness of the Government of India and lowered its stock values. What this meant was that the government would have to borrow money for the building project, when necessary, at closer to 4 per cent rather than 3½ per cent interest. This would drive up the cost of the new capital to something much greater than the proposed £4,000,000, perhaps as high as £10,000,000 to £15,000,000.[58]

Critics in the Commons, such as Colonel Charles Yate (member for Melton), were also critical of the large increase in the Government of India's positive budget balances because it created conditions for corruption in the India Office (see Table 4.2). With great suspicion, he examined the way the Secretary of State had lent with securities £10,000,000 to 'approved' borrowers. This troubled Yate who saw Crewe's loan activities as channelling the positive balances in the India Office to select individuals or institutions. As Yate declared, 'The money is public money, the property of the Government of India, not the private property of the Secretary of State.'[59] He questioned why Crewe had

Table 4.2 Government of India positive balances, 1907–1911[60]

Year	Balance (£)
1907	4,600,000
1908	7,000,000
1909	12,000,000
1910	16,000,000
1911	18,000,000

lent this £10,000,000 at 2½ per cent but then borrowed £3,000,000 at 3½ per cent from London. Additionally, Yate asked why the Secretary of State had been withdrawing £26,000,000 to £27,000,000 from India if the Secretary of State's annual budget required only £16,000,000 to £17,000,000 a year in expenditures in England?

Montagu responded to Yate criticism by explaining that the balances were coming out of a well-known financial and economic practice used by the Secretary of State to facilitate trade between Britain and India. The practice was typical procedure and had nothing to do with using Indian revenues to benefit preferred individuals and financial institutions or to manipulate London's money markets. The Government of India planned to allow the reserve to grow to £25,000,000 with £5,000,000 held in gold sterling. The large balances of the last several years were due, argued Montagu, to the large surpluses on the estimates and the under-spending of some departments. In addition, Montagu pointed to the great volume of trade between Britain and India:

> That is what distributes the government balance between the Secretary of State and the Government of India. The size of the balance there depends upon the sale by the Secretary of State of bills of exchange instead of granting transfers. He sells the bills in England to obtain the money in England required to meet disbursements there by the banks and merchants.[61]

In short, the brisker the trade between Britain and India, the more bills that were sold.

Montagu's response to Yate sheds light on the manner in which the Government of India and the India Office, though calling for reforms and using surplus revenues to fund government needs to ease the tax burden on Indians, used financial practices that eased the flow of money from India to Britain. Crewe's handling of the positive balances arising in India was not novel, as Yate wanted to suggest, but normal financial practice within the India Office that gave London's financial elite easier and better access to India's wealth. Hardinge's government and the India Office were not anti-merchant or anti-commerce. Indeed, they wanted to secure Britain's political economy in a rapidly changing India. Creating surpluses gave them the necessary flexibility to fund government in ways that were more difficult for Indian anti-colonial agitators to condemn. The system, in other words, helped obfuscate the economic exploitation of India by commercial elites, both in Britain and in India, and the role played by the Government of India, even one engaged in reform efforts, in abetting and easing this flow of capital between India and Britain.

The Government of India's difficult financial choices

The Government of India planned to seek British and Indian loans when surplus revenues were insufficient to build the capital. Opponents of the transfer were angry about this financial method as well. There was only so much capital that could be used to finance building projects and other commercial ventures in India, and the building of New Delhi would compete for these finite resources. For critics, moneys used for the new capital could be better invested in revenue-earning projects such as railways and canal colonies.

Wyndham once again linked opium revenues to the transfer and its accompanying reforms. Disparaging the government's budget decisions, he claimed, 'just as opium last year was the greatest source of revenue, so education next year is to be the greatest item of expenditure'.[62] 'Until there is a change in the opinions of India', he continued, 'it would not be wise ... to lavish money upon services, the value of which are not yet appreciated by the people of India, especially when there are services appreciated by the people in India upon which the money could be more usefully spent.'[63] For Wyndham, the Government of India needed to be smarter in how it generated and spent revenues. While the Indian desire for education was questionable, according to Wyndham, it was manifestly obvious that they liked railways. 'Now here we have a happy and complete coincidence between what we think India needs and what we know India wants. The population of India delights in using railways ... more than 400,000,000 travelled on the railway last year.'[64] For Wyndham the development of railways was one of the 'greatest functions of empire building and making ... Every penny we spend upon development ... is most certainly ... to bring the prosperity of India nearer than money spent in any other way.'[65]

It was clear to Wyndham that the cost to build a new capital and to fund its related reforms came at the expense of railroad building. In 1910, 32,398 miles of railroad had been laid in India, but only 701 miles were added to railway lines in 1911 and only 790 miles were budgeted for the year 1912.[66] As Wyndham argued, 'that increase is not very great, and I doubt whether it is great enough in proportion to the enormous task which we are only beginning in India – that is, to make it a great civilized community'.[67] Here, Wyndham was using the stadial logic of many of his predecessors where human progress was translated as economic development. The answer to the problem was simple for Wyndham:

> [Indians] like railways, but they do not care much for education, and as the modern view seems to be that we should govern India with the consent of the governed, and as the rule of Rome was that roads were the foundation of Empire, we should attack this problem and so build roads in India, and thereby please everybody, not only the population that requires them, but the reformer and reactionary in England as well.[68]

The fear that the transfer and its related colonial policies would hurt the building of railways in India became a common refrain in the House of Commons. MacCaw believed it squandered money for purely sentimental reasons. For him, the money could be much better spent on 'works of real utility'.[69] He reminded his audience that India's railways were starved for money and required new investments in rolling stock to move India's goods. 'If the government', according to MacCaw, 'would only meet this crying necessity, instead of squandering millions of money on a new capital which I believe will serve no good purpose, they will be doing a real service to the trade of the country and the wants of the people.'[70] Similarly, Ronaldshay complained that 'the rapidly growing amount of trade and industry in the country' required more railroad building and that it was 'notorious to those who have been in India ... that stations in all parts of the country are congested with goods, and that the amount of transport which is available is nothing like adequate for the present requirements of the country'.[71] Even members of Montagu's own party were upset with the potential loss of capital for railway building. Sir George Scott Robertson (member for Bradford Central) repeated Ronaldshay's concerns:

> It is a most pitiable fact that at present ... the railways were ... unable to cope with the business which they ought to have been able to

undertake. Feeder lines were blocked entirely, simply because the trunk lines could not take the traffic, and even if all that had been done away with we have this extraordinary position, that the ports themselves were not able to cope with the traffic which was supplied to them by the main line.[72]

The problem, for Robertson, was locating capital to finance railway building, 'Could we possibly in any other way than those methods which are adopted at present obtain capital in this country to build railways? I am afraid not.'[73] Thus, there was little way to avoid direct competition for limited financial resources between the non-revenue making new capital and revenue-making projects.

Similarly, in the Lords, Curzon reflected on the limited amount of capital for investment in India and the manner in which the building of a new capital would draw funds away from revenue-yielding ventures. Private investors, he noted, had taken up only 15 per cent of a recent Government of India issued £3,000,000 loan. For Curzon, this suggested an already unfavourable lending market for Indian loans, 'Will any Lord tell me if the money raised by ordinary loans in India and this country is to be shared between Delhi on the one hand and railways and irrigation works on the other, that the latter will not suffer.'[74] He reminded his listeners that a previous committee, led by Lord Inchcape and created to examine the state of railways in India, had concluded that India required £12,500,000 per annum to be raised by sterling loans in Britain and by rupee loans in India. However, this amount had never been reached. From 1911–12, only £9,500,000 had been found; in 1912–13 only £9,000,000. Because much of this capital needed to go into servicing existing rail lines, only around 70–80 miles of new track would be laid in the current year, according to Curzon. The fact that major amounts of capital would need to be spent on the building of a new capital that existed solely as a site of government was anathema to those imperialists who saw empire as a means to create wealth. As Curzon concluded:

> If this money which is so urgently required to carry us up to the limit fixed by the noble lord opposite [Lord Inchcape] for railways alone is to be taken for Delhi, it is inevitable that these works must suffer, and that you will be taking the money of the Indian taxpayer, not for the most remunerative of expenditure such as railways and irrigation, but for the purely unproductive object of building your new capital on the plains of Delhi.[75]

Lord Minto, who spoke immediately after Curzon, agreed. Focusing on what in the future must be a competition between the building needs of the capital and the needs of the assorted Government of India departments that made British rule possible, Minto announced, 'what I am most afraid of is that various departments, upon the success of which the future of India so largely depends, may be stinted in order that this money may be obtained' for the building of the new capital.[76] He added that Indians would suffer the most from insufficient financial support, especially in the areas of agriculture and railroads. Looking into the future, Minto asked, 'Is India to face the growing demands of future years with a millstone around her neck? ... if the revenues of the great Departments are to be curtailed in favour of Delhi expenditure, all I can say is that the result will be most unfortunate for the people of India.'[77] Like Minto and Curzon, Midleton was concerned about the new capital drawing moneys away from more remunerative building projects. He argued, 'I cannot contemplate without extreme apprehension the idea that for the next ten years the development of Indian railways is to be hampered in order to provide money for a change of capital.'[78] 'I look upon it', he continued, 'as a departure from the whole principle of economy on which we have been engaged in Indian finances for the last twenty years. The pace of the forward movement in the direction of railways and irrigation work requires to be quickened rather than retarded.'[79]

Crewe countered the broad criticism that he had faced in Parliament concerning India's current financial policies. For those who argued that the building of the new capital should be made part of the official budget, Crewe claimed, 'you can never venture to speak with certainty of what your available revenue may be in India for a year or so hence. To promise therefore that you would pay these varying sums as you go along would have been too bold a step for the Government of India to take.'[80] The other option, which seemed to be favoured by Curzon and most of his allies in the Lords, was to raise a single, large Delhi loan, which could be drawn on as needed during the building project. This option seemed unwise to Crewe, who asked in the Lords, 'what are you going to do with the money when you have got it until it is spent? Are you going to reinvest it somewhere? If so, that would be a rather strange and unusual operation for a Government to take.'[81] Crewe agreed with Curzon that Indian and London money markets were under-performing because capital was drying up in both places; this was precisely why the Government of India chose not to obtain a single loan dedicated to the building of the new capital. The Government of India's decided path for financing the building project – by drawing from revenue surpluses and ordinary loans when these surpluses were insufficient – was the safest way to finish the project with economy, according to Crewe. Rather than burdening the Indian taxpayer with a 'millstone' around his neck, as critics had claimed, these surplus revenues actually eased the weight placed on the Indian taxpayer. 'We are not', claimed Crewe, 'doing anything unfair or unreasonable by the people of India in saying that this charge, which is to a great extent of a nature which might fairly be placed upon posterity, yet should be met so far as you are in a position to do so from these transient and ... fortunate sources of revenue which exist at this moment.'[82] Crewe added, 'I venture to think we are adopting a common sense course in finding as much money as we can from our balances for the purpose of these annual payments and adding the rest to the ordinary loans, whether in India or here, which we raise every year for our current outlay.'[83]

In the Commons, Montagu was even more positive than Crewe about India's financial situation and its ability to meet its financial demands. India, he argued, was in a strong position to enact major reform. In response to a query by Bonar Law concerning India's proposed educational reforms, which were tied to the transfer, Montagu argued, 'Although he [Law] did well to draw our attention to the financial position of the Government of India with regard to its large commitments on education, the financial prosperity of India is so wonderful that I think we are entitled to take a little bigger risk than we can in a country like this.'[84] Montagu disagreed with those critics who claimed that railways had suffered under Liberal government. Yes, capital was hard to find, but the story was the same throughout the world. But even in this capital-poor climate, Indian railways had managed to make money in the last several years. 'I think this story may be taken as a symptom of the marvellous possibilities of our Indian Empire, and as a lesson that bold Government enterprise in the direction of helping and exploiting her resources by developing railways, or her irrigation works, or her wonderful forests, will lead to large national profit.'[85]

Trade protection or trade preference in Britain's world system

The debate between supporters of the Government of India's new policies and critics of its new direction reflected a larger discussion concerning the place of India in Britain's global system of trade. The question of how to achieve economic stability in the empire opened space for the proponents of either free trade or trade protection to raise their voices. The debate broke down along political lines with mostly liberals continuing to support free trade policies and conservatives calling for strong tariff protections and usually suffering at the ballot box in consequence. Indeed, the question was so important that John Morley, the Secretary of State for India under Asquith's liberal government, used it as a criterion for Hardinge's candidacy as Viceroy of India. As Hardinge and his wife waited at Windsor for the arrival of the casket carrying King Edward VII, who had died on 6 May, Morley took Hardinge aside and asked him if he was a 'free trader', to which Hardinge said that he 'was then and always had been'.[86] The Indian Protectionist Movement and the related Tariff Reform League, both of which had been encouraged by a small section of the commercial community in England, pushed for greater trade protections in the empire. Fleetwood Wilson argued that following these policies 'would mean to India that the United Kingdom and the colonies would give freer entry to Indian tea, coffee, sugar, wheat, and all Indian staple products, and it would mean to us [India] that the Indian import duty on a large number of British manufactures would be either abolished or reduced'.[87] Protection would increase trade between Britain, India, and the other colonies by forcing out foreign competition, but it would retard Indian manufacturing. As a colonial officer who took his charge to improve the conditions of the Indian peoples seriously, Wilson was sceptical of this type of trade relationship. Trade protection would encourage India to become a producer of raw goods and a consumer of British manufactured products. He was even more incredulous of the economics of protection. In response to calls for Britain to raise a tariff wall to protect Britain's trade with India, Wilson cautioned slowness and careful consideration on any protectionist policies in the Indian market. The real question, for Wilson, was who paid for trade protection? He answered that the cost was borne by the poor who paid more for goods since the loss of foreign competition eliminated economic conditions that kept prices down. As Wilson concluded, 'If you succeed in encouraging industry by a tariff, it can only ... be by raising home prices. That is an axiom on which all economists appear to be agreed.'[88] The increase in domestic prices would reverberate across the empire as colonial subjects, like their fellow subjects in England, paid more for necessary consumer goods. Wilson argued in front of the Legislative Assembly that this economic reality was disastrous for a country with high levels of poverty like India:

> We have here an enormous population of the very poor; and however limited their physical requirements may be, the cheapness of

the things they need is essential to their very existence ... Can it be denied that artificially produced dearness would be injurious to the wellbeing of a great majority of the people of this country?[89]

Making matters worse, much of India's poor were engaged in the agricultural sphere of the Indian economy. For those who argued that protection might encourage higher wages to meet higher prices, Wilson claimed, 'Where are the increased wages to come from which are to enable them [Indian agriculturalists] to face with equanimity any artificial increase in the cost of living?'[90] The operation of economic laws might eventually 'pull up the remuneration' of the rural poor, for Wilson, but 'in the interval an immense amount of hardship and suffering might be imposed on the great body of our Indian workers'.[91]

Wilson admitted that protection might rejuvenate old industries or even create new ones, but an artificially created industry was like a pauper that 'cannot continue to exist unless it continues to receive dole after dole, and thus it lays a lasting burden on the general consumer, and through him on the economic growth of the state'.[92] Wilson noted that there was some truth to the 'infant industry argument' proposed by Frederick List who argued that selective protection could help emerging industries that suffered from lack of skilled workers or technological problems. In these instances, tariff protection from foreign competition might be allowed for a short period to give the new industry time to repay what it had received in state protection. But, Wilson asked:

Can the advocates of protection in India satisfy the legislature that, under a protective tariff, it will be possible to establish industries in this country which will eventually be able to fulfil conditions thus laid down as a test of success ... Can you assure those responsible for the Government of India that these industries will be able to produce articles as, or cheaper than, the price at which they can be imported under a limited protective system?[93]

Wilson closed his 1913 Government of India financial statement with the words, 'I would earnestly ask all to study the inner history of the influence of protection upon political morality in the countries where it has been established for any length of time'.[94] Was protection 'a fair burden to throw upon the awakening political life of India', and what might be the unfortunate consequences, Wilson asked.[95] Here, he was making a pointed statement that economic philosophy must influence political systems since both were deeply intertwined. Protectionism, which could lead to such corrupt practices as economic collusion amongst a powerful producing class, damaged democratic principles and practices. Indeed, Wilson was suggesting that the market place, in whatever form it might take, acted as a breeding ground for political philosophy.[96]

What caused Wilson to discuss in detail the potential risks of protection was Sir Gangadhar Chitnavis, who moved a resolution in the 1913 Legislative Assembly to strengthen the financial resources of India by having it become part of an imperial-wide system of preferential tariffs. The reason for doing so was the impending loss of the opium revenue. Though Wilson disparaged Chitnavis as 'a perfect specimen of a Tory Squire', he supported the resolution because it was based on trade preference rather than trade protection. Wilson looked to a future where the different parts of the empire were more closely integrated in what he called the Empire Movement, a system of imperial trade preferences adopted by Canada in 1897, New Zealand in 1903, South Africa in 1906, and Australia in 1907. The Empire Movement had one major objective, to strengthen the empire by developing and linking together the economic interests of its individual parts under a system of preference.[97] Of course, India's relationship to the larger empire, especially the dominions, was not a new question. Indeed, John Robert Seeley had raised it in his famous series of Cambridge lectures.[98] The most influential part of Seeley's argument was that Britain and its settler colonies needed to be bound more closely together in a reciprocal rather than exploitative relationship.[99] This 'Greater Britain' was necessary to compete against emerging powerful international competitors, such as the United States and Russia, which had far greater mineral and natural resources than Great Britain on its own. For Seeley, India's different communities of race and religion made it an ill fit for his Anglo-centric Greater Britain, but Wilson saw an opportunity to bring India into the family of Greater Britain via a shared community of economic interests.

5
Competing Visions of Empire in the Colonial Built Environment

Most observers in India and Britain assumed that the new imperial capital would be built in or near Delhi's civil lines since it was the closest thing to a European community in the Delhi District. Using a golden trowel made especially for the occasion, the king and queen even laid commemorative foundation stones near the durbar site, which was located in the civil lines' northern sector.[1] To many people's shock and bewilderment, the Government of India and its official town planning committee selected a building site to the south of the existing Indian city of Shajahanabad, effectively separating the present European community from the future capital. Rural villages, farmland, and the ruins of the Tughluk, Lodi, and Mughal empires dominated the selected area. These characteristics and the site's dislocation from any British historical presence invited further criticism of the transfer.

When rumours began to reach London that the official town planning committee was investigating a building site that was far removed from the European civil lines, Sir Bradford Leslie, an eminent railway engineer with long experience in northern India, prepared a town plan that placed the capital back within the civil lines. Whereas the official town plan generated little or no revenue, existing solely as a site of imperial government, Leslie's town plan fused the work of imperial government with finance by using private companies and private investments to build certain important city spaces. The building of a weir across the Yamuna River was the most important of these areas. Built by a private company, it would generate electricity for sale to the local community. The weir also would create a large scenic and recreational lake. This was especially true on the western shore, which would include a pedestrian-only promenade flanked by restaurants, emporiums, and other water front commercial properties. Thus, in Leslie's plan, the new capital became both a site of government as well as a revenue generator that created wealth and opportunity for private investment.

The proposal was so powerful and had such strong support from important official and unofficial quarters that Hardinge was forced to ask his town planning committee to revisit and re-evaluate the civil lines as a potential building site. After a second examination, the town planning committee once again rejected the northern site, as it came to be called, on geographical, sanitary, and historical grounds. First, committee members determined that natural and man-made obstacles constricted the building area in the civil lines. Second, they deemed the northern site irremediably unhealthy especially in regard to malaria. And third, they were troubled by the area's history. While the civil lines carried recollections of three grand imperial durbars, it also contained memories of a far darker, far more disruptive history of British rule. Delhi had been a focal point of the Indian uprising of 1857 when acts of extreme brutality were carried out by both sides. This problematic history of British and Indian conflict countered the very political narrative that Hardinge hoped to achieve in the new imperial capital. The controversy over the exact site of the new capital highlighted early twentieth-century arguments over who should benefit from empire and the purpose of British rule in India.

New Delhi's official town planning committee

As debates continued in Parliament over the transfer of the capital, the Government of India and the Indian Office in London began determining who should serve on the official town planning committee. Made up of well-known architects and town planners, this committee would be responsible for selecting a building site and planning the general layout of the city. Initially, John Jenkins, Home Member to the Government of India, recommended Lt Colonel Popham-Young, the Deputy Commissioner of the Punjab, T. R. J. Ward, superintending engineer of the Yamuna Canal, and George Wittet, the consulting architect for Bombay. Hardinge and the rest of his executive council immediately discounted Jenkins' choices. As Fleetwood Wilson, Finance Minister to the Government of India, mockingly claimed, 'To hand over the planning of such city to the non-entities – for I can call them nothing else – a youthful Lt. Colonel who has something to do with a canal colony, an engineer who has dabbled in canal works, and an architect who has had experience of some large buildings in Bombay, seems to me to court disaster and discredit.'[2] If New Delhi was meant to be a grand experiment that reinvigorated the British Raj, then its planning and building required the best names that Britain had to offer. The cost of the project would almost certainly go up, but this was a risk that the Government of India was willing to take.[3] 'I feel very strongly,' again claimed Wilson, 'that this is an opportunity which has never yet occurred, and which will probably never recur, for laying the foundation of one of the finest cities in the world and certainly the finest city in the east.'[4]

Hardinge began pressing Crewe early in January 1912 to locate the best men in England to serve on his three-person town planning committee. The selection of the Liverpool Corporation's John Brodie to serve as sanitation engineer was relatively free of controversy, but the appointments of a town planner and an architect were more difficult.[5] For the position of town planner and chair of the committee, Crewe confidentially consulted Leonard Aloysius Stokes, President of the Royal Institute of British Architects. Stokes offered the names of Edwin Landseer Lutyens, John William Simpson, and Henry Vaughan Lanchester, all of whom were noted, highly accomplished architects.[6] Crewe also consulted members of the Local Government Board, who further suggested Professor Stanley Adshead of the Liverpool School of Civic Design. He was a leading expert on the science of town planning and had published numerous studies on the subject.[7] Captain George Swinton, who had been an aide-de-camp to Lord Lansdowne (Viceroy of India, 1888–1894) and who currently served as vice-chairman of the London City Council, actively pursued the position as well.[8] Though an unlikely candidate because of his lack of training as an architect, Swinton had powerful men that backed him. Cyril Jackson, head of the London City Council, for example, wrote on Swinton's behalf, inform-ing Crewe that if Swinton 'could get such a chance, nothing on earth would stop him'.[9]

By early 1912, the India Office had settled on two men, Swinton and Adshead, for the position of town planner. Compared to Adshead, Swinton's qualifications for being on the committee were remarkably slim. In a letter to Cyril Jackson, Swinton listed them as his lifetime interest in landscape gardening; his sightseeing in India as a member of Lansdowne's staff; his travels to every capital in Europe with the excep-tion of Lisbon; and drawing classes for two years in Bombay and in London since his return to England.[10] His only real training as a town planner was his work with the London City Council. Still, Crewe and other members of the India Office were impressed with Swinton's 'temper and attitude' toward town planning in general and his excitement about the new imperial city in particular.[11] Crewe wrote to Hardinge that Swinton impressed him as a man who saw town planning as a traffic expert and space designer rather than as an architect.[12] During his interviews and in repeated correspondence with the India Office, Swinton made it clear that he was a pragmatist who believed that healthy and organic expansion depended on how space was originally allotted. He argued that the most effective town planning committee would consist of a municipal sanitation engineer, a 'pure architect', and a civic expert like himself.[13] Frederic Hamilton, an influential British diplomat and writer, agreed.[14] For Hamilton, Swinton's lack of architectural and engineering training was irrelevant since the town planner was quite distinct from the architect and engineer, though the latter must always be close at hand to assure the planning of a healthy and sanitary community. The town planner, for Hamilton, did not design buildings; he chose sites for them: 'here government house; here a broad avenue; here a block of government buildings; here the public park'.[15] A planner who could visualize the scheme of an entire city would remedy the mistakes of the past. Every city in the British Empire had grown up 'higgedly-piggedly', Hamilton claimed, with no original plan and certainly no plan for future expansion.[16] They had become 'cramped, inconvenient, and architecturally a failure, owing to lack of presight'.[17]

In the end, Crewe and the India Office gave Swinton the appointment as town planner and chair of the official town planning committee. Adshead was passed over not for want of any skill or training but because he was not a member of London's inner sanctum. For all his academic training and publishing, Adshead simply and ineluctably was a 'Liverpool' rather than 'London' man. Commissioning Adshead, along with John Brodie as sanitation engineer, would have meant placing two provincials on the most important town planning committee in generations.[18] Indeed, arguing against Adshead, Leonard Stokes referred to the academic as the 'provincial type', and Thomas Holderness of the Indian Office did not think he was a 'big enough man for the job'.[19] In contrast, Swinton's clear amateurism as a town planner was seen as a great strength rather than weakness because it showed more than anything else that he belonged to that special class of gentleman who involved himself in civic or political responsibilities because he had the time and resources to do so.[20]

The selection of Edwin Landseer Lutyens as architect on the committee represented another example of the importance of having powerful friends in the right places. Lutyens was a well-known structural and landscape architect who had studied at the Royal College of Art, London. He was best known for designing and building country houses for England's elite. His most notable recent achievement had been the highly acclaimed British School built for the International Exhibition in Rome in 1911.[21] No name has become more attached to the building of New Delhi than Lutyens', but his appointment was a secondary consideration.[22] Hardinge was far more interested in locating the best town planner and sanitation expert that he could find because he saw the building of New Delhi as a two-step process.[23] The town planning committee represented the first stage in which experts decided on questions of general effect and sanitation. The second stage would consist of an architectural board that made decisions on architectural style.[24]

Still, it made considerable sense that the architectural member for the town planning committee would also serve on the later architectural board. Hardinge began to make inquiries on his own with this in mind. He contacted Valentine Chirol, foreign editor for *The Times* of London, about architectural style and the best architects in England to carry out the work on the new imperial capital.[25] In response, Chirol contacted Reginald Barratt, a painter of landscapes and architectural subjects, who advised that it was a mistake to go through Crewe to find an architect. Crewe, he argued, would contact the council at the Royal Institute of British Architects, who then would offer up one of its 'pet' architects.[26] Instead, Barratt offered the names Reginald Theodore Blomfield, Leonard Stokes and Robert Stodart Lorimer as excellent architects for the new capital. But his strongest recommendation went to Lutyens. For Barratt, Lutyens had the best 'temperament', was 'reasonable', and 'would take great interest in initiating the scheme even if he did no more'.[27] He even argued that Lutyens should be allowed to formulate the capital's scheme, to determine and design its general architecture style, to nominate others to assist him, and to be, in essence, 'the moving genius from the outset'.[28] Barratt concluded that 'an exceptional man is best, and Lutyens is a very exceptional man'.[29]

By early March, the members of the town planning committee had been selected and their fees determined.[30] Of the three, only Lutyens would see the building project through to its end. Along with Herbert Baker, his life and work became intertwined with the building of India's new imperial capital for the next two decades.[31] The work took its toll on friendships and perhaps family though Lutyens' relationship with his wife Emily, as Jane Ridley has shown, always seemed distant and strained.[32] The committee was charged with drawing up a preliminary scheme that addressed sanitation and water, drainage and waste disposal, defence and crowd control, and various traffic concerns such as congestion, right-of-ways, and road and rail connections.[33]

On 29 March 1912, the committee left England for its first visit to India to survey potential building sites in the Delhi District, to judge its climate, and to study its building traditions (see Figure 5.1). After spending two days in Bombay examining the town plan of Salsette Island, a suburb being developed to the north of the city, the committee arrived in Delhi where they spent the next five weeks. They studied suitable ground within a 10 sq. mile radius of the existing city of Delhi. As they

Figure 5.1   Map of Delhi, Gazetteer of India Atlas, 1909

did so, Swinton encouraged his committee to strike a balance between aesthetic and pragmatic concerns. While the selected site needed to lend itself to the architect's creative imagination, it also needed to satisfy the basic requirements of sanitation, defence, future expansion, and land use. As Swinton told his fellow members, they were looking for a space that would contain not just government buildings but an entire city with shops, offices, and residences 'for all classes and races; with their churches and temples, hospitals and schools, palaces, hotels and rest houses, markets, slaughter houses, refuse destructors, etc.'[34]

After their initial examination, the committee travelled to Simla on 20 May 1912 to draw up tentative plans for the new capital. There, they met with Hardinge and his executive council to discuss their findings and conclusions about the Delhi District's capacity to house the new imperial capital. Two building sites rose to prominence, the European civil lines and an area to the south of Shajahanabad. The civil lines offered certain benefits such as existing rail, telegraph, and road connections. It was near the Kalka rail line that served Simla, the summer capital of the Government of India from approximately April to October. A large number of European residential bungalows and administrative buildings already were present, and its filtered water supply and other municipal amenities had been improved for the 1911 durbar. In the end, however, the committee passed over the civil lines in favour of the southern site's expansiveness, its healthier conditions, and its tremendous opportunity to reimagine future British-Indian relations in the twentieth century.[35] As the town planners claimed in their final report, 'a well-planned city should stand complete at its birth and yet have the power of receiving additions without losing its character'.[36]

The town planning committee returned to England in August 1912.[37] During their absence from India, special committees examined railway connections for the south site and considered land reclamation in potential building sites. Arrangements were made by the government to hire a municipal forest officer, P. H. Clutterbuck, who determined the suitability of certain trees and plants for the city's many avenues and parks. He also began to develop a nursery.[38] T. R. J. Ward, who was now acting as sanitary engineer for the local building establishment, and Geoffrey de Montmorency, who was serving as interim Chief Commissioner of the Delhi District, drew up a preliminary estimate of the cost of the building project.[39] The estimate covered the cost of land acquisition, storm water drains, sewage and sanitary installations, irrigation, domestic water supply, roads, parks, buildings, lighting, and brick and mason works.[40] The acquisition of land also began in the civil lines where the temporary capital would be placed until New Delhi's completion.[41]

Swinton returned to Delhi in late November 1912 and Lutyens and Brodie followed a month later.[42] During their second stay in India, the town planning committee began to finalize their highly anticipated town planning report. Interest piqued in June 1912 when the Government of India published a press release that informed the public of the selection of the southern site. Critics who believed that the civil lines would be transformed into a capital at reasonable cost were incensed by the decision to build an entirely new city on the south site.

After months of heated debate in Parliament, it was clear to opponents of the transfer of the imperial capital that Hardinge's Government of India was not going to reverse its policy, and that, indeed, it would have been nearly impossible for it to do so since the king himself had made the new policy a royal proclamation. This placed it in the same rarefied status as Queen Victoria's Proclamation to India in 1858.[43] In this moment of parliamentary angst emerged a figure, Sir Bradford Leslie, who descended as a kind of saviour who would set the colonial world right again. On 12 December 1912, exactly one year after the king's proclamation, Leslie read a paper before the Royal Society of Arts in London titled 'Delhi: The Metropolis of India'.[44] His paper embraced the transfer of the capital but attempted at the same time to incorporate the commercial and financial concerns of men like Curzon and his allies in Parliament.[45] He did so by drawing on his own extensive experience as an engineer and a railway builder in India. Leslie's paper exacerbated the debate over the transfer of the imperial capital and raised the stakes by highlighting what British colonial rule had meant in the past.

'Delhi: The Metropolis of India': Sir Bradford Leslie and the meaning of empire

Leslie was born on 18 August 1831 in Portman Place, London. His grandfather, Robert Leslie, an American from Philadelphia and a friend of Benjamin Franklin, was noted for his mechanical and mathematical skills. The family later moved to London where his father, Charles Robert Leslie, was born. His father became a popular painter and illustrator of books and a Royal Academician.[46] His older brother, Robert, was a painter of ships and sea pieces, noted for their beauty but never quite capturing the public's taste due to their frank depiction of sea life. His younger brother, George, was more successful as a painter of gardens and girls and followed his father as a Royal Academician. As Leslie's obituary in *The Times* claimed, 'skill with pen, pencil, and paintbrush, as well as mechanical and inventive skills, ran in the family'.[47]

At the age of 16 Leslie was apprenticed to Isambard Kingdom Brunel, one of the nineteenth-century's foremost engineers. During his apprenticeship he served as an assistant engineer on the building of the Chepstow Bridge over the Wye and as the resident engineer on the Saltash Bridge. By 1858, he was entrusted with the inspection of materials for the Great Eastern, one of the largest ships ever built at the time of its launching. His Indian career began in 1865 when he was appointed chief engineer of the Eastern Bengal Railway and by 1876 he had become its agent and chief, overseeing an estimated 40,000 Indians, 1000 Europeans and 600 Eurasians who worked for the railway.[48] His skills as a railway builder, engineer, and administrator won him an invitation to represent the Government of India at the Railway Congress at Brussels in 1885.[49] One of his most notable works, which earned him a knighthood in 1887, was the building of the Jubilee Bridge spanning the Hooghly from Calcutta to Howrah.[50] That year, Leslie was invalided back to England. His work in India had tremendously advanced his career, his wealth, and his social status but at much personal cost. He lost his wife, a son-in-law, and three daughters in India within three years.

In England, Leslie became a notable intellectual and social gadabout who gave talks and offered advice on a diverse array of topics including preservatives in food, plague, salt on snow, and Willet Time (daylight savings).[51] Above all, he was recognized as one of England's foremost authorities on railway building and routinely appeared in the editorial or business sections of *The Times* as an expert examiner of prospectuses on publicly offered railway companies.[52] In these examinations he made it clear that the importance of colonial railways lay in their ability to better connect local markets to Britain's much larger maritime commercial empire.[53]

Leslie continued to be active in a variety of professional and financial organizations and railway companies after he left India.[54] But his greatest association was his directorship, beginning in 1895, of the Southern Punjab Railway. Under contract with the Secretary of State for India, Leslie and his partners formed the company to build a standard gauge railway from Delhi to Samasata 400 miles to the west.[55] The Southern reflected a typical model of colonial infrastructural development.[56] It was publicly traded, it advertised subscriptions from private investors, and it received important guarantees on those investments from the colonial government.[57] In return the Government of India received

52 per cent of the Southern's gross receipts and could purchase the railway after 21 years of operation.[58] Like other colonial building projects of the era, the Southern was a relatively safe investment in that the Secretary of State was required to pay back capital expenditures if the company failed to make a profit.

Leslie's success with the Southern and other business ventures was based on his understanding of the deep, reciprocal relationship between the world of finance and the world of empire building. This understanding was highlighted in 1912, near the end of his professional career, when he read his paper in front of the Royal Society of Arts, a study that was unsolicited by the Government of India. Using his tremendous experiences as a railroad builder, agent, and investor, Leslie designed an imperial town plan for the civil lines that allayed many of the fears previously voiced in Parliament. Its strength lay in the manner in which it brought government and commerce into an intimate relationship with each other both during and after the capital's building stage. Government and private business, just as they had always done in railway development, would form a mutually beneficial partnership. His plan for the new capital symbolized his own philosophy – gained through years of experience building railways in northern India and repeatedly expressed by him in editorials and as an expert consultant of business prospectuses – that government and private companies working in tandem best served the public need.

For men like Leslie, British rule seemingly benefitted all involved in the imperial project, from the Indian *ryot* to the London financier. The average Indian, perhaps a farmer in Leslie's eyes, benefitted from modern infrastructure that allowed him to travel in ways unimaginable to his forefathers and to engage in a much larger imperial economic system where his goods were sold worldwide rather than locally. Similarly, the average British and Indian investor financially benefitted from large public works projects, which carried guaranteed returns underwritten by the Government of India. Lastly, the Government of India benefitted by shifting some of the costs and much of the work of building infrastructure, which strengthened its colonial economy, to the private sector. Of course, the development of India's modern infrastructure was a double-edged gift to India in the colonial era. Yes, it allowed Indians a kind of mobility that they had never known, but this infrastructure also gave the colonial government, merchants, and anyone with access to capital more opportunities to exploit the material wealth of India for export abroad. When the global market for Indian goods was favourable, Indian farmers could do reasonably well raising and selling cash crops such as jute or cotton. In times when the market dropped for these goods or in times of famine, Indian farmers suffered severe financial duress and even death.

Leslie's plan reaffirmed the traditional relationship between government needs and private interests in the colonial built environment, and it offered a powerful alternative to the official town plan drawn up by Swinton, Brodie and Lutyens in council with Hardinge's government. The building of a weir across the Yamuna River made the scheme possible (see Figure 5.2). Placed just across from the southern-most gate of the old city (the Delhi Gate), it achieved two important tasks. First, the weir included a power plant, which would generate enough electricity to light the new and old city as well as to run area factories and tramways. Second, it created a large lake that improved the overall aesthetics of the area. The new government buildings and the residences of high officials, sitting on the west bank, would overlook the lake. In response to concerns that the civil lines was simply not large enough to accommodate the needs of the new capital, Leslie argued that land could be reclaimed by building a stone embankment that extended into the lake. According to Leslie this would add an additional two square miles for building purposes.[59] In addition, Leslie argued that the increased value of this reclaimed land, which would be rented to private businesses, would more than cover the cost of building the embankment, the weir, and the power plant.[60]

Indeed, the possibilities of economic gain were so great that Leslie believed a private company would take responsibility for building the weir, its power plant, and the embankment, freeing the Government of India to focus entirely on the design and erection of government structures. As Leslie claimed:

> The rental commanded for frontages on the boulevard, added to the value of the electric power generated at the weir, would be so considerable as to make it probable that a company could be formed for undertaking the construction of the dam and weir and of the dredging and reclamation in consideration of the revenue to be derived therefrom.[62]

Interestingly, Leslie already had a company in mind: his own. Before the decision to transfer the capital, Leslie and several other wealthy investors had invested in a London-based company, The United Provinces Power Company, which earlier had received a concession from the Secretary of State for India to satisfy Delhi's growing demand

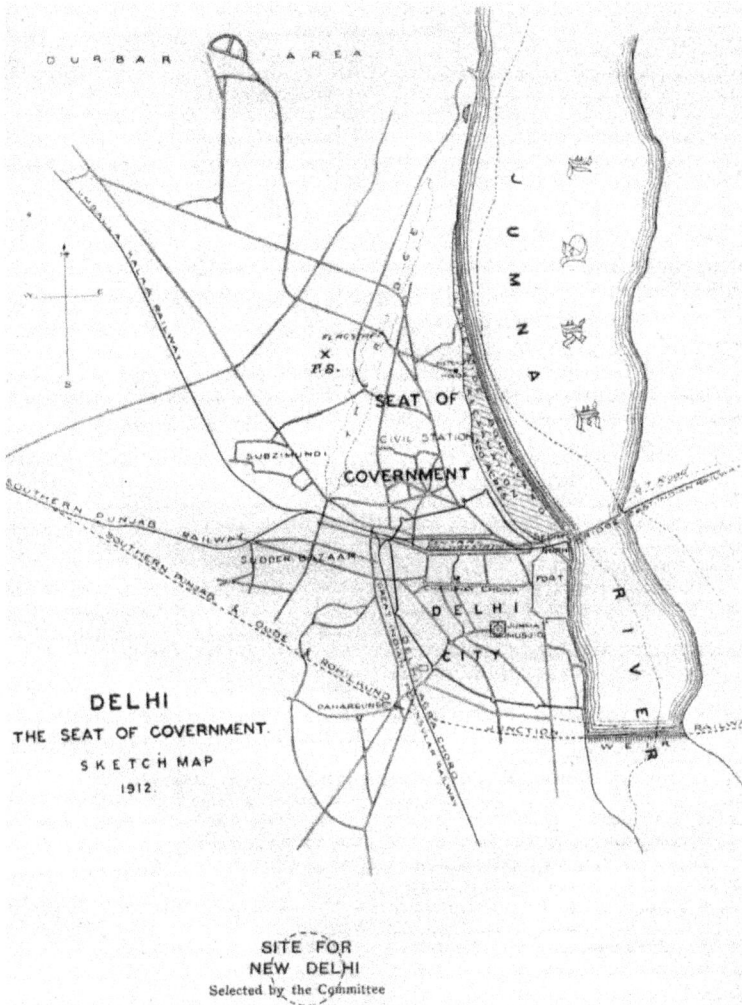

DELHI

THE SEAT OF COVERNMENT.

S K E T C H MAP

1912.

SITE FOR
NEW DELHI
Selected by the Committee

[The cross marked " F.S." indicates the site of the two foundation-stones laid by
His Majesty King George V.]

Figure 5.2   Leslie's plan for the northern site[61]

for electricity.[63] The building of a new capital in the Delhi area offered tremendous economic opportunity for well-positioned men like Leslie with access to investment capital. Leslie seemingly saw no contradiction in promoting a town plan that personally enriched him and his business partners. And why should he have felt any qualms about this union between a public building project and his own personal economic gain? After all, as Cain and Hopkins have shown, men like Leslie had been doing it in the open for years. In the end, for Leslie, both government and commercial interests would bear the burden of building the capital – benefitting government through reduced expenditures and providing private individuals and businesses with commercial and investment opportunities.

In addition, the lake would transform the new capital into something more than a place of government business; it would become a site of tourism through its various recreational and entertainment opportunities. A wide boulevard open only to pedestrians and passenger vehicles would run the entire length of the new embankment. Trees, shops, restaurants, theatres, clubs, hotels, and cafes would line this thoroughfare,[64] causing Leslie to claim that 'with so many and such varied attractions Delhi is certain to become a favourite rendezvous with tourists ... making Delhi the true Indo-European Metropolis'.[65] Simla, the government's summer capital located high in the Himalayas, was known as a place of refuge and relief from the hard work and heat of the plains. Leslie's lakeside city would do something similar, not only extending the amount of time government officials desired to spend in the capital but also attracting non-government individuals from all walks of life.

Furthermore, Leslie believed the lake created by the weir improved the general health of the Delhi area, which had a reputation as one of the dirtiest cities in northern India. The city was notorious for a particularly nasty boil that plagued inhabitants. Lord Lansdowne, when criticizing the decision to transfer the capital from Calcutta to Delhi, reminded the House of Lords that the boil could reach three to four inches in diameter and lasted five to ten months.[66] Far worse, the area was prone to malarial conditions due to poor drainage and the nearness of the Yamuna River, which rose and subsided with the seasons, creating breeding grounds for mosquitoes. Leslie argued that the lake created by the weir would help eradicate malaria by permanently inundating the swampy bed of the Yamuna River.

Leslie's plan for how the new capital would be financed and built exemplified the way in which his professional past influenced his town plan. Just as his Southern Punjab Railway was built using private investment but serviced by the Government of India, the building of a new capital would use private investment to build the new capital's most important features, the weir and the embankment. For those critics who feared that the new capital would be devoid of commercial opportunities, Leslie's plan once again brought the colonial government into intimate contact with commercial interests in India. A mix of private companies and private investments would bear much of the cost of building the new city, and subsequently they would reap many of the economic rewards. In this way, the cost to government to build the new capital at Delhi would be reduced, freeing government revenues for other, more remunerative building projects like railways.

In the end, the power and attraction of Leslie's town plan was that it made the new capital a revenue producer rather than a revenue consumer both during and after the building of the city. For men like Leslie, commercial and investment opportunities should be first and foremost in the minds of colonial officials. What caused Leslie to draft an alternative town plan was Hardinge's seemingly dangerous erosion of the traditional public/private model. The Government of India and its town planning committee had ignored or failed to recognize the importance of the private business sector in building and servicing the new capital. While Leslie's proposed capital could never fully imitate Calcutta's commercial success because of its distance from important ports that connected India to Britain's global commerce, the new capital at Delhi still could be a thriving city of government, commerce, and recreation if built in the civil lines.

Leslie's paper was followed by a long discussion chaired by J. D. Rees, who claimed that Leslie had been 'opposed to the change of the seat of government, but it having become *un fait accompli*, he felt it his duty, as a loyal subject of the king emperor, to do his best to show how it could best be carried out'.[67] For Rees, Leslie had dealt with the change of capital as a 'statesman' by transforming what he considered a bad policy into an opportunity to improve the health of Delhi and to create a city 'worthy of the occasion'.[68] J. F. Finlay, who had served as Under-Secretary to the Government of India's Department of Finance and Commerce as well as a member of the Viceroy's executive council as the Finance Member, also applauded Leslie's scheme, claiming that 'future generations would owe a debt of gratitude to Sir Bradford for improving the health and enhancing the beauty of the ancient historical city of Delhi'.[69] But, he argued, Leslie's hope that the new capital would one day become 'the commercial, trading, and manufacturing metropolis of India' was ill founded since Calcutta would always hold that position.[70] Sir Mancherjee Merwanjee Bhownaggree, member of Parliament for Bethnal Green North East, appreciated Leslie's plan to use a private company to help build city improvements because 'any scheme that resulted in such economy ought to receive a great deal of consideration'.[71]

The discussion was so lively and generated so much interest that the editors of the *Journal of the Royal Society of Arts* later allowed interested members to contribute further remarks that appeared in the next edition of the journal. In these later writings, members pushed the Government of India to take Leslie's proposal seriously. Capturing beautifully the connection between government and commerce, John Pollen claimed that the buildings of the new capital should be made of glass and steel. As he claimed, 'I have long held the opinion that, both here and in India, Government offices should be constructed on the same principle as banking houses, where those who pay for the labour can see their employees at work through the glass.'[72] Wilmot Corfield, a well-known philatelist who had been ill disposed to the transfer of the capital, was particularly upset about rumours that the new capital would be placed to the south of the existing city. For Corfield, 'the Delhi idea, as an idea, has a charm of its own; and much of that charm will be lost if not the romantic city of Delhi, but a brand new place somewhere else is to be India's new seat of government'.[73] He continued, 'the proposed site now holding attention would not contain a new Delhi, but a new place that ought to go by a new name, possibly Georgeabad ..."New Delhi" is too near to Delhi, and yet is not Delhi'.[74]

Leslie's paper renewed such impassioned debate in Parliament and in the press that the Government of India was forced to postpone the official town planning report so that the town planning committee could study Leslie's scheme for the civil lines and to prepare a second report on the northern site to be published alongside the official report.[75] Once finished, Hardinge had 1,100 copies of the official town planning reports printed at the Government Printing Office in Simla and shipped to England for use in Parliament.[76]

Morbidity and mutiny: the Government of India rejects the northern site

Leslie's paper added a new dimension in the criticism of the Government of India's new policy. For antagonists like Curzon, Hardinge's government had been wrongheaded in its policy to transfer the capital in the first place, and now its decision to place that capital far from the civil lines simply highlighted the government's irresponsibility. It was inconceivable for critics that the civil lines, a site of British residency and colonial memory, would be separated from the new capital by an Indian city. Curzon attacked the government's official building site as a 'region of stones and snakes'.[77] With questions being raised in Parliament concerning the official town site and with members of Parliament openly questioning the competency of the present leadership of the Government of India, Hardinge decided to take a decisive stand against Leslie's plan for building the imperial capital in the civil lines.[78] Though Hardinge claimed to be 'endeavour[ing] to keep an open mind' about where the capital should be built, in reality he used the debate over the civil lines as an opportunity to push back against the detractors of his scheme.[79] Hardinge had his official town planning committee systematically undermine Leslie's proposal by focusing on a variety of factors that ended the civil lines as a potential building site and in the process showed Hardinge's critics that his government was indeed threshing out the details of the transfer of the capital.[80]

The town planning committee took a diplomatic approach by arguing that though a town plan could be laid out in the civil lines it would be so reduced in size and so expensive to complete that the building project might fail, reducing the prestige and honour of the British Raj.[81] This remained true even after Leslie's land reclamation scheme along the western shore of the lake was included. They argued that five square miles was 'the absolute minimum space upon which you can start planning the imperial city, and we fail to see where even this minimum amount of suitable ground can be found on the northern site'.[82] Unmovable obstacles bordered the area and allowed no real possibility for future expansion. Old Delhi, one of the largest cities in northern India, lay immediately to the south. Wetlands and an extremely high water table stopped expansion to the north. The Yamuna River lay just to the east. Though the ridge offered splendid architectural opportunities, it required major land rehabilitation work. The vegetation was sparse and the over-abundance of rock outcroppings, which reflected the sun's rays, kept the area extremely hot especially during May and June. Lutyens, as a landscape architect, was concerned about trees being able to grow to maturity on the ridge, and he foresaw the need to bring in large amounts of topsoil.[83] The civil lines simply lacked the requisite space and soils to build the world-class capital envisioned by Hardinge's government and his town planners. If built in the civil lines, as Leslie desired, the capital would become 'merely a series of government buildings' and not a symbol of a new British-India for the twentieth century as Hardinge intended.[84]

It was at this time that Herbert Baker, who was not yet an official member of the architectural board but had been commissioned to evaluate the various building sites, had his first great impact on the city. In discussions with Swinton, Baker noted that the civil lines would give the new capital a strong British sentiment, foundation, and heritage, but it would be an imperfect city. Already familiar with the politics of large building projects from his work in South Africa under Cecil Rhodes, Baker warned of the 'cold fit' of later viceroys and Government of India officials who might be less willing to spend money and manpower on the new capital.[85] A capital built in the civil lines, small by necessity, could be allowed to suffer in its purpose by uninterested or even antagonistic viceroys; it could easily become a 'head without a body' – a capital in name only.[86] Building on the southern site, on the other hand, would mean that the 'die was cast'.[87] An imperial capital built here would have to be seen through to the finish 'over all obstacles and in face of all panicky fears', for it would be a catastrophe and an embarrassment for the empire if construction on the south site fell away 'from its high purpose'.[88] Though far riskier, the south site forced the government and its architects to create a city so great that its magnificence overshadowed the vast plains of Delhi.[89]

The town planning committee also attacked the central piece of Leslie's town plan, the weir, and the large lake it created. The impounding of a large body of water, they argued, would create more problems than it solved. Large portions of the Barari Plain north of the civil lines would have to be raised as much as eight feet to control the lake's back-flooding.[90] Much of this land, 'for at least half a mile from the margin of the inhabited area', would need to be set aside as a protective zone and could never be built upon in the future because of the potential for flooding. Furthermore, the civil line's present high water table problems would be made worse by the lake's percolation.[91]

Not wanting to leave any stone unturned, Hardinge formed a special health committee headed by Sir C. P. Lukis, Director General of the Indian Medical Service and the Sanitary Commissioner of the Government of India, to verify the findings of the town planning committee. Lukis was joined by H. T. Keeling, Chief Engineer of the Imperial Delhi Committee, which oversaw all aspects of the building of the new capital, and J. C. Robertson, of the Indian Medical Service and a Deputy Sanitary Commissioner.[92] After examining Delhi's civil lines, the health committee concluded that 'there would be a grave risk of excessive sickness from rheumatic affections and diseases of the respiratory system, including tuberculosis' caused by the area's damp conditions during the cold season.[93] Lukis' committee also examined the Delhi District's malarial survey, which was based on spleen counts – known as the splenic index – taken of children in the region.[94] In the mid-nineteenth century, health officers discovered that children who had been exposed to high fevers caused by illness such as malaria had enlarged spleens. The first examinations done in the 1840s were a response to the high levels of malaria in many canal colonies in northern India.[95] It was determined by Hardinge's health committee that two of the most dangerous malaria-carrying mosquitoes, *M. Culicifacies* and *Ne. Stephensi*, occurred in higher numbers in the civil lines than in the southern portion of the Delhi District. The committee captured and examined specimens throughout the district and found that in the civil lines 34 per cent belonged to the malaria-carrying class of mosquitos while in the southern, dryer parts of the district this number fell to 20 per cent. These differences in mosquito populations had led to different morbidity rates across the district. Delhi's malarial survey showed that 65 per cent of children tested in the northern portion of the Delhi District had enlarged spleens. In the south, this percentage dropped to 23 per cent.[96] The committee also noted that mosquito breeding grounds were extremely 'widespread and regularly distributed' throughout the northern site.[97] According to the committee, the area 'consist[ed] of extensive swamps and pools which would be extremely difficult to deal with effectively on account of the tendency to flooding, the general water-logging, defective drainage and the stiff retentive nature of the soil'.[98] The health committee concluded that 'Sir Bradford's proposal will have no effect whatever upon the incidence of plague ... [and would instead] intensify the adverse conditions already prevailing upon the northern site'.[99] Leslie's plan, the health committee determined, did not solve the civil lines' malarial problem; it simply shifted it slightly to the north where residents would continue to be in contact with malaria-carrying mosquito populations. This condemnation of the northern site by the health committee carried significant weight since Lukis was a noted specialist on malaria.[100]

The members of the town planning committee also concluded that it would be extremely difficult to provide adequate protection for a capital built in the civil lines. They estimated that perhaps 500 soldiers and officers could be accommodated in a half square mile area in the already constricted civil lines, but this number was certainly deficient for defending the city. The nearest location for a large military cantonment was 8.5 miles to the west in Sadr Bazaar, an industrial suburb.[101] The government's tremendous concern about the limited size of the cantonment and thus its inability to protect the new capital directly pointed to persistent memories of one of British-India's most transformative moments, the Indian uprising in 1857. Delhi quickly became a focal point of the uprising as Indian sepoys poured into the city to declare their allegiance to Bahadur Shah Zafar II, the nominal emperor of India who continued to reside in the Mughal palace at Delhi as a British pensioner.[102] Some of the most persistent and brutal fighting took place in the Delhi area.

Important monuments, buildings, and geographical features continued to carry memories of those eventful days. The ridge to the west of the civil lines, Flagstaff Tower, and Hindu Rao's House had served as important elements of the Delhi Field Force's defensive breastworks, which had allowed the British to hold out for months against repeated Sepoy attacks. Each time a new regiment of Sepoys entered Delhi they were asked to prove their commitment to the cause by attacking the British on the ridge. Flagstaff Tower served as a kind of beacon for British civilians and their families on the first day of the uprising when they huddled there in fear and confusion.[103] It later became an important defensive lookout because of its position on the ridge's summit. Hindu Rao's House and its Gurkha garrison faced some of the fiercest Sepoy attacks throughout the siege. These historic sites were ever-present reminders of British imperial heroism and the great sacrifices that British men and women and their Indian allies had made in defending and securing the British Empire in 1857. These sacrifices were later commemorated in 1863 with the erection of the Mutiny Memorial on the Ridge (Figure 5.3).

Early in the planning stages of the new capital, the town planning committee expressed reservations about building on the ridge because of its connections to 1857 and because planners feared that British public opinion would be offended. Building here would require severe restrictions. The only development that could occur among the ridge's sites of memory, as Jay Winter would call them, would be gardens with 'plain hallowed buildings'.[104] British sentiment might be appeased if, according to the town planners, 'the portion from Flagstaff Tower to Hindu Rao's House and the Mutiny Memorial ... remain[ed] sacrosanct'.[105] James Houssemayne Du Boulay, Hardinge's private secretary, believed that the area around Hindu Rao's House and the memorial could be transformed into a 'beautiful garden' with vistas cleared to the Kashmir Gate of the old city.[106] Within this garden, Hindu Rao's House could serve as a museum of the uprising, and the memorial replaced by a cathedral that housed the memorial tablets.

Figure 5.3   Old vintage antique print of Mutiny Memorial of 1857 Delhi, India

Before the uprising, relations between Indians and Europeans had been relatively cordial in the Delhi area with many European families choosing to live within the city walls in Daryaganj, a neighbourhood near the Mughal palace. This changed after 1857. According to Narayani Gupta, the British in Delhi, much as their fellow countrymen back home, 'fell back on stereotypes as short-cuts to understanding the Indians because the social contact between Indians and Europeans was decreasing'.[107] The demonization of Indians in the aftermath of the uprising encouraged European residents to live outside the city walls to the north and to become increasingly concerned about health and disease. In the process, they isolated themselves in a haphazardly designed civil lines inhabited by their own people. Their 'belief in godliness led them to zealously keep alive myths of 1857 and to nurse their fastidious distaste for degenerate Muslims and Hindus', according to Gupta.[108] In the immediate months after recapturing Delhi, some even called for the destruction of Delhi's Mughal palace and the neighbouring Jama Masjid, the largest mosque in South Asia. The latter, they argued, should be replaced by a cathedral. Instead, British troops were stationed within the palace grounds and in the suburb of Daryaganj, effectively transforming the heart of Delhi into a large military cantonment. This included the destruction of a number of residences around the palace to ensure open lines of artillery fire in case of another uprising. 'When the dust of the demolitions had settled down', Gupta poignantly writes, 'the people of Delhi rubbed their tired eyes and looked in vain for their familiar landmarks, and did not find them.'[109]

This remarkable history of British imperial trial and triumph pointed to perhaps the greatest flaw of building in the civil lines. It simply carried the wrong imperial history, one that was exceptionally ugly, fractious and a denial of Hardinge's vision of a new British-India for the twentieth century. The history of the civil lines was a story of conflict and division, and no lake or promenade could erase the life and death struggles that occurred in 1857 on the ridge overlooking the civil lines and within the city. Nor could it remove the clear animosity and fear that local European residents had for Indians in the uprising's aftermath.[110]

Leslie's town plan, which physically divided the European and Indian community, expressed this persistent anxiety. In his plan, the lake's west bank housed a highly developed metropolitan area of government buildings, places of entertainment, and European residences. A second residential colony for Indian clerks and their families was planned for the lake's east bank. These two communities, forced together during the day due to the work of colonial government, would be separated during times of rest.[111] Segregated into their own colony, Leslie argued, Indian clerks and their families would enjoy open-air bathing along newly built ghats and have their own schools, temples, and mosques. This type of division built into the new capital made perfect sense to an old India-hand like Leslie, but it expressed precisely the wrong narrative that Hardinge and other proponents of the transfer hoped to achieve as seen in the debates surrounding the transfer of the capital and its promise of future political devolution. Leslie's lake and its two segregated colonies, lying within a civil lines shaped by post-1857 imperial politics and fear, perpetuated the notion that Britain and India could not be mixed. Though Hardinge may have been sensitive to Leslie's desire to separate British and Indian residential blocs, he was far too talented a diplomat to settle for such a clumsy treatment, especially in India's existing political climate.

The problem with Leslie's vision for the northern site was that it did little to resolve the imperial problems that led to the transfer of the capital from Calcutta to Delhi in the first place. Indeed, Leslie's plan, though highly original, would do little to curb the forces of Indian anti-colonialism. Hardinge's new imperial vision demanded a different space and history altogether, one that was largely free of British and Indian antipathies and thus open for a new interpretation. A new imperial hegemony was required in India to replace the obsolete model espoused by Curzon, Leslie and others. Securing Britain's position in India, something John Darwin argues was essential to Britain's world system, meant winning back Indian cooperation with British rule, even if it meant major political concessions.[112] Based on his own pragmatism and years of work in diplomatic circles, Hardinge's new vision was not meant to weaken but to secure Britain's position in India by regaining the trust and loyalty of the Indian people. Building on the south site safely shunted rather than forgot the sacral memory of the ridge and civil lines, both of which represented the imperial past but not an imperial future. Thus, Leslie's arguments based on commercial concerns failed in the face of the south site's potential for rewriting the imperial relationship between Britain and India in the twentieth century.

What was needed was a new imperial vision that swung Indian opinion in favour of British rule. India's educated elite was not to be feared but to be won over by British good will and the promise of future political advancement. This new vision of empire was represented by the new capital's connection to political reform as evidenced by paragraph three of the official state paper that announced the transfer of the capital.[113] It could also be seen in the very words of Hardinge and his staunchest allies. Writing to Baker in 1913, Hardinge argued, '...the aim must be to achieve a style which will be symbolic of India of the twentieth century, with its British and Indian administration ... and it must be remembered that every year the Indian element in the administration grows in influence and learning'.[114] The goal was not simply to imprint British architectural ideals on an Indian landscape, as had been done at Calcutta, but to build a capital that represented a new era in British-Indian relations. As Hardinge explained to Curzon early in the planning stages, the city must reflect 'a broad classical style with an Indian motif ... the architecture must be combined with a spirit of the east such as will appeal to Orientals as well as to Europeans'.[115] And as he repeatedly reminded his planners, 'it must be remembered that it is not a British administration that is building the new city, as was the case when Calcutta was built, but a British-Indian administration that is charged with the task'.[116] Similarly, in the House of Commons in July 1912, Edwin Montagu claimed that the new capital would serve as an almost sacral symbol of a new British-India made stronger by merging what he saw as the national traits of both:

> The golden thread of Oriental idealism is being woven into and embellishing the drab web of our scheme of life, and our sciences and government, which we have so laboriously inherited and are handing down, is being offered to the Oriental to help him in material progress, and the East and the West together, united and assisting one another, are constructing in India ... the lasting temple of their joined ideals.[117]

Likewise, at his farewell banquet given by Indians in Simla in 1913, Fleetwood Wilson claimed that a new era was dawning in India where 'we shall have to resort to the more difficult arts of persuasion and conciliation, in the place of the easier methods of autocracy'.[118] He ended his farewell speech by quoting the words of Rabindranath Tagore, 'Into that heaven of freedom, my Father, let this country awake.'[119] For these men, the new capital symbolized an India that was unified and rejuvenated by the abiding loyalty of Indians to their king-emperor and by the Raj's rational response to their legitimate demands for a greater voice in the colonial government. Hence, New Delhi, for all its shows of imperial power, also represented a new kind of colonial project in India. The new capital would symbolize Britain's attempt to resolve the contradictory goals of giving Indians greater political power while at the same time strengthening Britain's paramount power in India.

The official town plan took on the contours of a large federal capital that symbolized the unity of India's diverse peoples under the supreme authority of the Raj.[120] During the second half of 1911, when the Government of India was debating whether or not to transfer the capital, high officials argued that just as Washington DC was not associated with any one state, India's new capital should not be intimately tied to any one province such as Bengal, Bombay, or Madras.[121] The concept of a federal capital again emerged during the planning stages of 1912 and 1913 when the official town planning committee and high officials in the Government of India examined the actual town plans of two other federal capitals, Canberra and Washington DC.[122] As Herbert Baker claimed when describing the Great Court's main intersection, 'These two roads gave the geometrical key of the ingenious plan of the new city, a noble development of the germ of L'Enfant's plan of

Washington.'[123] After Britain's problems in Bengal, the British Raj needed to redefine itself as incontestably strong yet benevolent enough to make concessions to deserving colonial subjects.

Federalism provided an attractive hegemony that better unified the diverse provinces of British-India and moved Indians toward greater political power in the provinces. Writing nearly two decades later in 1930, Herbert Baker claimed, 'Lord Hardinge and his government had a high, and in view of the [later] reforms even a prophetic, instinct when they decided to express in terms of architecture the common dignity and distinction of the Government of India as a whole.'[124] Within this colonial federalism, British officials were willing to give elected Indian officials more power in the provinces as long as the political centre, now at New Delhi, remained securely in British hands. Thus, while Britain devolved many political issues to increasingly Indian dominated provincial legislative assemblies, British colonial officials remained in control of the most important state functions including foreign policy, the military, and the police.

6
Hardinge's Imperial Delhi Committee and his Architectural Board: The Perfect Building Establishment for the Perfect Colonial Capital

While colonial officials alluded to an imperial future where Indians would one day have a much greater voice in their own governance, their reform rhetoric continued to be built upon traditional imperial assumptions not only about Indians but also about themselves. New Delhi's progressive vision, so well argued by Hardinge's government and its parliamentary supporters, began to fracture once those high ideals met the exigencies of British colonial rule in India. Much like the high modernist ventures that James Scott discusses in *Seeing Like a State*, a project that started with such high principles quickly fell prey to hubris and racial and cultural assumptions.

Hardinge, the greatest proponent of the transfer of the capital from Calcutta to Delhi, once again served as a catalyst for bringing promised political reform in line with continued British rule. As a sort of philosopher-king, he showed himself to be the absolute master builder who dictated the new capital's forms by continually haranguing his architects to build the capital that he envisioned. Hardinge's rejection of a competition to select an architectural board and his absolute control over the Imperial Delhi Committee, the government establishment responsible for building the city, point to his role as a priest of high modernism, a technocratic dictator. As Scott suggests, 'Technocracy ... is the belief that the human problem of urban design has a unique solution ... Deciding such technical matters by politics and bargaining would lead to the wrong solution. As there is a single, true answer to the problem of planning the modern city, no compromises are possible.'[1] Thus, even as Hardinge pushed for profound political changes in India, of which his new capital was a central component, his deep-seated commitment to an imperial hierarchy that simultaneously privileged western values and history while demeaning India's undermined the long-term security of British rule in India.

The Imperial Delhi Committee: Hardinge makes himself master of his city

Before any of Hardinge and his allies' high ideals could be realized, there had to be some kind of central authority to carry out the day-to-day tasks involved in a construction project of such magnitude. Its responsibilities would include the allocation and distribution of funds for various building projects and the assignment of human resources and building materials. It also would serve as an agent between the primary architects and the Government of India, its various departments, and private Indian contractors who physically would erect the new capital. Within weeks of the durbar ceremony, Hardinge began thinking about what this central authority might look like and, more importantly, how it could be used to advance his vision for a new British-India. Two interconnected problems had to be faced immediately, time itself and the colonial government's bureaucracy – a complex web of details, oversight, and competing interests. Hardinge's viceroyalty was scheduled to end in 1916, just four short years away. In that time he needed to design and begin building a city that would compare favourably to the great capitals of the world. Both of these tasks took time, a luxury simply denied to Hardinge because of his short duration in India.

The Government of India's traditional approach to public works projects did not help. The process was designed to move slowly, methodically, and with tremendous examination and oversight by the Secretary of State for India who ultimately approved or rejected project proposals. But the building of New Delhi was exceedingly different from India's typical public works project because of the new capital's political importance and because of powerful opponents who could apply continual pressure on the Secretary of State for India in London. Hardinge proposed a new procedure to expedite the planning and building of his capital. In a letter to Crewe, he pointed out that 'the Government of India by its constitution, and its procedure of departments, is not a suitable body to supervise the executive details of so vast a project'.[2] The project was too large for the Government of India's Public Works Department alone, and while the Delhi District had a local government, the project could not be turned over to it because of the 'far reaching imperial interests involved'.[3] Instead, Hardinge proposed the creation of a local central authority, the Imperial Delhi Committee, which 'could be entrusted the initiation and discussion of the multitude of issues which will arise in connection with the construction of the city'.[4]

The debates within the Government of India over this central authority, its membership, and, most importantly, its leadership reflected in many ways the same dynamics of old Indian hands versus new Indian men seen during the parliamentary debates that were raging simultaneously in Parliament over the transfer of the capital. Hardinge, an official with great diplomatic skills but little Indian experience and almost no patience for India's painfully slow colonial bureaucracy, pushed back against powerful Government of India officials whose entire careers had been in India and who had vested interests in maintaining the status quo. Where Hardinge dramatically differed from the traditional approach to public works projects in India was the way in which he by-passed the prerogative of various departments.

Reminiscent of his earlier career in the Foreign Office where he served as the eyes and ears of King Edward, meeting with him almost every week, Hardinge looked for a loyal official who could serve as his voice on the Imperial Delhi Committee.[5] He turned to Fleetwood Wilson, the senior member of his executive council, for guidance, ideas, and the names of potential candidates.[6] The right candidate was of utmost importance because he would relieve much of the pressure on Hardinge while still giving the viceroy tremendous control over the building project. Wilson agreed with the idea, and told Hardinge that a man who 'is someone to whom you can open your mind, and who loyally and successfully carries out your Excellency's wishes' should lead the Imperial Delhi Committee.[7] He strongly recommended William Malcolm Hailey, a deputy commissioner of the Punjab. Hardinge liked the suggestion since he had been impressed by Hailey's work as the representative of the Finance Department on the Central Committee charged with planning and managing King George's 1911 Delhi Durbar.[8] By February 1912, long before Hardinge hammered out the final contours of the Imperial Delhi Committee, he contacted Sir Louis Dane, Lt Governor of the Punjab, to inform him of his desire to have Hailey lead the Imperial Delhi Committee.

Hardinge remained committed to Hailey even in the face of heavy opposition from at least one member of his executive council and a powerful Secretary to the Government in the Public Works Department, Sir Reginald Craddock and W. B. Gordon, respectively. They opposed Hailey because of his relatively junior status and, more importantly, because they saw his selection as a missed opportunity to advance one of their own officers. The Indian colonial service had been plagued by lack of advance and opportunity for years. So much so that Parliament had established in September 1912 a special Public Services Committee, chaired by Lord Islington, to study the problem and to make recommendations. Colonial officers increasingly were concerned about their salaries, which did not keep pace with India's rising cost of living, and their poor prospects for advance within the service. At the same time, their work was becoming heavier due to parliamentary demands for oversight.[9] Thus, the Imperial Delhi Committee was a rare opportunity for officers to win recognition and promotion, and men in powerful positions attempted to shape the committee in ways that benefitted their own colonial departments.

None were more assertive than Gordon of the Public Works Department. He strongly advised that an engineer from the Public Works Department, working independently from the local Delhi administration, be made the presiding officer of the Imperial Delhi Committee. Gordon used the port trusts of Bombay, Calcutta, and Madras as examples of separate bodies that directly worked under the Government of India in isolation from local civil administrations.[10] The building of the new capital, like the port trusts, required the skills and knowledge of an engineer, a Director-General of Works, who was capable of handling all construction and administrative responsibilities, according to Gordon. A small central committee, free of any association with the local Delhi District, could serve as a mediator between the Director-General and the Government of India, which would be responsible for the overall design of the capital. This presiding engineer, working through the central committee and using his establishment's unique skills and expertise, would realize the architects' and government's vision. Suggesting just how disconnected Gordon was from Hardinge's general thinking, he suggested that the viceroy could be the president of the committee, with an honourable member as vice president. Other members could be the Public Works Secretary, the Finance Secretary, and the Chief Sanitary Officer to the Government of India. An additional officer of the Public Works Department could serve as Secretary to the Committee.[11]

Wherever possible Gordon not only worked in appointments for officers of his own department but also placed the Public Works Department at the centre of the building project by giving it control over construction and administration. The Director-General of Works would prepare a general estimate that would then be passed to the central committee for scrutiny and approval. After this was done, the estimates would be passed to the Public Works Department, which would forward them to the Secretary of State for sanction. After the

Secretary of States' acceptance of the estimates, the central committee would be empowered to handle all matters involved with the project, using the Public Works Department as the 'channel for communicating the sanction of Government to the Director-General of Works'.[12]

In his note to the viceroy, Gordon explained that he was not necessarily opposed to a non-Public Works officer managing the building project but that,

> In the distribution of work and appointments, some regard should be had to the reasonable claims of the various departments. The Department which *prima facie* has the first claim to be entrusted with the work of arranging for the design and construction of the new capital is undoubtedly the Public Works Department.[13]

He argued that there were a number of senior Public Works officers who had the necessary engineering skills and administrative acumen to handle the entire project. Gordon ended with the following caveat. He promised that no matter the final decisions made concerning leadership, Public Works' officers would 'work wholeheartedly and to the best of their ability to make the arrangement a success'.[14] But, he strongly warned, 'if they are to work with a civil officer in executive control, they will do so under a dispiriting sense that injustice has been done to their department, and that the main credit which will be due to the department if they make the work a success will go in the usual course to the head controlling authority, and not to an officer of the[ir] department'.[15] However, members of the Public Works building establishment would work more 'cheerfully and contentedly' if they felt the 'supreme control' was a 'brother officer' who would 'appreciate their difficulties'.[16] Realizing that their department had been given leadership of such an important task, they would work with greater energy and zeal, knowing that the accolades would fall solely to them, 'and the fact will be evident in the result', claimed Gordon.[17] When the Government of India ignored his advice about selecting a Public Works officer to head the building project, Gordon responded with an angry note. After describing his experiences in South Africa organizing an irrigation department, drafting and helping to get passed a large irrigation bill, and encouraging land owners to carry out his land irrigation schemes, he claimed, 'I could find you half a dozen Public Works men who would have done as well or better than I did, but in our own country we are without honour and not considered fit to be let out of leading strings.'[18]

Reginald Craddock, Home Member for the Government of India, also questioned the selection of Hailey to head the Imperial Delhi Committee because this meant advancing him over other officers who had seniority.[19] Hailey's official rank in the Punjab was a Deputy Commissioner of a District, but at New Delhi he would be heading the local government as Chief Commissioner. Craddock argued that,

> Other much more senior candidates have been put forward by the Punjab Government, and the selection of Hailey, involving the rejection of other officers of greater seniority and possibly equal merit, but who had not had the similar opportunities of showing their capabilities to the Government of India, is bound to cause considerable dissatisfaction and disappointment.[20]

Additionally, senior ranking officers whose skills were being enlisted for the building of the new capital might be upset by having to take commands from a junior officer, according to Craddock.[21] In the face of Hardinge's strong commitment to Hailey, Craddock acquiesced and promised to support the viceroy's decision on two conditions. Craddock asked that Major H. C. Beadon, who recently had completed the Delhi District Settlement Report in 1910 and who had been managing the initial land acquisition proceedings for the new capital, be kept on as the Deputy Commissioner of Delhi.[22] 'To turn him out of Delhi at this juncture,' argued Craddock, 'would be a poor reward for the help he has given us, and would be to throw away the benefit of the special knowledge which he has acquired.'[23] Craddock also strongly recommended the appointment of Geoffrey deMontmorency as Hailey's personal assistant and as secretary to the Imperial Delhi Committee. Hardinge had hoped to appoint deMontmorency as Deputy Commissioner of Delhi because he was impressed with his work on how best to compensate dispossessed Indian landowners in the Delhi District.[24] This, of course, would have removed Beadon from his current post. Craddock, however, remained firm, 'to man the enclave at the top with a not very senior Deputy Commissioner [Hailey], and to select an Assistant Commissioner for the respectable appointment of Deputy Commissioner and District Magistrate (deMontmorency), would be a combination of appointments which I could, under no circumstances, recommend to Your Excellency'.[25] Much like his reservations about Hailey, Craddock believed deMontmorency's relatively junior status would cause anger amongst overlooked but senior officials. Craddock closed his comments by suggesting that he be made president of the

Imperial Delhi Committee with Hailey as Vice President though he admitted that such an arrangement might not commend itself to all members of the Viceroy's executive council. Clearly, while the transfer and building of a new capital were generating heated debate in London amongst political and business circles, men in India were doing everything possible to get attached to the building project.[26] Hardinge followed most of Craddock's advice except the last since this would have minimized the viceroy's control over the Imperial Delhi Committee.

By November 1912, after receiving advice from the Public Works Department and from Wilson, Hardinge proposed to his executive council that the committee be made up of four-members, including a presiding officer, a chief engineer, an architect, and a finance officer. Rejecting Gordon's suggestion to separate the building of the new capital from the local civil administration, Hardinge urged that the presiding officer be the Chief Commissioner of Delhi since as the head of the local administration he would be able to exert greater influence. The chief engineer would be accountable for all questions regarding construction. The architect would be responsible for designing all buildings other than those entrusted to the as yet unnamed architectural board. The government architect as well as the chief engineer would be in close contact with this architectural board throughout the building process to ensure integrity of vision. The finance member of the committee would be responsible for overseeing funds for specific projects, and was essential, according to Hardinge, 'if rapid and efficient working is to be secured'.[27] Along with being responsible for initiating and discussing problems connected to the building project, the committee would have relatively strong financial powers and authority over all but the most important questions concerning general design. Its members, with the exception of the presiding officer, would be unattached to any government department and should consider their work on the committee a full-time commitment. Four consulting members would advise and aid the Imperial Delhi Committee on special matters: the Director General of the Indian Medical Service, the Sanitary Commissioner of the Government of India, a railway officer, and an officer representing military concerns.

Hardinge then asked the Public Works Department to submit an operational plan that put to paper his general ideas for an Imperial Delhi Committee.[28] Gordon did exactly what he said officers in the Public Works Department would do regardless of committee leadership. Working as a team player, he drew up two plans since he was not entirely clear about how funds would be sanctioned by the Secretary of

State for India. Typically, as Gordon explained to DuBoulay, Hardinge's private secretary, the Secretary of State refused to sanction any funding on building projects before detailed plans and estimates were drawn up and submitted to him. 'His orders in this respect are very strict,' claimed Gordon, and only recently had been waived for the imperial coronation durbar and its related pavilions, both of which were temporary works.[29] However, in discussions with DuBoulay it became clear to Gordon that Hardinge desired a different procedure altogether. Gordon's first plan was based on the assumption that the Imperial Delhi Committee would follow normal protocol concerning project funding and construction. It was designed to be a long process that assured thorough discussion and oversight with the Secretary of State sanctioning only a detailed estimate. The second plan was based on the Secretary of State breaking normal procedure and approving a 'more or less rough estimate' before detailed plans and estimates were completed.[30]

Hardinge, not surprisingly, selected the second plan, assuming that Crewe would sanction rough building estimates that had not been exhaustively examined by the departments of Public Works and Finance. The Imperial Delhi Committee would prepare a general square foot and cubic foot estimate for direct submission to the Government of India, which would then submit the estimate to the Secretary of State for India. This process by-passed the Public Works and Finance Departments, which typically reviewed building estimates and assured their detail and accuracy before they were sent to the Secretary of State for approval. Only later would the Imperial Delhi Committee prepare and sanction detailed plans and estimates against the rough estimate already sanctioned by the Secretary of State.[31] Though breaking protocol, the attractiveness of the second plan was that it allowed the Imperial Delhi Committee to perform much of the preliminary work that needed to be done before any ground was broken. This included acquiring necessary lands for the project, building access roads, locating building materials, setting up nurseries for shrubs and trees that later would be used in the city, and developing estimates for the general size of government structures based on current needs and the size of residential compounds based on rank. While the committee's total expenditures could not exceed the estimate sanctioned by the Secretary of State, it would have 'the full powers of the Government of India under the Public Works Department code and the Civil Service Regulations' which gave the committee financial powers and the authority to temporarily appoint or depute officers.[32] Because the committee would acquire relatively strong powers over finance and appointments, Gordon included the following reservations. The Imperial Delhi Committee could not sanction any specific project that exceeded 12½ lakhs (1,250,000 rupees). Additionally, though the committee was given the financial powers of the Government of India, it needed to exercise them under the Civil Service Regulation's Article 81, which authorized the committee to allocate funds as 'a local government in respect of provincial expenditures'.[33] Lastly, the salaries and perquisites of committee members would be closely monitored by the Government of India to avoid any suspicion that committee members were personally benefitting from their increased financial powers.[34]

Hardinge forwarded Gordon's second plan to his executive council for an official vote, but not before he added important reservations that assured his overall control of the project. In most instances, the Imperial Delhi Committee was given a 'free hand' in executing approved construction and building policy, but Hardinge made sure to retain the power to question or alter any decisions or policies made by the committee concerning the most important issues. These might include alterations to the approved layout of the city, size of compounds for different classes of officers, or architectural styles to be adopted.[35] As Hardinge claimed in his proposal to Crewe:

> Over all the actions of the committee His Excellency the Viceroy will exercise general control. All proceedings will be at once reported to him, and he will have an unrestricted discretion to call upon the committee to reconsider any point which he may deem to be open to criticism or to demand departmental scrutiny in the Government of India.[36]

In this manner, Hardinge made himself the master of his new city while the Imperial Delhi Committee became a workhorse that executed the vision of his architects who worked in remarkably close consultation with him.

In the end, Hardinge received nearly everything he asked of the Secretary of State for India. Hailey, the man Hardinge always wanted to head the Imperial Delhi Committee, was selected as presiding officer.[37] Because Crewe was just as anxious as Hardinge to get the building project started, he broke protocol and sanctioned the rough estimate in March 1913 and gave Hardinge full powers to select Imperial Delhi Committee members.[38] With this sanction, Hardinge was allowed to by-pass India's colonial bureaucracy and its endemic delays. Hardinge now had in place a powerful committee empowered to administer the building of New Delhi and to ensure economy and promptness in carrying out the numerous tasks and diverse needs of a construction project of this magnitude.

The final shape of the Imperial Delhi Committee's duties, its membership, and its financial powers reflected Hardinge's political needs and his personal desires. He wanted supreme authority over the most important aspects of the new capital – its style and its vision – but wanted to avoid dealing with the multitude of lesser tasks that would have to be accomplished on a daily basis. The committee also hastened the building of the new capital's main structures. This was an important step in assuring the long-term success of the project. The transfer of the capital already had faced tremendous criticism in certain parliamentary circles, especially from Lord Curzon and his allies. There was no guarantee that a later viceroy would not reverse the policy, just as Hardinge had reversed Curzon's partition of Bengal. But physically standing structures rather than structures merely on paper would make this possibility much less likely.

Hardinge's fears were immediately born out at the end of his viceroyalty. As Hardinge approached his imminent departure in 1916, demands to either reduce the scope of the capital or to stop the building project altogether became more vocal. In particular, Curzon continued his pressure on the Government of India by circulating to the cabinet in London a memorandum that asked that the building project be stopped until further studies could be made about costs. The political problem caused by Curzon's memorandum became so acute that Lord Chelmsford, who replaced Hardinge in autumn 1916, was forced to publicly support the project. However, in private correspondence with his Secretary of State, Joseph Austen Chamberlain, Chelmsford admitted that he was not attached to the project in the same way as Hardinge.[39] But he felt compelled to continue the project, not only because of the royal nature of its original announcement but because the city was already rising on the plains of Delhi. As Chelmsford stated to Chamberlain:

> In as much as there had been seven cities of Delhi in the past which had been completed by the monarchs who had established them, it was impossible to conceive of an eighth city of Delhi commenced under his Majesty's auspices and abandoned. It would be a fatal blow to the prestige of the British Raj to leave ruins as colossal as any of the old cities and as an example for all time of the inability of British rule to create a new Capital.[40]

Until the project was completed in 1931, succeeding governments continued to support the project out of necessity. Failure to do so would have expressed not only imperial weakness but also a serious lack of resolve by the British, something the Raj could not afford to do in the existing nationalist climate in India.

Edwin Lutyens and the search for an architectural style

At the same time as Hardinge created a central authority to oversee the building of his new capital, he sought an architect or architects who could design government buildings that reflected the new imperial hegemony created by the transfer of the capital and its related political reforms. There was tremendous debate in Parliament, in the press, and amongst members of important intellectual and artistic circles, such as the Royal Society of Arts, over the type of architecture to be adopted and the architects best suited to carry it to a successful conclusion. Generally, the debate over architectural style reflected the concerns and aesthetic values of two camps: those who saw the building project solely as an opportunity to promote and display India's architectural genius and those who desired to express a western neo-classical building tradition that was broad enough in scope to allow for Indian architectural elaboration and ornamentation. The latter argument won out in the end. It did so not only because colonial officials and intellectuals were conceited about the superiority of western aesthetics but also because the neo-classical building tradition better served to reflect the high modernist goals set out by Hardinge and his allies in India and England.

One solution to the question of architectural style, which was repeatedly heard in Parliament, was to hold a competition to select the architects that would serve on the architectural board.[41] However, high-ranking officials and intellectual elites strongly disparaged the notion of a competition. Leonard Aloysius Stokes, President of the Royal Institute of British Architects and an early recommender of Lutyens for the town planning committee, argued in June 1912, that competitions tended to attract younger architects seeking opportunity while experienced architects tended to ignore them.[42] The latter, he argued, were well established in the field, had active practices, and thus had no time for competitions. Furthermore, competitions reflected an element of risk. Candidates had to put in a great deal of work on their submissions with no guarantee that this would lead to a successful award at the end.[43] Lastly, Stokes claimed that competition judges could simply make mistakes and give the award to the wrong architect.[44] Similarly, *The Times* was extremely disparaging of a competition to select an architect for the new capital. Drawing readers' attention to recent construction projects in London and in Australia, *The Times* lamented that most of these had been unsatisfactorily conceived and realized. In the case of Australia, where a competition had been held for the building of a new capital at Canberra, supposedly no experienced British architects submitted proposals and the award went to two Chicago architects, Walter and Marion Griffin. For Stokes and *The Times*, the Government of India would be better served by hand picking the best architect(s) it could find. If, however, the Government of India was determined to hold a competition to appease critics, Stokes argued that six to eight experienced architects could be invited to submit plans for the main government structures, which included Government House and the Secretariats, and given money to personally visit Delhi. Unsuccessful competitors could be given the secondary buildings at the end of the competition. Thus, every architect in the competition would win some type of commission, which would encourage experienced architects to submit proposals when invited to do so.

By October 1912, the Government of India had yet to nominate an architect, and *The Times* began to get openly nervous about the implications. The paper complained that it had been ten months since the king's proclamation to transfer the capital and yet there had been no official announcement about architects or architectural style. Looking back to what it considered past colonial building mistakes, *The Times* bemoaned that 'a wrong choice of method at the inception of the scheme will ruin one of the greatest architectural opportunities that history has known'.[45]

An important reason for the delay in publicly announcing an architect was that Hardinge already had the man he wanted to build Government House, Edwin Lutyens, who was already serving as a member of the official town planning committee sent to India to examine possible building sites for the new capital and to draw up the town plan. Hardinge was drawn to the architect's clear genius and had made him the most important member of the town planning committee by having him design the earliest town plan. As early as July 1912, when the town planning committee still was investigating the site for the new capital, Hardinge wrote to Crewe about having Lutyens design and build Government House, the most important structure in the future imperial capital.[46] Indeed, Lutyens already had made drawings of the structure even though he had not yet received an official commission. For Hardinge, Government House 'should be placed in the hands of one man who would have the knowledge and skill to make it a success'.[47] But Lutyens was controversial for a variety of reasons. He was well known for designing extravagant and expensive estates for Britain's elite, and this reputation gave critics political opportunities to attack the project's high cost and the way in which it drew away precious capital from more remunerative colonial investments such as railroads.

Perhaps worst of all, Lutyens had little regard for Indian architecture. His letters to his wife Emily and others showed him to be a man of tremendous wit and creativity who saw the world of architecture through a unique lens, but his personal correspondence also reflected a great deal of bigotry and disapproval of Indian architecture, once calling it a 'pile of stones with an onion thrown on top'.[48] He was just as sceptical of the Government of India's stress on devolution. Concerning political reform in India, Lutyens wrote to his wife, Emily, that 'India, like Africa, makes one very Tory and preTory feudal'.[49] The problem, for Hardinge, was that the new capital's architectural style needed to reflect the new India that political reform would create. Thus, Lutyens' reluctance to adopt Indian architectural styles in his designs caused Hardinge a tremendous amount of anguish. At one point calling Lutyens a 'philistine',[50] Hardinge complained that Lutyens was 'the most uncompromising and quite irreconcilable on the subject' of architectural style for the new capital.[51]

Lutyens' well-known architectural proclivities as well as his outspoken criticism of Indian architecture led many to believe that he was the wrong architect to design and build a capital that represented a progressive India where Indians had a greater share in responsible government. While Lutyens had strong supporters, such as Reginald Barrat, there were many who were not fully convinced that he had the artistic desire or the flexibility to overcome his architectural conceits to create a new architectural style for modern India. This concern was best reflected in the persistent claim heard in Parliament throughout 1912 that Lutyens, if given the commission, would build a capital in the style of the Italian Renaissance. This rumour had stemmed from a series of articles in *The Times*, which are discussed below, and even by Hardinge, who encouraged Lutyens to examine the fusion of Mediterranean and Indian architecture since both had been shaped by sunny climates. As he explained to the architect, the British School at Rome, which Lutyens had designed, could be adapted for India by 'orientaliz[ing]' it.[52] He continued his pressure on Lutyens to discover some sort of fusion, arguing, 'I wish you would study the question, for herein, I believe lies the solution of the style of architecture for the new city.'[53]

Hardinge even offered Lutyens one possible direction, 'my belief is that the Pathan style, with its rectangular or hexagonal columns, its breadth of treatment with big walls, buttresses, flat domes and few windows, would lend itself to a composition with Italian architecture that would inspire beauty, solidity, and originality'.[54]

Lutyens responded by sending Hardinge some of his conceptual drawings of Government House with an accompanying letter that captured Lutyens' interpretation of a new style for British-India:

> The drawing will show how natural and Indian a western motif can look, treated for the Indian sun, with Indian methods applied, without throwing away the English tradition, and clinging too much to the curiosities of a less intellectual style. Except for the column, I do not believe that public opinion in India would know it was not Indian. You could employ every Indian artist, wood and stone carver, in the country, to decorate; and of course the fabric itself would be built by Indians, so it could only be Indian, and India must be as open to new methods as all other countries.[55]

Remarkably, even after tremendous pressure from Hardinge, Lutyens was still hesitant to truly fuse Indian and western architecture. Instead, he provided Hardinge with an architectural sleight of hand that seemed Indian but was actually western at its foundation. A kind of Indian sentiment would be incorporated in the form of labour since Indians would physically build the city, but that would be the extent of Lutyens' *stated* attempt to blend the two building traditions.[56] Clearly, Hardinge and his government needed an additional voice on the architectural board.

Herbert Baker and the spirit of British rule

Herbert Baker, relatively unknown in Britain but a British architect of tremendous ability, suddenly appeared in this moment of scepticism concerning Lutyens. His October 1912 editorial in *The Times*, 'The New Delhi: Eastern and Western Architecture: A Problem of Style', captured the aesthetic germ that many sought for the new capital.[57] Striking a nerve in the English public, his editorial caused a tremendous flurry of conversation, partly because of its ideas about what modern British colonial architecture should reflect, partly because of its deeply philosophic and beautiful prose. George Swinton immediately sent Hardinge a note that described the letter's impact on the public, saying it was the most interesting news item in the week.[58] Swinton claimed that in Baker 'we have a man who is a successful architect and speaks not only like a poet, but like a statesman'.[59] Indeed, Baker was an architect of acute political understanding, a trait learned from his most important client in South Africa, Cecil Rhodes.[60] He repeatedly manifested this talent during the New Delhi building project.

Baker's letter was introduced by an editorial from *The Times* and was followed by editorial responses from Lord Curzon,[61] Thomas Jackson, an influential architect known for his many buildings at Oxford, and Ernest Binfield Havell, one of England's foremost authorities on Indian art and architecture. The editorials, rich in their thoughts about architectural meaning, captured the dilemma faced by the Government of India when determining a colonial architectural style for the twentieth century. Sir George Birdwood, another authority on Indian art and architecture, reflected the complexity of the problem when he claimed during a Royal Society of Arts debate that though he was 'in no sense an opium eater, the whole question of the new Delhi rose before him in a sort of Apocalyptic vision'.[62]

Yet Baker seemed to have the answers to the questions that so troubled Birdwood. In his editorial in *The Times*, Baker argued that while the new capital's architectural style should be shaped by the climate and physical characteristics of its immediate surroundings, it was even more important that the government structures evince core imperial values. This was precisely what he had achieved with his highly acclaimed Union Buildings in Pretoria, South Africa. After examining images of these structures for the first time, Swinton wrote to Hardinge that Baker seemed to revel in rock faces that made 'his buildings rise off and apparently grow out of rocky foundations'.[63] Though the Union Buildings seemed cemented to Pretoria's rocky substrata, it was the spirit of British rule that gave them shape. For Swinton, this was exactly the kind of architectural fusion that the Government of India required for the new capital at Delhi. The main government structures – Government House and the Secretariats – needed to be 'the sculptural monument of the good government and unity which India, for the first time in its history, has enjoyed under British rule' while seamlessly rising from their Indian environs.[64] Thus, while Baker claimed that New Delhi should represent a 'civilization in growth, a blend of the best elements of east and west', his overriding concern was with symbols of British law and order. An Indian presence should be felt, but it was the spirit of British rule that must be 'imprisoned in stone and bronze'.[65] The key to the question of the new capital's architectural style, for Baker, was determining which architectural tradition was broad enough in scope to be adapted to both

Indian material conditions and the political needs of the colonial state. The answer was clear: only the western neo-classical tradition, with its reliance on geometric principles, could realize the universal truths that Hardinge sought in his high modernist ambitions for a new India.

Baker's letter mirrored an older and larger feud between Havell and Birdwood. While the former believed that India had a *broad* fine arts tradition that shaped its civilization and culture, the latter felt that India reflected many *local* art traditions that were disparate in meaning, content, and context. Though Birdwood had been a great promoter of Indian art and had published an influential study, *The Industrial Arts of India* (1884), he claimed at a Royal Society of Arts meeting in January 1910 that India had no all-encompassing fine arts tradition that shaped the spirit of Indian culture. Instead, numerous village communities, which produced distinct crafts and goods, characterized Indian art. The claim was made after a paper read by Havell, who became so upset that he helped found the Indian Society, a group dedicated to bringing western attention to Indian art by sponsoring exhibitions and publications, including Havell's own study of Indian art, *A Handbook of India Art* (1920). Using his past experiences with the Bengal School of Art, which based its curriculum on Mughal rather than western traditions, Havell argued that only an Indian or an Anglo-Indian with sympathies toward Indian art could understand Indian building conditions.[66]

Thus, Havell strongly disagreed with Baker's focus on the western classical tradition. For him, the Government of India needed to draw its architectural inspiration from Indian master builders and be a school for Indian artists and craftsmen. Directing his ire at men like Lutyens or the philatelist Wilmot Corfield, who claimed that 'No Indian artist has yet designed even a decent postage stamp for an Indian state',[67] Havell claimed that 'the real issue to be settled in the building of the new Delhi is whether British architects have the same capacity as the amateur court officials of the Great Moguls for adapting to modern times this living tradition of Indian craftsmanship ... or whether we must prove the righteousness of British rule by continuing to stamp it out'.[68] He continued, 'I would join with Mr. Roger Fry in saying that all other issues are "polite archaeological humbug".'[69] 'The *raison d'etre* of the modern architect,' claimed Havell, 'is to bring archaeology up to date, and even if there is no living building tradition in India, there should be no more difficulty in adapting Mogul palaces to modern requirements than the architects of the 15th and 16th centuries had in adapting Greek and Roman temples to the secular requirements of their own day.'[70] The new capital offered a wonderful opportunity to energize and preserve Indian art 'by using the artistic resources of India practically and artistically. This is not so much a question of style as of spending Indian revenues honestly for the preservation of Indian art,' Havell argued.[71]

Havell was not alone in his criticism of adopting the western classical tradition in the buildings at New Delhi. Joseph King, member for North Somerset in the Commons and another major proponent of Indian arts and crafts, similarly questioned whether it was 'fair that the Indians, who have great genius, a great history, and a great tradition, should be asked to pay out of their revenue in order that some architects ... may have the opportunity of erecting in the new Delhi palaces of Italian art'.[72] Robert Fellowes Chisholm, a leading practitioner of the Indo-Saracenic architectural style that fused Moslem, Hindu and British building traditions, joined Havell in soundly disparaging the adoption of a neo-classical architectural style for the new capital. During a meeting of the Royal Society of Arts, he claimed that 'So called scholastic "Renaissance" is as dead now, and out of place, as the Greek language would be on the posters of a kinematic peep show. If it is a fact that Renaissance is to be the official architecture of the new Delhi, the outlook is appalling.'[73] As for Hardinge's seeming reluctance to use architects practising in India, Chisholm claimed, 'Are all the earnest workers in Indian architecture, both native and European, a mass of useless "poggles" that they should be ruthlessly set aside?'[74]

Even Bradford Leslie, who created such tremendous problems for the Government of India over where to place the new capital in the Delhi District, raised questions about architectural style in his paper read before the Royal Society of Arts.[75] Arguing against those who promoted a western neo-classical tradition as well as those who argued for a purely Indian style, Leslie looked to advancements in building technology to create an entirely new architectural aesthetic freed from its underlying 'constructive methods'.[76] Not surprisingly for a railroad builder whose specialty was building bridges, arguably the most difficult and expensive element in any railway line, Leslie turned to steel rather than stone and concrete as a building medium. For Leslie, steel opened up new worlds of architectural expression where 'walls ceased to carry weight and became mere partitions' that hid the load-bearing steel skeleton underneath.[77] He was adamant against adopting an architectural style allied with the past saying that it would be like 'putting new wine into old bottles'.[78] Hinting at the need for employing Indian architects and craftsmen, he argued that the Raj could not depend entirely on its own genius. What British-India needed, for Leslie, was a new 'Indo-European' style.[79]

These voices of dissent, however, were far outnumbered by those who agreed with Baker and Birdwood. The argument over architectural style was not about material aesthetics or beauty. Indian architects and craftsmen understood how to interpret beauty as well as anyone in the world. The problem was that – according to Baker and his supporters – India's architectural traditions lacked the necessary breadth to capture the spirit of British rule. Only the modern western classical architectural tradition of Wren and Jones, adapted for India by an architect like Baker, had the expansiveness to enshrine 'the solid, open, and orderly conceptions of the King Emperor's rule' as well as to 'embrac[e] many of the nobler features of Indian architecture'.[80]

The Times argued that Indian architecture was designed and meant for uses that were uniquely Indian and thus alien to Britain's political culture. As the paper described, 'There is grandeur and splendour about the Pathans; they built like giants, though they finished like "goldsmiths" ... But they gave us only tombs and fortresses and mosques; and how is a modern seat of government to take its line from these?'[81] As for the Mughals, *The Times* claimed that 'they built tombs in the form of splendid enclosed gardens, with lofty portals, formal paths and fountains, and a storied pavilion in the midst – a pleasant retreat from care for its builder until he ended all his cares and was borne to it for the last time'.[82] The Mughals, in essence, specialized in designing beautiful monuments for a particular individual and a particular time that had ended with the death of the ruler. This focus on individuals or particular religious institutions led to an aesthetic telescoping by Indian builders who simply could not conceptualize, for many British intellectual and political elites, 'large constructive designs' such as entire cities.[83] As Wilmot Corfield explained, Indian craftsmen had built beautiful temples and mosques, but they had done so on 'severely restricted lines'.[84] 'Where is, or has been, the "Indian Master-Builder" capable of planning a glorified Delhi of secretariats, railway termini, free libraries, banks, fire engine stations, and other attributes of civilization', Corfield asked?[85] *The Times* agreed, 'Indian architecture has spent itself entirely on palaces, temples, and tombs; and none of these are kindred enough to the architectural problem we have in hand'.[86] India's indigenous traditions could never 'hope to embody the distinctive spirit of British rule', its timelessness, its universal truths, its secularism, and its modern methods of government, which the transfer of the capital promised more fully to establish in India.[87]

But what precisely was the eternal spirit that *The Times* and Baker wrote about? They described it by using a dichotomy based on well-worn cultural assumptions. For *The Times*, Indian architecture represented 'ideals of life and government as alien to ourselves as to the conquered races among whom they were reared, and they are all most distinctively themselves'.[88] While past Indian emperors encased their most important state structures – halls of audience for example – behind 'battlemented walls', the British built civic institutions such as railroad terminals and post offices.[89] *The Times* readily accepted, in fact celebrated, Britain as a conquering imperial nation, but it also proudly proclaimed Britain's differences from previous Indian empires:

> Most of the Indian conquerors have destroyed the old in order to make the new; but that has not been our way. What Akbar sought as an individual, we have sought as a race – the union of new principles with what is best in the old. Let us leave, like him, an architecture that truly embodies that ideal.[90]

Hence, while Baker and *The Times* celebrated what they believed to be the permanence of British rule in India, they also described how that permanence was made possible, not by force, which had won the Indian empire, but by good government that benefitted Indian society. A key component of the new capital would be that its most important structures would not be hidden behind walls. So while *The Times* asked, 'why should we, the greatest of Indian conquerors, who hold sway and mean to hold it for all time, be other than ourselves', it also proclaimed:

> The building of [the new capital] is part of the process to which we committed ourselves with MacCauley's famous Minute on Education in 1835, and our architecture cannot be noble nor even sincere unless it be a reflection of our own period and our own minds. We are endeavouring to place before the peoples of India our distinctive British ideals, and to adapt to their use the principles of government on which British power has thrived. The new capital has been decreed to carry on and consolidate those aims, and it should bear the impress of them in its stones.[91]

Baker and *The Times'* reliance on orientalist dichotomies even as they called for a fusion of eastern and western architecture reflected the deep ambiguities that shaped the meaning and design of the new capital's architecture. *The Times* concluded:

> Eastern and western art may meet together in the colonnade, the deep portal arch, the open court of audience, the dome; and into these

may be blended all that India has to give of subtlety and industry in craftsmanship. Such a conception ... will speak of our own time and government, as the older Delhi's speak of other times and rules; and it will give full expression to Lord Hardinge's desire that the new capital should have in it the spirit of the East as well as of the West.[92]

Sir William Lee Warner, an experienced Government of India official who spent much of his career in Bombay, summed up the main point of the architectural debate appearing in the pages of *The Times*: 'to get the best of both hemispheres – the taste of the east and the practical knowledge of the west – applied to the building of the new city at Delhi was what everyone hoped'.[93] Baker, for many, seemed to be the architect best suited to make this happen.

With his influential letter to *The Times*, Baker's name began to be discussed by powerful people interested in the new capital. F. H. Lucas, Private Secretary to the Secretary of State, forwarded to the Government of India a letter from Herbert John Gladstone, Governor General of South Africa. In the letter, Gladstone, who was familiar with Baker's work in South Africa, urged the Government of India to commission Lutyens and Baker since the latter's genius lay 'in adapting his buildings to the scenery. In this he never fails'.[94] Furthermore, Gladstone showed that Baker and Lutyens had a history of collaboration. They worked together on the new Art Gallery at Johannesburg and discussed plans and sites for the future university at Grooteschurr. Most importantly, for Gladstone, Baker's pragmatism would help rein in Lutyens' overly extravagant ideas and designs.[95] Even Reginald Barratt, one of Lutyens' strongest supporters, expressed his 'sincere hope' that Lutyens with Baker would be given the commission to build Government House and the Secretariats and to control the general architectural scheme of the new capital since the two men made 'an ideal combination'.[96] Baker's ability to adapt architectural style to a given location would help silence critics who worried that Lutyens, if left to his own devices, would create an architectural style totally foreign to India. Barratt was not alone in this opinion. Leading architects, engineers and intellectuals believed that Lutyens' genius, in cooperation with Baker's pragmatism, would create a city that was 'epoch-making'.[97] Crewe was so impressed by Baker that he declared he would approve of Lutyens' appointment only if he collaborated with Baker.[98]

By early January 1913, Hardinge had talked with Lutyens about collaborating with Baker on the architectural board with George Swinton serving as an advisor on Indian architecture.[99] As members of the architectural board, they would be responsible for designing and carrying out plans for Government House and the Secretariats, assisting in the selection of designs for other government buildings, and acting as general architectural advisors to the Government of India. Barratt, for his part, was ecstatic with the make-up of the new capital's architectural board, and congratulated Hardinge for commissioning Lutyens and Baker. 'You will have stamped your viceroyalty', Barratt claimed, 'with an advance in taste, hitherto unknown in India, which cannot fail to bear much fruit in the years to come.'[100] His many letters to Hardinge had been done with one goal in mind, according to Barratt, 'to show to the world, in this new century, [the role that] imperial rule can lead in art and cultural taste, as well as science and justice and truth'.[101] Indeed, these high modernist ideals would re-energize Britain's imperial vigour and leave no doubt that the empire was a force of good not only in India but also in the world.

Easier said than done: Baker goes into the desert to 'fast and pray'

Baker visited India in early 1913 to study India's architectural traditions. He followed the advice of the architect and intellectual Thomas Jackson, who advised in the pages of *The Times* that function needed to come before style. Architects, for Jackson, needed to approach the design process more like typical artists. An author who intended to write a book, for example, would never say I want it to be in the 'style of Swift, Carlyle, or MacCauley', he claimed.[102] An author would know these masters, but his style would be 'natural to himself and not imitated from any one of them'.[103] For Jackson, an architect, like an artist, 'should study works of art, not copy them, but to be impregnated with their principles'. 'If our study has done its work', he continued, 'we should be so saturated with the true principles, not of this or that particular style, but that of architecture itself.'[104] An architect with such studies behind him would be able to meet any of the unexpected conditions that Delhi and India might offer. 'The first considerations should be purely utilitarian: what sort of architecture is demanded by the climate, the social habits of the inmates, and the functions the buildings are to fulfil', explained Jackson.[105] An architectural style should arise from these basic principles. 'To think first of the style, and try to bend and warp an old to suit the case, is to begin at the wrong end, and will only ensure another of the many disastrous architectural failures of which India has been the field', argued Jackson.[106] He ended by claiming, 'we cannot forget the past, but [architects] must not be fettered by any conventional formula'.[107]

Yet actually creating a new architectural style that blended the spirit of India with the spirit of Britain proved difficult for Baker, who admitted to Hardinge, 'I confess I have not yet seen a clear and complete vision of our new style, which is to give expression to British rule in India.'[108] Part of the problem was that Baker was looking to capture a general feeling that was easier to talk about than to actually illustrate in the built environment. In July 1913, he told Hardinge, '... we should certainly fail if we set out consciously to be "stylish" and, like the archaeologist who makes a bad architect, lose in a maze of detail the breadth and spirit we set out to obtain.... one cannot create a living style *consciously* any more in architecture than in literature'.[109] This style, he claimed, would not be found by copying 'the accidents of style of any old architecture ... more than India can be ruled by following the actual laws of Chandragupta or Akbar. But there is nevertheless very much to be learnt of the architect, as perhaps also by the ruler, from the spirit of what the old builders and kings left behind them.'[110] Baker informed Hardinge that he would follow these masters in the greatness of their methods rather than in the 'superficialities and prettiness of their style'.[111] He affirmed that it was his 'desire to recognize Indian sentiment to the fullest extent compatible with our object, which is to embody in our building the idea of the British administration in India'.[112] The new capital of course needed to be magnificent and beautiful, but it also needed to express the ideas of the colonial state. Baker was no different than other architects, past and present, who were commissioned to create public structures that modelled the state's deepest meanings. This was precisely what he had accomplished, many believed, in his Union Buildings at Pretoria. As he explained in a letter to Hardinge, his experiences in South Africa had 'strengthened my conviction that art has something more than purely objective motives, and should be inspired, as far as possible in the comparatively material art of architecture, by human and national sentiments'.[113] For Baker, his Union Buildings expressed the modern unity of South Africa's British and Boer communities.[114] But the search for a style for modern India, with its British administration and Indian subjects, was a task that Baker found so challenging that he claimed he needed to go into 'the desert and fast and pray'.[115] For, of course, what was missing in South Africa's Union Buildings and what was giving him such difficulty in India was how to adopt indigenous building traditions.

After a deep study of Indian architecture in the first half of 1913, Baker's earlier assumptions about India's building traditions remained unchanged. Baker explained to Hardinge in March 1913 that the problem with Indian architecture was that:

> The direction is often superb in detail but, as a whole, it often lacks coherence and unity of conception. The great ingenuity of the designs is too often spent, not on fine planning and construction, but on superficial fantasies and elaboration. It suggested the expression of their life and so was right. But their life is not ours.[116]

By August of that year, Baker still had not found a solution and whether or not he ever admitted it to himself or others he stopped looking. As he wrote to Hardinge:

> We must not try to be purely English, nor purely Indian; still less purely Roman, Venetian or any other style, or a mixture of any two. But we must aim at expressing, within the limitations of architecture as a medium and of our own powers to use it, the British Government of India, with its history, ideals, and practical achievement. We must try to build our city in the same spirit which animates those who are building up the fabric of modern India.[117]

Baker intended to create a novel style that fused India and Britain. Yet where he ultimately ended after months of deep study of Indian architectural traditions was precisely where he began when he first wrote his letter to *The Times*.[118] India's contribution to the new capital's architectural style would have to be ornamental, elaborative, and superficial rather than foundational.

By 1914 the Government of India believed it was time to send out a press release stating its progress on the new capital. After giving a mental tour of the layout, the Government of India directed readers' attention to the new capital's style of architecture. It admitted that the buildings would not be built in any 'special Oriental character' and would reflect few of the features 'commonly known as the Indo-Aryan and the Indo-Saracenic style'.[119] As the press release explained:

> The task set to the architects was not to produce a group of buildings of any particular style, but to design a capital which should be structurally adopted for the uses for which it is required, and at the same time in keeping with the great monuments of India's past with which it is surrounded. It was not necessary to imitate these remains in order to be in keeping with them, success in this direction lay rather in giving

to the new buildings a sense of dignity and a breadth of treatment which would ensure their effective harmony with the old.[120]

Indian sentiment, according to the news release, would be included later in the form of enrichment since 'the peculiar genius of the Indian workman lies in ornament and decoration'.[121] To ensure that this would happen, the Government of India announced its intention 'to collect at Delhi a body of craftsmen suitable for employment on this work, and the Indian craftsmen should therefore have every opportunity of contributing to the scheme those features in which he is best qualified to show his skill'.[122]

Here, George Swinton was particularly important. His primary role on the architectural board was to keep Lutyens and Baker informed about Indian architectural matters.[123] Swinton even suggested that Indian builders be asked to contribute to the design of the new capital's most important buildings. However, William Hailey, now Chief Commissioner of the Delhi District and the president of the Imperial Delhi Committee, believed the proposal was 'an expensive and ineffectual sham' since Baker and especially Lutyens would be reluctant to change their designs because Indian builders had a different idea about a particular building.[124] Additionally, as Hailey reminded the viceroy's private secretary, DuBoulay, no Indian architects submitted building plans when an open competition was held for bungalow designs for the new capital.[125] The reason for the competition was to engage Indian architects in the building project, certainly not as members of the architectural board but as designers of residences. They would not have any say over the new capital's vision, but they would serve as decorators of the new city, dressing the suburbs with residences for officers and government workers. Reflecting his pragmatism as well as his imperial conceit, Hardinge declared to Swinton, 'I do not anticipate that any Indian architects would be able to send in a satisfactory architectural plan, but I do feel very strongly that the door must not be shut in their faces. It satisfied their vanity and can do no harm.'[126] Similarly, he explained to Lutyens, 'the new capital at the present moment enjoys popularity in India, but that popularity would very soon disappear if it were discovered that India was to have nothing to say to its construction beyond paying for it'.[127]

Swinton's second idea to employ greater numbers of Indians in the decorative aspects of the building project was far more sensible to Hardinge and Hailey. He suggested that the Government of India create a Studio of Indian Art. Students trained here would be responsible for adding the final touches to the new capital's buildings. The idea of a studio for training Indian craftsmen was so attractive that Hailey and Hardinge kept a variation of it even after Swinton had resigned from the architectural board in August 1913.[128] Hardinge even had two Indian builders in mind, Bhai Ram Singh, the Principal of the Lahore School of Art, and Lala Shankar Lall, currently working in the Indian state of Bikaner.

The active pursuit of Indian builders and craftsmen was meant to silence critics such as Havell and King who claimed that the Government of India was ignoring Indian art or missing an opportunity to encourage it. Yet Baker's failure to find in Indian architecture elements that could be used to actually shape the new capital's structures as well as Swinton's idea for a school of Indian craftsmanship reflected the basic relationship between western architecture and Indian art in the new capital. The former served as the general foundation and the latter as mere decoration. Likewise, this relationship where an Indian spirit would be part of the city but never the dominant inspiration pointed to the inherent problem of Hardinge's new hegemonic vision for India. Though deserving greater involvement in the colonial government, India always would be a junior imperial partner.

By early 1913, Hardinge had made tremendous strides toward achieving his signature policy of building a new capital at Delhi. He had formed a town planning committee that had selected a general building site. He had put together an Imperial Delhi Committee that would serve both as a liaison between the architects and the actual builders of the new city and as his official voice piece, giving him mastery over the entire planning process and early building stages. Lastly, he had formed an architectural board to draw up plans for the major government buildings. All of these steps had been characterized by tremendous controversy and criticism, and still Hardinge had prevailed, suggesting his talent and abilities as a statesman.

7

'A New Jewel in an Old Setting': The Cultural Politics of Colonial Space

In many ways, the planning of New Delhi shared much in common with other twentieth-century high modernist building projects that sought to create a particular image of the ideal nation. Hardinge, his town planners, and his architectural board used the geometric precision of their town plan and their government structures to express the universal and timeless truths that inspired the spirit of British rule. These truths were none other than Britain's professed love of reason and science, enlightened values that the British believed were the basis of their colonial rule. This enlightened foundation had led to a colonial government based on rationalism, a system of colonial justice based on the rule of law, and a political-economy that brought rural India into Britain's larger maritime global economy, all of which, officials argued, had improved the lives of the Indian subjects in their care. As a well-planned city based on rational lines, New Delhi represented the highest ideals of the high modernist project. The apparent negative impacts of colonial rule were either ignored or understood as part of the painful process of making India modern.

Yet in other important ways the new capital drastically diverged from the high modernist project. Master planners like Le Corbusier, one of the great high modernists of the twentieth century, often negated a city's previous history once it fell under their planning and architectural gaze.[1] The history that had come before was either eradicated or overwhelmed by the high modernist impulse to represent a new, rational, more productive national ethos. As James Scott argues, for men like Le Corbusier 'No compromise is made with the pre-existing city; the new cityscape completely supplants its predecessor.'[2] Hardinge and his planners, in contrast, were compelled to capture and reinterpret Delhi's various imperial pasts. They did so to relegitimize the authority of British colonial

135

rule, which had been undermined by Indian anti-colonial agitation. Hardinge wanted his city to represent both a continuum of imperial history, where Britain was the rightful descendant of past Indian empires, and a break with the past, where loyal and educated Indians were given greater access to the workings of a rational colonial government.

Delhi's Indian history influenced the choice of buildings sites for the main government area, often called the central forum or acropolis after Rome and Greece. Rather than disavowing the area's Indian history, Hardinge and his planners sought to embrace and reinterpret it. Planners literally wove this history into their new city by incorporating the best examples of Indian imperial ruins in the area. The newest of Delhi's imperial capitals would sit proudly amongst other ancient and not so ancient Indian capitals. Thus, Humayun's *Purana Qila*, the Lodi Mausoleums, and Safjardang's Mausoleum, for example, were blended into the town plan as important vista points for the new capital. As 'a new jewel in an old setting', the new capital helped to legitimize British colonial rule by placing Britain within a long lineage of imperial rule in India. Additionally, positioning the new British capital of India against a backdrop of decayed Indian cities helped to contrast Britain's enlightened, more rational view of the world with India's indigenous imperial history which lay in ruins.[3]

Similarly, the new capital and its vision were juxtaposed against the existing city's (Shajahanabad's) chaos. This living Indian city with its myriad streets, densely populated neighbourhoods, and daily cacophony of sounds and smells served as a foil for the new capital. New and old Delhi were meant to be seen together, the one vibrant and progressive, the other corrupted and stagnant.[4] Writing in December 1911 to John Jenkins, John Hewitt stated, 'It [old Delhi] is at present the most unsanitary city that I have seen in northern India, and my personal opinion ... is that one of the chief difficulties will be to get rid of the unhealthy reputation of the place.'[5] In contrast, with its massive administrative buildings and broad boulevards, rationally designed and laid out, the new capital would symbolize Britain's colonial vitality and western rationalism. If New Delhi was designed 'to be an appropriate backdrop for an autocracy as mighty as Rome of the Caesars', according to Robert Irving, it was also meant to signify a new imperial hegemony where Indians consented to British colonial rule because of the benefits it brought.[6]

Yet the new capital also represented the harsh realities of colonial rule. Its promises of devolution were matched by the need to retain Britain's absolute authority at the centre, now located at Delhi. This balance, an imperial exigency in India's current political climate, became clear in the selection of a building site for New Delhi's main government area. Even progressive political policies designed to politically empower Indians suffered from long-held imperial assumptions about colonial subjects.

Mapping colonial power: a town plan in search of a focal point

The general layout of the town plan and its axial direction went through at least four major stages, but whatever the layout or direction, three government structures served as the fulcrum for the new city. These included a massive Government House, which contained the viceroy's residential quarters, chambers for the Imperial Legislative Council, and a princes' chamber. This massive structure was flanked by two additional structures, the Secretariats, which housed various Government of India departments. Together, the buildings made up the central forum. Initially, the official town planning committee closely merged the old city and the future capital. This is best reflected in Lutyens' first town plan, created before the arrival of Herbert Baker, which faced the forum into the heart of the old city. The main processional route, placed to the side of the main government buildings, led from the new capital's forum to the Red Fort and the Jama Masjid, the heart of the old city.

Hardinge was not entirely impressed with Lutyens' first town plan. The main view from Government House was 'a fine conception', according to Hardinge, but he saw serious impediments.[7] After examining the layout, Hardinge concluded to Reginald Craddock, his Home Secretary, 'there has been a singular lack of common sense in the plans of the Delhi Committee ... it is extremely fortunate that I went to Delhi and looked into the matter myself'.[8] The city spaces adjoining the main avenues were much too large and would require enormous buildings to fill the emptiness. Lutyens' original plan was to dress the main avenue with large palaces belonging to Indian princes, but Hardinge thought this would keep princes away from their states.[9] Only about half the space was filled when these palaces were excluded. Additionally, because the government buildings that would line the main avenue were only two stories high, they would 'present a puny appearance across the great open space in front of Government House'.[10] Hardinge was particularly concerned with Lutyens' planned road grid. The main processional way was much too large at 464 to 484 feet wide.[11] This caused Hardinge to call for information on the widths of main avenues in other cities such as Paris, Berlin, and Vienna.[12] By August 1912,

Hardinge had learned that the width of the Champs Elysees varied from 230 to 260 feet; the width of Berlin's Unter den Linden was 193 feet; and Vienna's Ringstrasse was 188½ feet.[13] The Royal Commission in London recommended 140 feet in main avenues and 100 feet in major arterial streets.[14] Lutyens' axial layout for the new capital was also problematic. Though it provided picturesque views of the old city from Government House, the main processional way ended at a 45-degree angle into a blank wall of the Jama Masjid.[15] After seeing the proposal, Sir Louis Dane, Lt Governor of the Punjab, suggested in a letter to Hardinge that he was not certain that it was 'a good thing to have the main avenue of a British capital ending on the rear of the mosque'.[16] Hardinge also did not like the way the processional way was placed to the side of the main government buildings because, he argued, 'by adopting the line of the committee the main avenue does not become the centre of the layout of the new imperial city, but forms one of its flanks'.[17]

By the end of July 1912, Hardinge concluded that Lutyens had conceptualized a town plan and road system that was 'far too spacious a scale to fit in with any harmony of proportion to the material with which these conceptions are to be fulfilled'.[18] The spaces and avenues were 'too hopelessly big and the buildings too hopelessly small', and that 'insignificance coupled with inconvenience would ... be the inevitable result'.[19] 'We must study economy a little,' Hardinge told his town planners.[20] Hardinge revealed his deep scepticism of Lutyens' original plan by confiding to William Malcolm Hailey, the president of the Imperial Delhi Committee, 'I am quite convinced that, if we allow the town planners to have their own way, they will make our city ridiculous.'[21] In response, Hardinge turned over Lutyens' town plan to Henry Vaughan Lanchester, who had been hired by the Government of India as a consulting architect for the new imperial capital.

Lanchester was an experienced architect and town planner. As an academic, he lectured on civic design at University College, London and was an outside examiner on civic design for the University of Liverpool. As a professional, he had designed town plans for Madras and Zanzibar. As a writer, he had published several books on town planning and edited *The Builder*.[22] The India Office had offered his name as a potential member of the official town planning committee, but Hardinge and others found his personality difficult. Hardinge admitted as much to Richmond Ritchie, Permanent Undersecretary of State for India and a man with deep roots in India, when he claimed that Lanchester would probably be the perfect choice for finding a British-Indian form of architectural expression for the new capital, but 'the first impression that he makes upon one is not a very favourable one, owing ... to the roughness of his manner'.[23] Lanchester, who was later commissioned to design the new capital's city extensions, had a profound impact on the general layout of the city. Hardinge asked Lanchester to draft a second town plan that kept the forum in its current location but turned the axis of the layout by 30-degrees. This would face the forum toward the Yamuna River rather than the Jama Masjid.[24] He also asked Lanchester to constrict Lutyens' town plan to bring the structures more in line with the space they would occupy.[25]

Lanchester's modified town plan focused on four principles.[26] First, he wanted to show an 'obvious and organic relationship between Government House', and the rest of the new city. Second, the new capital required a better processional route. Third, the Secretariats and Government House needed to be placed more closely together to ease communications between officials. And fourth, the entire scheme required 'a simple and comprehensive means of allocating various parts of the city to the communities that would live there'.[27] Lanchester shifted the main processional way to the centre of the layout, 'making the official group the real focus of the new city scheme'.[28] He also revised Lutyens' road grid by adding curves and better connecting the new city to the city extensions of Sadr Bazaar, an industrial neighbourhood. Lastly, he developed a railway station for purely ceremonial purposes and designed a bathing *ghat* near the Red Fort for the residents of old Delhi.

Lutyens, upon seeing Lanchester's modifications, quickly wrote to Hardinge and asked him not to adopt any of Lanchester's ideas until the town planning committee had had a chance to submit their final plan.[29] The town planning process was moving so slowly that T. R. J. Ward, the Imperial Delhi Committee's sanitation engineer, asked that Lanchester be placed on the official town planning committee to aid Swinton, Brodie, and Lutyens.[30] Geoffrey deMontmorency, who was serving as interim president of the Imperial Delhi Committee, argued against this since it would suggest to critics that the Government of India had lost its focus and control over the project. Matters were not helped by rumours that Lanchester was telling people in England that he had 'upset Lutyens' apple-cart'.[31] Hardinge, in a show of frustration, finally exclaimed that the main goal of everyone should be to concentrate on creating the best plan and 'not on such petty puerilities as apple-carts'.[32] Swinton agreed, writing to Hardinge that 'I should not myself deride a suggestion which came from a globe-trotting Yankee, if it was sound'.[33]

While Hardinge liked many aspects of Lanchester's new scheme, such as his treatment of the area that fell within the walls of the old city between the Red Fort, the Jama Masjid, and the Delhi Gate to the south, he remained unsatisfied with Lanchester's general layout. In particular, he thought Lanchester's town plan failed to place Government House, a symbol of Britain's supreme authority, in an advantageous position that would give it proper command of the area. Finding the best location for this structure was essential since it served as the fulcrum of the new city. Construction was stalled until the site for Government House was determined. No main avenues could be built since they all emanated from this structure.

Lanchester and Lutyens' failure to place Government House at a higher elevation had more to do with poor soil conditions along the southern ridge than with a failure of imagination. Both had rejected higher ground because of poor soil quality and concerns about excessive heat that radiated from the southern ridge's rock outcroppings. The selected site lacked elevation but it did have good soils for growing trees, shrubs, and gardens. Still, Hardinge remained unconvinced by their arguments for placing the new capital's most important structure at an elevation equal to much of the Indian city. Hardinge asked M. Nethersole, Secretary to the Department of Public Works, and C. E. V. Goument, Chief Engineer for the United Provinces, to evaluate and report on Lanchester's scheme as well as the tentative layout designed by the town planning committee. Their findings profoundly changed Hardinge's thinking about the placement of Government House and the forum. Goument and Nethersole showed that the southern ridge's soils could be improved at an affordable cost, about £3,000 per acre.[34] P. H. Clutterbuck, a Government of India forest officer, also inspected the ridge and came to the same conclusion. With these new findings, Hardinge realized that the most important reason for not situating Government House at a higher elevation on the southern ridge – its rocky surface, heat radiation, and poor soil – was no longer an issue. Hardinge told his town planners to seriously consider placing Government House on the ridge since its elevation offered remarkable views and opportunities for a skilled architect to build an awe-inspiring structure.[35] This shift in the placement of Government House, and consequently the Secretariats that flanked it, did not entail reconceptualizing the town plan, just the placement of the forum. In a letter to Swinton in August 1912, Hardinge informed him that the whole question concerning the site of Government House needed to be reconsidered, especially now that Nethersole, Goument, and Clutterbuck had determined that it was feasible to afforest the southern ridge. Hardinge wrote:

> I can picture to myself the approach to Government House from the plain below with terraces and fountains and gardens along the

hillside that should be a reproduction of Versailles and its gardens. Such a Government House would appeal greatly to the Indians, who would be able to point to it from miles away as the residence of the Lord Sahib. While being seen from the whole town below, it would command the town and the plain beyond.[36]

Still, Lutyens, who was an experienced and exceptionally talented landscape architect, had his doubts about afforestation on the southern ridge.[37] He aired his concerns at a meeting with Lord Crewe, Secretary of State for India, and Thomas Holderness, Permanent Undersecretary of State for India, at a meeting in September 1912. The meeting was held at Crewe Hall to discuss the progress of the committee as well as to consider Hardinge's most recent concerns and criticisms about the location of Government House and the axial direction of the town plan's layout. In a letter to Hardinge written shortly after the meeting had taken place, Lutyens argued that while trees could be grown for perhaps a decade or two, if the original holes were deep and wide enough, there would be tremendous risk of die-off after several generations.[38] This possibility countered the very timelessness the new capital was supposed to express since the image of dying ornamental trees did not speak well for the permanence of the British Empire in India. Additionally, Lutyens argued that the Viceroy's House could not be built too far up the ridge because it then would have views of old Delhi's industrial neighbourhoods.[39]

Swinton also sent a letter to Hardinge after the meeting. In it, he claimed that he had always questioned Lutyens' original location of Government House and that, like Hardinge, had always believed the southern ridge offered better architectural opportunities. However, he never pushed the point because Lutyens was so keen on the current location of Government House and had already begun to prepare, with Hardinge's encouragement, drawings of the structure. 'Personally,' Swinton apologetically claimed, 'I thought that you were both putting the cart a little before the horse, and that we were hurrying too fast, but it was natural zeal.'[40] Swinton had also accepted the tentative site, though reluctantly, because at least it meant rejecting the civil lines as a building site, and thus the project was partially moved forward. Yet to a certain degree this once again stalled the town planning because 'we got anchored on to one special site for Government House, with a layout mainly to suit that particular site and house'.[41] In short, Lutyens' excitement to begin designing Government House and Hardinge's desire to begin building as soon as possible had gotten in the way of sound town planning.

A new site for Government House needed to be found, one that had good soils, some elevation, and was reasonably close to the old city. Two sites rose to prominence, Raisina and Malcha, two rises in the southern part of the district. While Hardinge leaned toward placing Government House on Raisina, Swinton was committed to the Malcha site further southwest. Thus began a debate over the connection between the new capital and the old city. For Swinton, '[Government House] must have the best and the most suitable site within the ten square miles [of the general building area], and space for a great house with numerous subordinate houses for staff and other purposes, a beautiful garden and a park sufficiently extensive to ensure privacy.'[42] As such, the best site for building the new capital was 'absolutely on Malcha village, facing east-northeast on Raisina Hillock', Swinton argued.[43] It was large enough to accommodate the main government structures, and it had good soils for planting trees, shrubs, and lawns for beautification. Most importantly, its elevation provided a commanding view of the area. This was key for Swinton, who believed a commanding presence gave the capital its motive. As he claimed:

> The British Raj has come up at last to range itself alongside of the monuments of past rulers, and it must quietly dominate them all, Tughlakabad and Siri as well as Indrapat and Shajahanabad. And the note must ring right down. Correct style in architecture and artistically laid out gardens will help to produce beauty and dignity, but we have to try and express also something quite outside of art and penetrating far beyond the few genuine art lovers; our inheritance of, and our dominion over, the traditions and the life of India.[44]

Swinton argued that Raisina was not high enough to give a commanding presence and that it was too close to 'man worn ground'.[45] For Swinton, 'At Delhi dust is the great enemy; the surface of the ground, save where it is actual rock, is by nature a dusty waste', and man worn areas were particularly prone to dustiness.[46]

Hardinge agreed with most of Swinton's points, but there was one problem that made Malcha an impossible location as the main focus of the town plan. It was too far away from the existing Indian city. The new capital was meant to express not simply British power, as Swinton suggested, but the Government of India's historical place in the life of India. This alone caused Hardinge to reject Malcha as a site since, as he claimed, the two cities were meant to be a 'joint concern'.[47] Raisina, on the other hand, had 'the advantage of being nearer to all the great landmarks and to be surrounded by ground with splendid soil, while it would be easier to fill up our main avenues with good buildings not too far extended'.[48] Though he had his misgivings, Swinton eventually acquiesced, writing, 'I am bound to give you my real opinions as a town planner, but equally bound to listen to words of wisdom on political considerations such as the linking together of the cities.'[49] Hardinge ordered Swinton to have Lutyens draft a new town plan that placed Government House and the forum on Raisina. Concerning the axial layout of the town, Hardinge told Lutyens that it needed to face the river toward Indrapat, have the Jama Masjid to the left, and Safdarjung's Tomb on the right. 'In this way,' according to Hardinge, 'the view would comprise all the ancient monuments and objects of historical interests in one comprehensive panorama'.[50]

Lutyens made two layouts based on the Raisina site.[51] The first faced east-northeast from Raisina and provided a good ceremonial avenue and other state roads. It also had good drainage, the potential for good water effects, space for varying ranks and classes of officer residences, good communications, and the rail diversions were easy to accomplish. The second layout faced Indrapat, the most ancient of all Delhis. It had many of the same benefits as the first layout, but water effects would be slightly more difficult. On the other hand, Indrapat would be given considerable recognition. In the end, the latter layout was selected because it provided a wonderful opportunity to connect the imperial present with India's deepest imperial past. The incorporation of Indian ruins in the new capital's town plan reflected a particular vision that the Government of India wanted to project to both Indians and the rest of the world: Britain was not only the benevolent caretaker of Indian culture but India's legitimate imperial heir. This Indian imperial past, woven into the new capital's town plan, not only gave the British Empire greater legitimacy in India but also highlighted the rightness and benevolence of British rule in India. As Hardinge wrote to the members of his executive council, 'Delhi is to be an Imperial capital and is to absorb the traditions of all the ancient capitals ... It has to convey the idea of a peaceful domination and dignified rule over the traditions and life of India by the British Raj.'[52] The Raj would be part of Delhi's long history but only as the culmination of a much larger process that had begun long ago. The historical nature of the southern site became as great a determining factor as the more mundane concerns of drainage, health, and size. Not surprisingly, some of the first expenditures on New Delhi concerned stabilizing and restoring Indian imperial ruins and monuments such as the *Purana Qila* where Indrapat lay.[53]

Raisina had become the heart of Britain's Indian Empire. Raised slightly above the rest of the city, the forum's main government structures symbolized the operation of colonial power in India. It was, according to the town planning committee, 'the keystone of the rule over the Empire of India; this is the place of Government in its highest expression; this is the seat of the Governor-General in India and his Council ... Thus the imagination is led from the machinery [the Secretariats] to the prime moving power itself [Government House].'[54] Raisina served as the locus of British imperial power in India, the platform upon which state power flowed from the imperial centre to the rest of India. In their final report, the town planning committee claimed:

> Looking from the centre of the site towards the river there is Shahjahan's Delhi on the left, and following down the river frontage Ferozshah's Delhi, Indrapat and Humayun's tomb fill the outlook in front, while outside the site itself Tughlakabad, Siri, Jehanpanah, Kila Rai Prithora, Lal Kot, and the Qutb complete the panorama ... Right and left the roadways go and weld into one the empire of today with the empires of the past and unite Government with the business and lives of its people.[55]

Almost mystically, especially for an empire that prided itself on its material view of the world, New Delhi focused space and time into a single point on Raisina's raised platform. As the town planners claimed, '[From Raisina], there is a wide outlook over its demesne – ridge, river, and plain, the Delhi of to-day and the Delhis of the past.'[56] In a single glance, one could imagine the power and breadth of British power over not only the present but also the past. A complex, interconnected road system consisting of straight, broad avenues tied together by large traffic circles linked this new vision of empire with the remains of past Indian empires. Travelling from the new city outwards along one of the new avenues one always seemed to be heading toward a vista of Indian history. The new capital was at the centre of this imperial environment, clearly reaffirming colonial relationships of power. In a straight surveyor's line, the oldest of all Hindu capitals, Indrapat, was connected to the newest imperial capital, and in the relatively short distance between the old and new cities was represented the long lineage of imperial rule in India. Indeed, the imperial capital, as 'a new jewel in an old setting', temporally and spatially unified India under British rule (see Figure 7.1).[57]

But what kind of rule did New Delhi precisely represent? The following case studies of specific areas in the town plan help to answer this question.

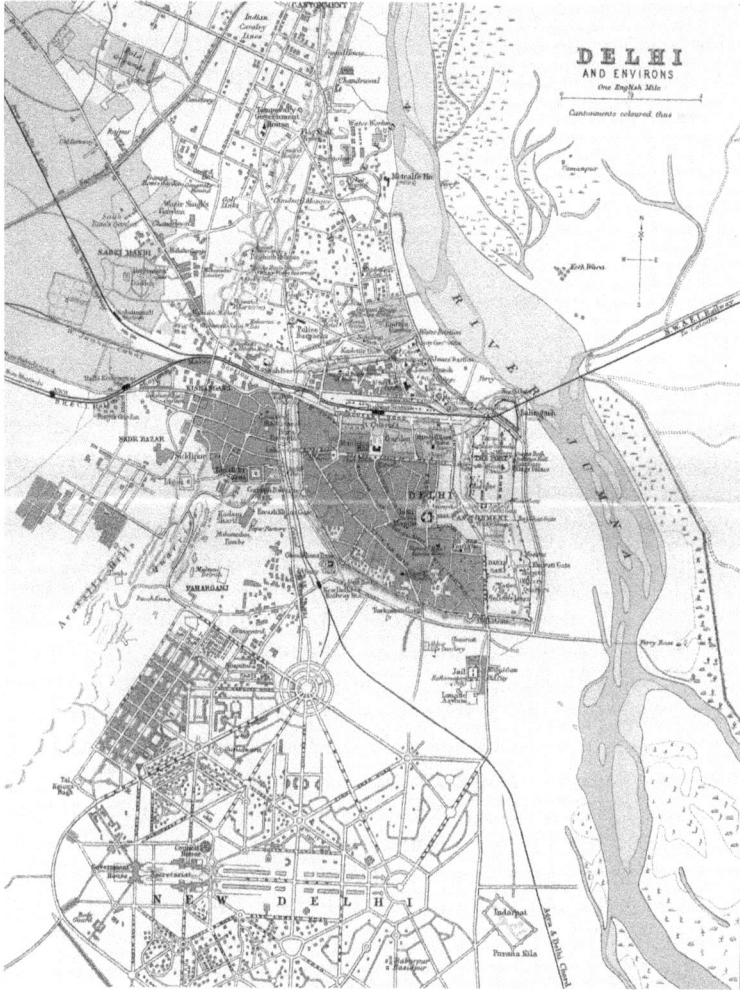

Figure 7.1   New Delhi and its environs

Lutyens' Bakerloo: the colonial meaning of an architectural gradient

The push by Hardinge to begin building as soon as possible led to a bitter argument between Edwin Lutyens and Herbert Baker who had been made a member of Hardinge's architectural board in early 1913 and given the commission to build the Secretariats. The quarrel centred on the gradient of the Kingsway, the main processional route that connected the central forum to the All-India War Memorial in the eastern quadrant. Lutyens, who was always ready with a turn of phrase or witticism, later called it his 'Bakerloo', the site of his greatest defeat. The debate reflected the growing strength of Hardinge's hegemonic vision – based on coercion and consent – and the subsequent decline in purely coercive colonial models.

As 1912 moved into 1913, Hardinge became concerned about the slowness of the process by which the architects submitted their plans to the Imperial Delhi Committee, which examined the architects' proposals and estimated their costs. These estimates were then passed on to the Secretary of State for India who sanctioned them. Baker, as he so often did during the building project, offered a solution based on his past experiences as a state architect in South Africa. His suggestion followed the lines of the Secretary of State for India's previous sanction of the rough estimate for the entire project. While Baker 'realised the necessity of estimate and financial caution', he believed that it was possible to approve a general plan and estimate for specific buildings so that work on the basements and foundations of his Secretariats could begin at once.[58] Later, the departments of Public Works and Finance could draw up more detailed estimates of the building costs. If this meant later changes due to alterations in the general scheme of the structures, then 'we will loyally help, time being an object, and will not complain of altered drawings', Baker promised Hardinge.[59] Following Baker's idea for the basements, the Imperial Delhi Committee devised a scheme that would speed the building of Government House and the Secretariats. The cost to build the outer walls of these structures could be given rough estimates, which then would be divided between (a) the cost to build the outer shells and (b) the cost to decorate them.[60] This would allow the Government of India to begin building almost immediately after they had received the architects' plans. Contracts were drawn up with Baker and Lutyens that stipulated extra payments for any major alterations of previously approved plans. Believing the need to begin building as soon as possible outweighed the risk of greater payments to the architects, the Imperial Delhi Committee claimed, 'it is better to face the expenditure thus entailed than to risk the waste of time'.[61]

By December 1914, construction was beginning to move so rapidly on Baker's Secretariats that the supply of stone could not keep pace, and the Imperial Delhi Committee was forced to ask Hardinge to intercede with the state of Bharatpur where the stone was being quarried.[62]

The Imperial Delhi Committee needed 300,000 cubic feet of stone just for the months of December 1914 and January 1915.[63] This amount, according to Colonel Bannerman, the British political agent for the state, was far beyond the abilities of Bharatpur, which could produce about 33,000 cubic feet a month at maximum output.[64] The supply could be doubled perhaps if the Imperial Delhi Committee lessened its requirement for a particular shade of stone.[65] Hardinge, too, demanded that his two architects be less particular about the shade of stone in their buildings.[66]

Though the Imperial Delhi Committee's financial strategy had expedited the building of the Secretariats, it ultimately created the conditions that led to Lutyens and Baker's argument over the Kingsway's gradient. The architects prepared and submitted their plans at very different speeds. Baker, the consummate state architect, was fully aware of Hardinge's need to have the main government structures rising above the ground by the end of his viceroyalty since standing structures would make it almost impossible for future governments to ignore the building project. Thus, he had submitted rough drawings for the Secretariats in December 1913, not long after his appointment to the architectural board. Lutyens, meanwhile, still had not done so, much to Hardinge's annoyance.[67] As he explained to Thomas Holderness, Lutyens had given 'endless troubles' and that while Baker had been practical, Lutyens was 'artistically the reverse'.[68]

It was only when Lutyens saw Baker's Secretariats rising on Raisina that he realized there was a problem with his conception of the central forum, especially the relationship between Government House and the Secretariats (see Figure 7.2). As one travelled down the Kingsway toward Raisina, Government House descended behind the lip of the Secretariats' massive platform. Baker's Secretariats, in contrast, remained in full view becoming larger and more powerful as one neared them. Visually, the Secretariats rose as Government House sank. For Lutyens, this simply was the wrong imperial message as well as an aesthetic catastrophe. He wanted Government House to rise majestically above the rest of the capital.[69] He proposed an impossible solution that required making a long, deep cut between the Secretariats. This would lower the gradient of the Kingsway as it passed between the Secretariats, making Government House visible at all times along the main processional avenue.

In the end, and much to Lutyens' dismay, his proposal to lower the Kingsway's gradient was rejected by the Imperial Delhi Committee with Hardinge's full support. Indeed, as both the committee and Hardinge

Figure 7.2   The approach to the central forum from the Kingsway, now called Rajpath, New Delhi, India

concluded, Lutyens had already signed off on the gradient several years before, during the cold weather of 1913–14, and this gradient 'formed the basis of all designs and work executed up to date'.[70] To change plans at this point would have been not only exorbitantly expensive but also harmful to Hardinge's scheme of the town plan, architecturally as well as symbolically. Accepting Lutyens' proposal would mean, according to Hardinge, 'the complete disruption of the Government House and the Secretariat buildings as a harmonious whole, which ... is a most important and vital object of attainment'.[71]

Baker's conception of the relationship between Government House and the Secretariats was much more in line with Hardinge's new vision for India. These most important government structures needed to sit on the same elevation, not necessarily as equals but as equally important elements of British rule in India. As a correspondent for *The Times* explained as late as 1930, 'It is characteristic of the change in times that the term applied in Delhi parlance to the palace of the Great Mogul is applied in New Delhi today not to the Viceroy's House but to the Secretariats. The sword has been beaten into the pen.'[72] A symbol of coercion, Government House, was balanced by the symbols of good government, the Secretariats, which advanced the development of India. Britain could regain its footing in India not by simple force but by creating an imperial partnership. The planning and placement of a new structure, the Council House, best expressed this new sense of cooperation.

Remapping colonial power: the Council House and imperial unity

The building of a large government structure to house the new Central Legislative Assembly, the Council of State, and the Chamber of Princes exemplified Britain's new imperial vision.[73] The political changes brought by the Government of India Act of 1919 forced the Government of India to rethink the imperial capital's central forum. A new structure, the Council House, was designed and erected to signify this latest step in India's political advancement.

In the early planning stages, Hardinge had been adamant that the Chamber of Princes and the Imperial Legislative Council, which had an expanded number of Indian representatives after the reforms brought by the Indian Councils Act, be housed under the same roof as the viceroy. He even warned Swinton to 'please dismiss from your mind any question of the council chamber not being in Government House. Wherever Government House may be, there must the council chamber be.'[74] The close link between the viceroy and the Imperial Legislative Council was necessary in order to avoid any notion that India was heading toward something as radical as an independent parliament. Hardinge may have pushed for political reform in India, but he did so to ensure the stability of Britain's Indian Empire. For Hardinge, the council played an advisory role and did not make policy free of the viceroy's influence. India, in short, was not England.

Not everyone agreed with Hardinge's stance. As early as August 1912, Captain Arthur C. Murray (member for Kincardineshire) stood in the Commons and asked Edwin Montagu, Undersecretary of State for India, about rumours that the Imperial Legislative Council would be housed in Government House. While Murray rejected the notion that India should be given a parliamentary government immediately, he encouraged the Government of India to recognize that India was heading in that direction. As he argued, 'It cannot be gainsaid that in India the old order is changing and giving place to the new ... I submit there is a new spirit abroad in India today.'[75] This political evolution should be allowed to continue, Murray argued, and be symbolized in the new capital by giving the council its own building. 'In my humble opinion,' according to Murray, 'no more fitting monument for the commencement of this new era could be devised than the erection in the new city of Delhi of a council chamber in which the meetings of the reformed Imperial Council would take place.'[76] Though India was not yet ready for an independent parliament, the building of a separate chamber free of the viceroy would be 'an outward and visible sign of the new era of political development in which the peoples of India must be wisely guided to take an increasingly larger share'.[77]

Montagu responded to Murray's suggestion by describing Government House's tentative building plan. The viceroy's residential quarters would sit between the prince's durbar hall and the Imperial Legislative Council. Each wing would have its own entrances so there would be no possibility, as some members of the press had warned, that council members and princes would run into the viceroy's servants. Like Hardinge, Montagu saw the imperial council as an extension of the viceroy's office. If India was governed by a Governor-General-in Council, the official title of the Viceroy of India, then the building scheme served to mirror this reality. While Murray's plea was rejected initially, events beyond the control of the Government of India and the India Office forced changes to the building scheme along lines that closely paralleled his suggestions in 1912.

Britain's entry into the Great War in August 1914, its catastrophic human and material losses during the first years of the war, and its subsequent need to maintain India's support of the war effort encouraged Lord Chelmsford, who had replaced Hardinge as viceroy in 1916, and Montagu, who was now Secretary of State for India, to forge an agreement that promised India major political reforms after the war. The 1919 Government of India Act made this promise a reality by transferring a great deal of legislation from the central government to the provinces, whose provincial legislatures had large numbers of elected Indian officials. The deep paternalism of the Act was evidenced by the powers given to British governors or lieutenant governors who were given veto powers over legislation passed by provincial legislatures. While the Act potentially empowered provincial Indian legislators, it also reaffirmed Britain's monopoly over the most coercive powers of the state. All matters that concerned the police and national defence, for example, were reserved for British officials.

The Act also transformed the office of viceroy, which traditionally had held both executive and legislative powers. For the latter, the viceroy received advice from a council. Before 1919 this role was played by an Imperial Legislative Council that had an expanded Indian presence due to the 1909 Indian Councils Act. After the passage of the later 1919 Government of India Act, the viceroy's legislative functions were taken over by a higher house, the Council of State, and a lower house, the Central Legislative Assembly, which had a large number of elected Indian officials.[78] These significant political changes in the colonial administrative structure needed to be reflected in the new capital. Thus, the viceroy became separated from the Central Legislative Assembly and the Council of State. The Chamber of Princes was also given its own quarters, but much of this had to do with reducing the cost to build Government House.

Herbert Baker, who was given the commission to build the Council House, designed a neo-classical structure that was circular in shape and bounded by columns all around (see Figure 7.3). Inside this circular structure, three chambers housed the Council of State, the Central Legislative Assembly, and the Chamber of Princes. The central dome, which covered a common library for all three chambers, was particularly important for symbolizing Britain's new vision, for it served as the site of joint sessions called by the viceroy. Hence, as Baker claimed, the Council House's central dome symbolized the essential unity of the three estates of India: the Raj, the princes, and Indian subjects.[79]

The Council House was a remarkable symbol of Britain's new hegemonic model. On the one hand, it represented Britain's attempt to encourage Indians to consent to their colonial status by offering greater political reform such as expanded numbers of Indians on legislatures. On the other hand, the Council House was placed physically to the

Figure 7.3 Herbert Baker's Council House

side and below the forum's Secretariats and Government House, now called the Viceroy's House after the 1919 Government of India Act. Baker argued that the Council House's diminutive location was due to the fact that the Secretariats and Viceroy's House, which were already being built, fully occupied the raised platform at Raisina.[80] However, his explanation rings slightly hollow in that the Viceroy House's compound covered 200 acres. Certainly, some of this large area could have been used for the Council House, but that would have disrupted the meaning of the Central Vista where the focus of symbolic power remained on the Viceroy's House and its flanking Secretariats, all of which rose above the Council House by virtue of their position on Raisina. With striking ambiguity, Britain used the Council House to create an image of consent, but this consent was subordinated symbolically to the business of British rule. The Council House and its relationship to the other main government structures was a perfect rendering of Hardinge's vision. Indians could have greater political power in the provinces as long as their political decision-making did not harm the ultimate power of the British Raj.

Schematizing race and class in New Delhi's residential quarters

Traditional assumptions about race and class in the imperial project proved exceptionally hard to break even though Hardinge had insisted to his planners and architects that the new capital was being built for a British-Indian administration. The arrangement of residential quarters is an apt example of the way in which the Government of India failed to live up to the language of political reform heard in paragraph three of the official dispatch to transfer the capital.[81] In the first half of 1912, well before the town planning committee had finalized the city's layout, Hardinge's government began to examine the fundamental spatial relationship of different residential quarters to each other and to their places of work and recreation. Geoffrey deMontmorency, Secretary of the Imperial Delhi Committee, was given responsibility for preparing estimates of the residential and office space needed by each government department. He claimed in spring 1912, 'It does not matter ... whether the eventual layout, which may be adopted, should differ in *toto* from this or not. The difficulty of the interrelation of the various items, for which accommodation is to be found, applies equally *mutatis mutandis* to any layout.'[82] In the Government of India's hypersensitivity to social status, one's official civil service rank determined the size of their office and residential compound. Town planners could theoretically estimate how much office and residential space was needed once the rank and number of officers were determined for each Government of India department. For deMontmorency, any work done on the spatial lay-out of the city, even if later rejected by the town planning committee, helped the government to begin thinking about the physical relation-ship between government offices and residences. DeMontmorency drafted a report that described the primary principle to be followed in laying out residential areas: the distance between residence and work should be based on official rank. In descending order of rank, residen-tial quarters were laid out in a fan shape with the central forum acting as the hub. Members of the Viceroy's executive council were placed nearest the central forum in large residential compounds, followed by secretaries and heads of departments, then by deputy secretaries and undersecretaries, then by registrars and superintendents. The clerical establishment, with its sizeable Indian and Anglo-Indian populations, lay at the farthest edge of the residential fan. These clerical residences were segregated into different quarters based on race and pay grade.

The responses from high officials in the Government of India to deMontmorency's report are telling. Unconsciously accepting that the city should be divided along racial and class lines, their main concern was the size of acreage that should be allotted based on one's rank. Of central importance was the size of executive council members' com-pounds because all other ranks would be adjusted accordingly along a descending scale.[83] Other than the Viceroy's compound (200 acres) and the Commander-in-Chief's residence (35.5 acres), both of which housed unique offices and thus were not part of the residential equa-tion, the size of compound reflected the imperial hierarchy. Any changes in the size of the council members' compounds would directly alter the size of all other compounds. Reginald Craddock, Hardinge's Home Member, believed that there should be no less than six and pref-erably eight or ten acres for members of council. For him, New Delhi's residential compounds were a chance to remedy some of the 'evils' found in European enclaves in India. As an old India hand, Craddock wrote, 'There has ensued a multiplication of servant's houses to hide which too thick a vegetation has grown up, involving stuffiness and encouraging mosquitoes, and hiding improper bestowal of rubbish, and unsanitary practices.'[84] A minimum of six acres, however, would provide enough space to maintain a good distance between the main house and the servants' quarters 'on account of noise and on sanitary grounds'.[85] 'From long practical experience of this very subject,' claimed

Craddock, 'I have found that this question of outhouses in Indian stations is a very difficult one. They may not offend the occupant, but they offend his neighbour, and your neighbour's servants are very much more unpleasant than your own.'[86] If the planners of New Delhi were not careful, warned Craddock, the city would become a series of native *bastis* (slums) between each row of official residences.[87]

The key was finding just the right balance between a compound that was large enough to accommodate the various needs of the council member and his servant's quarters but not so large that it would be impossible to maintain an attractive, well-ordered appearance.[88] After consultation with engineers from the Public Works Department concerning the amount of land that could be reasonably irrigated, the Government of India finally settled on six-acre compounds. All other compounds were reduced accordingly.[89] In minute detail, each department within the Government of India closely examined its personnel and issued the information to the Government of India, which then allotted residential and office space to each department.[90]

If the sliding scale for European residential housing began at the top of the colonial civil service with members of the viceroy's executive council, the sliding scale for Indians employed in the imperial government began at the bottom with menial servants (often called government peons) who swept and cleaned government offices, restrooms, and other facilities. These government menials were so below other workers, British and Indian, that Baker, for example, designed hidden service passages throughout his Secretariats so that government clerks and officials would not have to see them. To house these workers, the Imperial Delhi Committee's sanitation engineer, T. R. J. Ward, devised a scheme by which menials would live in 10 square foot rooms grouped into 50 room barracks. Each barracks would have two rows containing 25 rooms placed back to back with front doors opening to the outside. An air space of 45 feet would surround the barracks. Within these barrack compounds, according to Ward, the government could house 350 peons or 75 peons per acre.[91] For junior clerks, who were also relatively low on the imperial social scale, Ward determined that one clerk would require 'the space of five peons' or 25 junior clerks to the acre.[92] Upon reading Ward's report, the Sanitary Commissioner for Delhi suggested that Ward had underestimated the area required by menials: 'These quarters will practically be permanent ones and it is hardly to be expected that the menials will not be accompanied by their families ... This will reduce these barracks to the condition of very densely packed *bastis*.'[93] The commissioner recommended that the number of menials per acre be reduced and the allotted area increased roughly by a third either way. The final calculation meant that residential allotments for menials would consist of approximately 50 peons per 1.33 acres.

The town planners' apportionment of residential areas for the clerical establishment reflected British assumptions about race and class. Clerks were divided into salary groups to determine the size of their residential compounds: those who made less than Rs 100, those that made Rs 101–200, those that made Rs 201–300, and those that made Rs 301–500.[94] There was a marked discrepancy between race and salary where Indians were well-represented in the lower salary categories but were nearly absent at the highest clerical pay scales. Anglo-Indians and a few British civil servants usually filled the higher ranks of the clerical establishment. As salaries decreased, the number of British and Anglo-Indians declined and the number of Indians rose.[95] On average, the highest paid Indian clerk (Rs 301–500) was expected to live in quarters that were inferior to the lowest paid Anglo-Indian (Rs 200 and under).[96] Conversely, the highest paid Anglo-Indian (Rs 301–500) lived in quarters that were twice the square footage as the highest paid Indian who made the same salary. One clerk, Chandra Narayan Mathur, sent a memorial to Lord Hardinge detailing the inferiority of the Indian clerks' quarters. With measured civility he stated that the Indian quarters were 'insufficient and unsuitable', that it was 'invidious to draw a distinction in respect of quarters' for clerks who made the same salary, that the 'better quarters of Anglo-Indians came at the expense of Indian clerks', and that 'this unequal treatment [was] felt as a mark of inferiority of Indians as a class'.[97] The clerical establishment's unequal government housing reflected New Delhi's ambiguity as a symbol of a new imperialism for the twentieth century. Racial and social assumptions about Indians and Europeans continued to shape the imperial project even after high colonial officials, such as Hardinge and Montagu, called for a more progressive direction in India. New Delhi spatially reflected the colonial order. Its layout served as a schematic that traced the flow of imperial power from the viceroy's 200-acre compound to 50 menials residing on 1.33 acres (see Figure 7.4).

The new capital's recreational facilities also reflected the colonial order. Club life was particularly important for Europeans. The club's intimacy, its rules, its games, its decor, and its alcoholic drinks gave them a home away from home. Whether in Calcutta or a small hill station, whether a government official or a tradesman, Europeans had been sharing the same private clubs for some time. In Calcutta, the Government of India had felt little need to sponsor government clubs since the large number of European trades people living there had developed a rich

Figure 7.4   Edwin Lutyens' Government House, later called the Viceroy's House

club life that European colonial civil servants were welcome to join. The transfer of the capital from Calcutta to Delhi posed problems for this traditional club structure since the new capital, in comparison to Calcutta, would have far fewer European trades people. Comparing the two cities, one official wrote, 'In Delhi the case will be quite other and Government must provide ample ground for many separate clubs – for there are many strata of society and many races – and must provide ground not only for Government servants but for the trades peoples.'[98] Any existing European clubs in the civil lines would be too far away for residents of the new capital, and thus the Government of India would have to provide new clubs in the new capital. By July 1913, high-ranking officials had applied for an exclusive club titled the Gymkhana Club Limited, which would serve primarily the elite European community. Located between the new capital and the cantonment to the west, both military and civilian officers could take advantage of its clubhouse, large golf course and polo grounds. Lord Hardinge was made the first president of the club.

Other clubs were needed as well. The Department of Revenue and Agriculture serves as an example of how recreational areas were allotted.

The department decided that there should be different tennis and cricket grounds for its officers and staff based on the following racial and social designations: superior staff, clerical establishment, Indian establishment, tradesmen, European subordinates, Europeans in Survey of India Offices, and Indians in Survey of India Offices. While the superior staff would most likely be members of the exclusive Gymkhana Club, other golf courses would be provided for European tradesmen, European clerks, and European subordinate departments. There was some discussion of whether Indian clerks needed clubs as well. It was finally decided by the Imperial Delhi Committee that Indian clerks did not need official clubs like British officials. Rather, unofficial space would be provided in the form of evening access to one of the new capital's schools since, as the committee argued, they would rather spend time with their families than at the club.[99] Thus, even recreational venues were shaped by imperial assumptions of race and social status in the colonial world.

Though town planners successfully divided the capital's residential spaces and clubs along racial and social lines, the realities of the Delhi District made a clean break between Europeans and Indians impossible. The following examination of Paharganj, a large and densely populated suburb that lay between the old and new cities, exemplifies how Britons and Indians were pressed together, whether they wanted to be or not, in the colonial world.

Paharganj: *Metis* (indigenous knowledge) and the colonial world

Rebecca Brown has argued that colonial urban planners not only failed to completely segregate Indian colonial cities into European and Indian spaces but that any attempt to do so would have failed due to the realities of colonial life.[100] In the case of Paharganj, the town planning committee and especially Lutyens called for the acquisition and demolition of major sections of the suburb. They did so because Lutyens' original main processional route ran through the middle of Paharganj and because the community was considered a massive slum. They also wanted to acquire Paharganj to create an isolation zone to ensure that the old city's natural growth would never encroach upon the new capital to the south.

By the end of July 1912, however, Hardinge had determined that the removal and compensation of Paharganj's residents would be extremely difficult and costly. The community was too heavily populated, it would be too expensive to demolish the numerous houses and shops, and the complexity of property rights were almost impossible to decipher.[101] The latter was perhaps the most damning aspect of acquiring the community since an imperial state that celebrated its rule of law could not simply force people out of their homes and residences without compensation. As British officials believed, the sanctity of private property as well as the rule of law separated the British Empire from past Indian empires.[102] The Government of India estimated that it would cost the government 27 lakhs to acquire the neighbourhood, a number that was far too expensive in the context of parliamentary debates about the cost to build the new capital.[103] Instead, Hardinge and the Imperial Delhi Committee determined that the suburb would have to be improved 'gradually and tactfully' over time through municipal authorities 'for a few lakhs of rupees'.[104]

The Imperial Delhi Committee dealt with the problem of Paharganj's uncontrolled growth by placing Connaught Place (New Delhi's major commercial centre) and the New Delhi Railway Station between this community and the new capital. The committee also purchased a strip of land at Paharganj's southernmost edge nearest the capital. These three areas created an obstacle for the old city's growth and ensured that New Delhi remained distinctly separate from the Indian city, a division that has remained to the present.

Though the town planners stopped the growth of the old city to the south, no plan could stop the movement of people. Thus, the government's racial and social schematic for the new capital immediately began to break down not for want of effort by the new capitals' planners but because the local realities of maintaining one's European respectability required the help of Indians.[105] For most Europeans, life in colonial India required a certain number of low-paid servants who cooked and served meals, cleaned the house and compound, ran errands, and carried or taxied their employers about town. In an age before air-conditioners, they even provided the main means of cooling. The punkawallah, as he was called, manually worked a large swinging ceiling fan that blew air on his employers. Old India hands like Craddock realized that a space for Indian servants, who catered to the domestic needs of the European community, needed to be set aside near the new city, close enough for menials to do their daily work but far enough away to not have to deal with them and their families in the evening. As he claimed, 'Even if the climate of Delhi is good, India is not England. Sanitary appliances do not make sanitary men ... You cannot keep Indian servants perpetually separated from their families, and families of Indian servants should not be too close to houses.'[106] Menial servants living in Paharganj were particularly important to the domestic needs of those low and mid-level colonial officials whose smaller residential compounds could not accommodate servant housing. Hence, New Delhi came to require Paharganj for practical reasons. European residents needed their privies cleaned, their floors mopped, their sidewalks swept, and their ceiling fans operated, and the Indians doing these chores needed a place to live near, but not in, the new capital. While Paharganj was seen as one of the worst examples of an Indian *basti* and, according to the town planners, should have been destroyed under modern town planning principles, the reality of imperial life in India made its removal impossible. As James Scott claims, 'Formal order ... is always and to some considerable degree parasitic on informal processes, which the formal scheme does not recognize, without which it could not exist, and which it alone cannot create or maintain.'[107] New Delhi and Paharganj had a symbiotic relationship in that the latter's unplanned and informal reality sustained New Delhi's exceedingly planned and greatly formal high modern idealism. Thus, the Government of India dealt with Paharganj by working around the edges of this complex community. The internal logic of the Delhi District saved Paharganj from demolition and, as Scott suggests about similar neighbourhoods, 'provided a vital margin of political safety from control by outside elites'.[108] The power of this local, indigenous logic became apparent when town planners attempted and failed to acquire Paharganj. Hardinge could manipulate many aspects of his future capital – its style, its spirit, its purpose – but he had limited control over this large, densely populated neighbourhood not because he lacked the authority to acquire the entire community but because his new capital could not exist without it.

Hardinge and his town planners' decisions about the general town plan, the relationship between government structures, residences and recreational facilities, and what communities to acquire and not to acquire were examples of the imperial state's over-schematization and over-simplification of a highly complex colonial social life. Some scholars have argued that Britain painted itself into a corner in India with the offer of political reforms that it could never fully live up to. While the claim is certainly compelling, Scott offers an additional explanation for the end of British rule, namely, that political reform made India's colonial world increasingly more rather than less complex. At its heart, Britain's offer of devolution was about splintering or fracturing the energy of the Indian nationalist movement and to drive a wedge between moderate and more radical nationalist elements. Britain did so by promises of future political reform through the constitutional process and by creating reserved seats in provincial legislatures for minority religious groups, classes and ethnicities. This schema for controlling the power and energy of Indian nationalism slowly eroded the colonial state not by political reform but by the colonial government's misunderstanding of how those reforms would be felt and indeed used by local Indian communities and their leaders.

8
Land Acquisition, Landlessness, and the Building of New Delhi

As architects and high officials debated the symbolic relationship of architecture to empire and as town planners worked out the final details of their town plan, land acquisition officers from the Government of India began the tedious process of assessing and acquiring lands for the new capital on a monumental scale. With the aid of the Delhi District's Land Revenue Office, town planners designated approximately 40,000 sq. acres to the south-west of the existing city of Delhi. The proceedings represented a moment when British abstract notions about imperial legitimacy, about the architectural aesthetics of empire, and, indeed, about the contribution of the British Empire to India's progress ran up against material reality. This chapter examines the manner in which New Delhi's *abstract* imperial vision was played out against and made possible by *real* people on the ground. In particular, it focuses on the colonial mechanisms of domination and subordination inscribed in New Delhi at its most basic level – namely, the land upon which the city itself was actually built. It does so by looking at the enclosing of lands and the removal of Indian communities for the building of New Delhi. Most dispossessed agriculturalists were given cash awards for their Delhi lands and offered the opportunity to purchase new lands in the neighbouring Punjab districts of Karnal and Rohtak or farther away in the new canal colonies of the Punjab's Lower Bari Doab.

The colonial government's acquisition of lands for the new capital sheds light on the growing divide between Britain's new, more progressive vision of empire and the potentially harsh consequences of its free market principles at the turn of the century. This disconnect between opportunity and disruption points to the limitations, or possibly the logical endpoint, of the colonial project, reformed or otherwise. One of the greatest of New Delhi's many ironies was the manner in which a city designed to silence Indian criticism of British rule actually highlighted systemic problems in Britain's political economy and, subsequently, its approach to colonial land policy in India. In short, the colonial government's construction of its progressive vision at Delhi required the exploitation of the very people it claimed to protect and advance.

The permanent land settlement and Britain's political economy in India

The enclosing of land for the building of New Delhi took on characteristics similar to but also quite different from earlier land enclosure movements. Unlike powerful English landowners who privatized common lands in England to increase their personal wealth, the Government of India enclosed lands near Delhi as part of the process of reinterpreting the meaning of empire in twentieth-century India. New Delhi was not meant to enrich private individuals but to reinvigorate, collectively, the British imperial project in India. Britain's enclosing of land for the building of New Delhi followed land policies long used in British-India. The Land Acquisition Act of 1894, which gave the British government the authority to enclose private lands for public purposes, had its antecedents in an earlier East India Company land law, the Permanent Settlement of Bengal. Passed in 1793 under Lord Cornwallis's government, this Land Act 'settled permanently the revenue to be paid by landlords to the state, giving them immunity against revenue increase in addition to security of ownership'.[1] According to Ranajit Guha, the ideas and values behind the settlement drew on French and British enlightened economic thinking, particularly regarding free trade and the perceived social and economic benefits brought by securing individual property ownership.[2] The latter ineluctably led to the improvement of lands according to Philip Francis, an influential author of the Bengal settlement.[3] Individual property ownership, and thus a direct stake in the land's productive potential, created, in theory, a more stable, satisfied, and wealthy rural India. However, as Thomas Metcalf long ago showed, rather than improving their private property, as Francis argued they would, many Indian landowners became burdened by crushing debt as they sought loans from local *banias* (bankers), merchants, or wealthy neighbours to meet their land revenue obligations, their family responsibilities, or simply to purchase the following year's agricultural necessities such as seed.[4] One problem, for many agriculturalists, was that the East India Company initially set a high revenue demand on permanently settled lands to ensure that the company received the highest revenues the lands could bear in perpetuity. Another problem concerned introducing the free market to the rural economy. Whether agriculturalists or not, Indians with investment capital accumulated land while many cultivators became tenant farmers. This connection between land and capital created precisely what Francis wished to avoid in his enlightened and progressive land reforms, a feudal-like agricultural economy.[5] Though later Land Alienation Acts were passed by the British to impede the transfer of land from agriculturalists to non-agriculturalists, 'the result ... was that the moneylending business was taken over by the wealthier agriculturalists, who stepped into the *banias'* shoes'.[6]

The Permanent Settlement was repeated throughout British India via periodic settlement reports drawn up by local District Collectors and their staffs. These reports and the occasional District Gazetteer, which attempted to draw a general picture of a district's social and cultural life, exemplified the state's simplification of complex rural communities. Local colonial governments measured only what was of interest to the colonial state's revenue streams, the most important of which was land tenure which determined who would bear the burden of taxation. Often relying on the fieldwork of Indians who worked in his office, the District Collector drafted reports based on static aggregates that grouped people in ways that allowed 'collective assessment', as James Scott has shown for other communities.[7] His primary administrative goal was to 'measure, codify, and simplify land tenure', a process of 'heroic simplification of individual freehold tenure'.[8] The British Raj's simplification of the relationship between the land and the people who worked it gave the state access to what Scott calls 'synoptic facts' that made taxation more efficient and predictable into the future.[9] In the case of land acquisition for the new capital, the land acquisition office remapped and reassessed Delhi's rural land holdings, considering 'only the dimensions of the land and its value as a productive asset or as a commodity for sale'.[10] As such, the land acquisition officer followed long-held protocols concerning land tenure in India, namely that 'each holding be held in full proprietary title by a single owner', as Metcalf claims.[11]

The decision to build a new capital gave the colonial government an opportunity to further modernize property relations in the Delhi District, but the colonial government's firm commitment to free market principles, which shaped its land acquisition laws, made landlessness for many Delhi farmers a near certainty. Additionally, Britain's reluctance to forego free market principles even during moments of natural disaster, such as droughts, not only failed to slow the financial ruin of many Delhi agriculturalists but also, in many ways, hastened it in the years just prior to the building of New Delhi. Though the colonial government was committed to offering fair compensation and resettlement to Indians who lost their property for the building of the new capital, it was also faithful to official land policies. Certainly, larger Delhi landowners with disposable capital or deep connections with the British government were able to leverage the process of land enclosure for economic benefit. But Britain's political economy, which above all valued property, made no allowances during the land acquisition proceedings for the rights of those without title to the land. The land acquisition office's static picture of private property ownership ignored local customs regarding labour and its compensation. In so doing, land acquisition officers chose not to recognize that 'customs are better understood as a living, negotiated tissue of practices which are continually being adapted to new ecological and social circumstances', as Scott claims.[12] Even after a century of British rule in the area, Delhi's adaptable rural environs allowed a complex reciprocal relationship to develop between landowners and non-landowners where they had 'no difficulty in grasping its subtleties and using its flexible provisions for their own purposes'.[13] But the government's acquisition of land for the new capital, based on a myopic view much like a cadastral map, led to a compensation system that left both landowners and non-landowners alike in vulnerable positions. Thus, the colonial state set adrift many rural residents who did not own land near Delhi but worked for the dispossessed residents that did. Many Delhi agriculturalist, who had lost either their lands or their livelihoods for the building of New Delhi, were swept away by British land policies that privileged private property and the free market over community and social cohesion.

An understanding of the influence that Britain's political economy had on the process of land acquisition and its impact on Delhi's rural communities is more important than ever in light of an emerging trend in scholarship on the British Empire. Several recent studies have attempted to re-examine the benefits brought by British colonial rule. Most notably, Niall Ferguson has argued that British imperialism introduced liberal economic theories to the colonial world, making it better prepared for the modern global economy.[14] Pushing the point even further, Michael Mandelbaum has argued that the spreading of the free market to undeveloped or developing parts of the world is the first step toward their democratization.[15] He finds India a particularly interesting test case for his theory, arguing that Britain's long inculcation of free market thinking during the colonial period created a remarkably stable democracy in independent India.[16] Certainly, both Mandelbaum and Ferguson would concede that British colonialism caused tremendous damage in some areas of colonial life, but both conclude that the British Empire brought more good than harm.

John Gray provides a far more convincing approach that counters Ferguson and Mandelbaum's arguments. He posits that 'democracy and the free market are rivals, not allies'.[17] The free market, for Gray, must end in what he calls a 'politics of insecurity' for an overwhelming majority of people.[18] Contrary to what many of its proponents claim, the free market does not arise from natural economic conditions – the invisible hand as Adam Smith would proclaim – and it is most certainly not encouraged by deregulation. In fact, according to Gray, 'free markets are creatures of state power, and persist only so long as the state is able to prevent human needs for security and the control of economic risk from finding political expression'.[19] In the case of India, colonial officials rigidly held to free market economic principles that led to some of the greatest failures of British rule in the late nineteenth and early twentieth centuries. As the following examination of land acquisition shows, Delhi's rural communities were well down the road of agricultural ruin when George V declared his desire to build a new capital in the district. A similar free market philosophy that stayed the hands of the colonial government to ease the economic stress caused by late nineteenth-century droughts now would be employed to dispossess Delhi farmers of their land and to resettle them in potentially higher revenue yielding canal colonies in the Punjab.

Physical geography and social make-up of the Delhi District

What did the area in and around Delhi look like just prior to the transfer of the capital? What were its settlement patterns and how did these patterns influence relations between Indians and British administrators as well as relations between Indian landowning agriculturalists and Indian village proprietors? What was the quality of the soil and how much land was irrigated by wells or canals for these were the two most important criteria for determining land value in the relatively arid district? By knowing what the Delhi area physically and socially looked like before land acquisition began, we gain a better sense of the material and cultural transformations that took place in consequence of the decision to transfer the capital.

Demographically, the Delhi District was characterized by one large city amidst many dozens of small agricultural villages averaging 1,100 acres.

The average village population was 900, and village revenue payments yielded Rs 1,500 per year on average.[20] According to the *Third Regular Settlement, 1906–1910*, 67 per cent of the district's land was cultivated, 18 per cent was culturable waste used for grazing, and 15 per cent was unculturable waste often occupied by non-agricultural industries such as brick kilns.[21] As Thomas Metcalf has shown for the neighbouring lands of the United Provinces, which shared similar soils, climate, and rainfall patterns, the Delhi District was characterized by low agricultural yields.[22] Consequently, there were few rich and powerful land magnates in the Delhi District because the soil could not support them. Instead, the average farm was only 2.2 acres.[23]

The agricultural quality of the land, and thus the revenue due the Government of India, was determined primarily by irrigation improvements and secondarily by the basic composition of the soil and the nature of the substrata.[24] As David Ludden argues, 'Everywhere (except at very high altitudes), the calendar and the rhythms of farming in South Asia [were] pegged not to temperature but rather to moisture.'[25] Hence, the local government was responsible for two agricultural improvements: bands and canals. Located on hills, bands were artificially flattened areas of cultivation made possible by building down-slope retaining walls that trapped rain water during the monsoon and winter rains. Approximately 2,400 acres of hill country in the Delhi District were irrigated by bands, or less than one per cent of the cultivated area.[26] Much more significant were two canals, the Agra and Western Yamuna, which ran through the west and south-west portions of the district. Dating back to the Mughal period, the two canals irrigated 98,519 acres, about 18 per cent of the cultivated area of the district.[27] The most common and most economic land improvement, however, was the building of wells at the landowner's expense. In the Delhi District, 105,976 acres, or 19.5 per cent, were irrigated by wells.[28] This left over half of the district's rural lands dependent on the summer monsoons, a fact that made the district prone to agricultural crises during drought years.

Two harvest periods, the *kharif* (October–January) and the *rabi* (April–May), defined rural life. Both were determined by two wet periods – the more predictable summer monsoon between July and August and sporadic winter rains.[29] Dry weather prevailed between these two wet periods, creating a season of cultivation during the monsoons and a season of circulation during dry weather. Crops during the season of circulation, according to Ludden, 'take new life' by assuming 'new material forms as moveable measures and piled-up stores of grain, fruit, pulses, and vegetables, in stocks, carts, trucks, bags, head loads, and shops'.[30] In short, they became commodities to be priced, traded, and speculated. Hence, the trader of agricultural goods was just as important to the health of the agricultural system as the farmer scraping a living from the soil. 'Agrarian wealth [arose],' claims Ludden, 'from the social powers that articulate[d] these two great seasons – of cultivation and circulation – in the life of agricultural produce.'[31]

Almost the entire rural population depended on agriculture in one way or another.[32] Seasonal labourers often belonged to traditionally non-agricultural castes. Two of the most common were *chamars* (leather workers) and *chuhras* (sweepers). Other villagers who seasonally worked in the fields or were closely tied to landowners were *khatis* (carpenters), *lohars* (blacksmiths), *kumhars* (potters), *dhobis* (washers), and *sakkas*, *jhinwars* and *kahars* (all three water carriers). Lastly, nomadic peoples such as *Kanjars* or *Saperas* were sometimes used as agricultural workers during the harvest. In the Delhi District, much like the neighbouring districts across the Yamuna, village tradesmen were often cultivators as well.[33] Seasonal labourers regularly asked to be paid in kind rather than in cash, especially during the *rabi* when wheat was grown and when food stores were less predictable due to the sporadic nature of winter rain. Small land holders, whose lands did not produce enough food to feed the family a whole year, also often asked to be paid in kind when hiring themselves out to wealthier neighbours. The amount of grain paid to agricultural workers was typically four *pulis* (sheaves) of wheat. The Settlement Officer for Delhi estimated that nomadic peoples earned from 2 to 8 per cent of the harvest in lieu of cash wages.[34]

Land tenure and land occupancy in the Delhi District, as in much of India, could be difficult to gauge precisely though Government of India District Collectors made committed efforts to penetrate the haze. In general, rural lands in the Delhi District fell under three occupancy categories: owners, tenants, and tenants-at-will (see Table 8.1). Lands often

Table 8.1 Land tenures in the Delhi District, 1911[35]

Land tenures	Percentage of district
Occupied by owners	56
Occupancy tenants:	
Free of rent	2
Cash rents	9.25
In-kind rents	0.25
Occupied by tenants-at-will	
Cash rents	25
In-kind rents	7.5

were held by individuals or by *Bhaiacharya*, a system of tenure in which a group of men, often brothers, owned a single unit of land. Occupancy tenants and tenants-at-will, both of which averaged less than two acres per holding, either paid no rent to a *zamindar* (landowner) or paid rents in cash or kind.[36] Cash rents were by far the most common. Individuals who fell within the two forms of tenancy were in a strong occupancy position and their rents to landowners were often low because they were determined by long-standing custom or traditional rights. More importantly, landowners tended to avoid demanding higher rents from their tenants because it meant recourse to the courts. Much like other regions of India, it was in the best interest of landowners to keep the true nature of their land holdings vague in order to protect themselves from the demands of British revenue officers. As P. J. Marshall has argued, 'To set all [property] down on paper would make all vulnerable.'[37] *Ryots* (peasants) and *zamindars* 'had more confidence in their own powers of concealment and evasion than in the good intentions of government and the working of the courts'.[38] Vague land tenures were particularly important for rural residents living in a district where the average landholding was a bare two acres and where it was often difficult to determine who was a *ryot* and who was a *zamindar*. Thus, the Delhi District's land tenure structure reflected the difficulties the colonial state faced when attempting to codify and simplify its understanding of the relationship between individuals and land. In the Delhi District, as Scott claims for other cities, 'the actual practices of customary land tenure were frequently so varied and intricate as to defy any one-to-one equation of taxpayer and taxable property'.[39] Delhi's rural residents had resisted to some degree the incursions of the District Collector and his staff because many of them would be damaged by 'the unified and transparent set of property relations desired by the state's fiscal agents'.[40]

The rural lands around Delhi had been extensively farmed for many generations. This is made clear by comparing the *Regular Settlement Reports* from 1880 and 1910. The area under cultivation in 1880 was 519,417 acres; in 1910 the cultivated area had risen to 544,055.[41] This represented a relatively small 4.6 per cent increase over a 30-year period suggesting that the district's arable land had been settled at near maximum capacity since at least 1880. The rural villages around Delhi were relatively small with the landowner at the centre of a complex labour and social system. Community members were bound not only by cash wages but also by payments in kind during certain times of the year. There was certainly a considerable flow of people in and out of the village, particularly during harvests, but there was also a great sense of reciprocity between, say, the ploughman and the *zamindar* or the *zamindar* and the *chumar* (sweeper). 'Social commitments within families, communities, sects, castes, and other groups ... enable[d] farmers to acquire what they need[ed] to plough and plant' and subsequently survive from one year to the next, according to Ludden.[42]

After several generations of detailed Settlement Reports that exhaustively mapped land ownership for revenue purposes, the local colonial government still failed to fully appreciate the social makeup of village life in the Delhi District. The problem was not due to any lack of information. Indeed, Delhi's Deputy Commissioner, Major H. C. Beadon, had just written a detailed Gazetteer on the district that examined social and geographical features as diverse as marital rites to soil types. Aided by a cadre of local Indian civil servants, Beadon knew a great deal about rural communities in the Delhi District. The problem was that this cultural and social information was irrelevant to the needs of a state whose primary concern was revenue. Minutia like the fact that the village barber oversaw weddings in some communities, and was thus an important agent for social cohesion, was inherently interesting to an anthropologist perhaps but not of overriding significance to the District Collector's revenue accounts. The rich texture and diversity of traditions that brought people and the land together in a sustainable and productive way were 'reduced to a convenient, if partly fictional, shorthand' that gave the local government a better sense of land holdings in the district.[43] Subsequently, the state's focus on property holdings and assessments erased the complexity of village social life and ignored the glue that held people together. These village communities, bound by ties of reciprocity between individuals and loosely held together by vague rights to the land, were difficult to recreate elsewhere.

Land enclosure under the Land Acquisition Act of 1894

Tracing the various processes by which Britain enclosed lands underscores the ambiguities of the symbolism posed by New Delhi. The gap between the harsh realities of land acquisition and the rhetoric of reform damaged the new imperial vision Britain worked so hard to create in its new capital. Two important impulses shaped land acquisitions for the building of New Delhi: the need to keep costs down and the desire to take possession of Indian lands under the rule of law. Both impulses worked toward the same ultimate goal, enclosing Indian lands for British imperial purposes. The acquisitions would have to be carefully handled since the Government of India wished to avoid creating hostility over the acquisition of land for a building project meant to silence Indian agitation. Yet, in the end, Britain's new imperial vision, built on a foundation of shattered rural communities, collapsed under the weight of its own contradictions.

The Government of India turned to the Land Acquisition Act of 1894 to reapportion property rights from the private sector (controlled by Indians) to the public sector (controlled by the colonial government). It authorized the colonial government to take control of lands deemed necessary for public purposes, in this case a new capital, and to compensate dispossessed individuals. The Act provided various descriptions of interested parties, listed the appropriate procedures for assessment and acquisition, described the rights of the dispossessed, and offered terms of compensation. The Act also set the price of land at its value on the day that its acquisition was announced in one of the official government gazettes of British-India. In the case of acquiring lands for New Delhi, this notice was issued in the *Punjab Gazette* on 21 December 1911, just nine days after the king's proclamation to transfer the capital from Calcutta to Delhi.[44] This ensured that land acquisition officers purchased lands at prices that had not been driven up by speculation, as many feared in Parliament.

The enclosing of lands for New Delhi required a special establishment drawn from the district's Land Revenue Office, which had the most detailed knowledge of the Delhi District's agricultural communities. H. C. Beadon and later J. Addison were selected to run the new land acquisition establishment. Indian members, however, were far more essential to the process of land acquisition since they were more intimate with the district's farmers than their British officers. An Assistant Commissioner and two Extra Assistant Commissioners worked closely with their British superiors in the Land Acquisition Office. Four *naib tahsildars* (revenue deputies in charge of district subdivisions), fourteen *patwaris* (keepers of revenue accounts), and seven field *kanungos* (field assessors) made up the rest of the Land Acquisition Office. Field *kanungos* and *patwaris* did most of the measurements on the notified lands and had the greatest interaction with landowners. Additionally, a Special Indian Pleader, who acted as a liaison between the Government and local residents, was essential to the process of land acquisition. The need for an Indian pleader was a good example of just how alien the British land tenure model still seemed to many local Indians, even after years of dealing with the British revenue system and the District Collector. As Scott claims, 'What was simplifying to an official was mystifying to most cultivators.'[45] Rai Sahib Lala Mool Chand, who held this position, worked hard to minimize Indian discontent and to encourage them to accept the government's compensation.

In the final land acquisition report, J. Addison, who took over as the head of the Land Acquisition Office in late 1912, spoke glowingly of his Indian staff singling out the two Extra Assistant Commissioners, Rai Bahadur Lala Daswandhi Ram and M. Khazan Singh; the *naib tahsildars,* M. Amir Singh, M. Raghbir Singh, and M. Mohamad Saddiq; and the *kanungos,* M. Fazal Din, M. Arjan Singh, P. Tej Kishan, and L. Kali Ram. Addison wrote that the arduous work of acquisition required 'delicate and tactful handling' and that 'success was only possible with the loyal help of all the staff'.[46] British officials may have held the highest offices, but Indian civil servants made the acquisitions possible.

The Land Acquisition Office divided the designated area for New Delhi into five main blocks.[47] Block A, the military cantonment, was an area to the south-west of where New Delhi would eventually be built. The cantonment also included the areas of high ground demanded by the military. Block B, where the government buildings would arise, lay adjacent to old Delhi.[48] Blocks C, D and E represented future imperial city extensions and were important for controlling the city's growth. Using the guidelines of the Land Acquisition Act, lands to be acquired were measured, valued, and acquired on a village-by-village basis within these five blocks (see Table 8.2).

The average cost per acre of enclosed lands shows the government's wisdom in selecting a largely agricultural rather than urbanized area for the building of New Delhi. The average price for privately owned agricultural land acquired for the imperial city, its future extensions, and the cantonment was a little over Rs 156 per acre. This rate included the compulsory acquisition fee of 15 per cent of the assessed value of the land. In comparison, urban lands averaged a little over Rs 7,903 per acre. The lands closest to Delhi generally cost more to acquire

Table 8.2 Total expenditure for all lands acquired (in rupees)[49]

	Awards	Misc.	Court increases	Total
Land acquired for Imperial Delhi	3,399,524	3,729	8,209	3,411,462
Land acquired for cantonments	1,263,490		474	1,263,964
Land acquired for New Delhi Railway Terminal Station	151,220			151,220
TOTAL	4,814,234	3,729	8,683	4,826,646

since farmers in this area often produced cash crops for local markets, which were assessed at higher amounts. The villages of Khandrat Kalan, Banskoli, Jurbagh, and Narhola, for example, averaged between Rs 271 and 473 per acre because of their proximity to Delhi whereas the villages of Alipur Pilanji and Malcha, because of their long distance from Delhi, cost between Rs 44 and 55 per acre.

Disruption, compensation, and the failures of the free market

Under the Land Acquisition Act, the Government of India had a variety of ways to compensate dispossessed landowners. It could offer single cash payments or revenue remissions on properties not acquired by the government. The government could also offer lands of equal value in exchange for acquired lands. Government discussions about compensation for lands acquired for New Delhi began as early as December 1912. Hoping to avoid any controversy that might undermine his plans for New Delhi, Hardinge encouraged Geoffrey deMontmorency, the interim president of the Imperial Delhi Committee, to seek the most equitable compensation for dispossessed Delhi landowners. A heated debate began over which form of compensation – land, cash, or revenue remission – would be most satisfactory for dispossessed Delhi landowners. Yet in many ways, the debate was not about compensating Indians but about the relationship between the rule of law, land, and the free market.

In March 1912, deMontmorency sent a memo to both the Home Department and the Revenue and Agriculture Department suggesting that Delhi's dispossessed landowners should be compensated in lands located as close as possible to Delhi and suggested that they also receive small sums for restarting their farms on new lands. As deMontmorency claimed in his memo, 'His Excellency [Hardinge] is anxious that the foundation of the new Capital at Delhi should not lead to any feelings of soreness or fancied injustice among those who are expropriated.'[50] Reminiscent of earlier debates concerning the permanent land settlement, ill feelings would be reduced by giving good farmland to people who knew how to use and improve it.[51]

However, deMontmorency's initial estimates tremendously underestimated the amount of land needed to compensate dispossessed Delhi landowners. In his original design for compensation, deMontmorency determined that only Indians who lost all their property for the building of New Delhi would be entitled to land awards. Large landowners, in contrast, would be compensated either in cash or through revenue remissions. Believing that there were greater numbers of large landowners in the district, and thus far fewer landowners requiring compensation in land, deMontmorency wrongly estimated that about 8 square miles of land in the Delhi and nearby Rohtak and Karnal Districts would satisfy the compensation needs of land acquisition. By June 1912, however, land acquisition officers realized that dispossessed Delhi farmers would require much more land than was available for resettlement in the Delhi, Karnal and Rohtak Districts.[52] In the end, the British government turned to the Lower Bari Doab Canal Colony for nearly two-thirds of its resettlement needs. Five thousand acres were set aside in the Rohtak and Karnal Districts, and the rest was found in the Lower Bari Doab.[53] Few dispossessed farmers were resettled in the Delhi District due to the unavailability of land.

The Lower Bari Doab Canal Colony posed a new problem for resettling Delhi's dispossessed landowners. As noted earlier, land acquisition officers assessed Delhi lands at Rs 156 per acre on average and sometimes far less. In contrast, land in the Lower Bari Doab Canal Colony cost a little over Rs 400 per acre on average between 1912 and 1927[54]. As H. J. Maynard, an official of the Lower Bari Doab Canal Colony, made clear, '...some of the Delhi claimants are entitled to only a few hundred rupees a piece; and I do not see what they are to do with an acre or so of land on the Lower Bari Doab Canal'.[55] Recognizing this predicament and still desiring to keep hostility to a minimum, deMontmorency claimed that Delhi's dispossessed landowners should receive land compensations that were in excess of the lands they lost. It was 'hard on the farmer', he claimed, 'to go halfway across the province [for] 4/5 of an acre of canal land in a strange country, to which we know [they] are disinclined to go in any case, for the same money'.[56] Consequently, deMontmorency drafted a land transfer scale in which dispossessed Delhi farmers received liberal amounts of canal acreage for their relatively poor Delhi lands.[57] As deMontmorency claimed, 'We do not want an outcry that we have pared down the awards to the lowest possible figure, while the charge for the new land is assessed at an extravagantly high figure', deMontmorency argued.[58]

Other officials, however, had a different view about compensating Delhi farmers for their loss of lands. H. B. Holmes, for example, argued that deMontmorency's plan set an extremely bad precedent. Delhi's dispossessed landowners, according to him, should not receive any preference because it would open the doors to further demands by Indians who had had their lands acquired by the British government for other building projects. 'It is of the greatest importance', argued Holmes, 'to emphasize that ex-proprietors of land required for Delhi should not be more favourably dealt with than the ordinary ex-proprietors whose land is acquired under the Land Acquisition Act'.[59] He continued, 'If we were once to admit that the 15% given under the Act was not really adequate compensation for the compulsory nature of the acquisition under the Act, we should lay ourselves open to claims for further consideration in every case of acquisition under the Act.'[60] Holmes realized the uniqueness of the situation – that the land acquisitions were intended for a new capital meant to silence Indian disapproval of British rule – but that it was of the utmost importance to follow to the letter the policies of the Land Acquisition Act. Dispossessed Delhi landowners should be treated like typical Indian farmers seeking to purchase new lands for agricultural purposes. Holmes ended his response to deMontmorency's resettlement plans by stating, 'Personally, I have grave doubts about the wisdom of attempting to find land for anyone in these circumstances ... It is better to give them their money and let them do the best they can with it.'[61]

In the end, Holmes' argument won the day because it was rooted in what British colonial officials believed was their firm commitment to the unbending principles of the rule of law, which, according to many of them, made the British Empire unique in the history of India.[62] Britain's rule of law, which had been shaped by enlightened reason and maintained by indifferent colonial officials, had given India stability because it supposedly made no distinction between colonial subjects. In contrast, the Indian empires of the past were characterized by fluid, unpredictable, and arbitrary systems of justice since the rule of law was in essence the will of the emperor. Thus, the rule of law was shaped and reshaped with each successive imperial rule. DeMontmorency's liberal compensation plan, though certainly more compassionate, simply reflected the wrong imperial tradition in India. The supposedly inflexible rule of law as set forth in the Land Acquisition Act would be arced in favour of Delhi's dispossessed farmers by deMontmorency's preferential treatment. It was simply dishonest and contrary to the spirit of the law to say that an acre of Delhi land was equal to an acre of canal land.

Based on Holmes' thinking, the Government of India authorized the Land Acquisition Office to offer cash awards as full compensation for lands acquired for the building of the new capital. No lands would be given in compensation. Instead, lands would be *reserved for purchase* in the Karnal, Rohtak, and Lower Bari Doab. The Land Acquisition Office advised dispossessed residents to bank their cash awards and to report on a specified date to the courts of Deputy Commissioners where resettlement lands were located. The Land Acquisition Office kept a register of awards and informed Deputy Commissioners in the Karnal, Rohtak and especially Lower Bari Doab, of when to expect a new resident and how much land should be reserved for them. Their Delhi cash compensations became, in a sense, irrelevant. 'As there will be no obligatory payment of purchase money in such cases,' wrote the Land Acquisition Office, 'it will not be necessary to arrange that the value of the land given should bear any strict correspondence with the sum allotted as compensation for the Delhi lands.'[63] Instead, dispossessed Delhi residents would be required to purchase new lands in a new District, and their Delhi awards could be used to offset these costs. If these were insufficient, as most were, they would be eligible for agricultural loans.

A brief examination of a typical compensation case serves as an example of the Land Acquisition Office's process of compensation and resettlement. Bhola, a farmer from the village of Mubarikpur Reti, owned 0.20 acres of Delhi land assessed and compensated at a little over Rs 25.[64] Like other agriculturalist seeking lands in the Lower Bari Doab, he needed around Rs 10,000 to purchase one rectangle (25 acres) of canal land, the average size of an allotment.[65] Clearly, he was in no financial position to purchase canal lands outright with his Delhi compensation. However, this did not necessarily mean that Bhola could not be resettled here. With Bhola's approval, shown by a thumbprint, the Land Acquisition Office asked for and received one rectangle of land from the canal colony officer. What seems like a tremendously liberal compensation by the British – 25 acres of arable canal land for 0.20 acres of poor Delhi land – was actually a smart long-term, low-cost investment in the raw potential of an Indian farmer. The land was not given to Bhola as compensation. It was reserved for his immediate agricultural use, and he would pay for this land in future instalments 'on such terms as may be generally prescribed' by the British government.[66]

The process of resettling Delhi farmers in the Lower Bari Doab Canal Colony had mixed results. For the most part, the few large Delhi landholders who lost all their lands chose to resettle in the canal colony. Larger landowners, typically, were connected to or on intimate terms with the Government of India before resettlement. Some large landowners had worked for the colonial government, using their incomes to expand their family's landholdings. Other landowners held *muafis* (lands free of revenue) or *jagirs* (lands where the revenue went to the owner rather than the government) in the Delhi District. The British, as had the Mughals before them, gave these special land grants to individuals for meritorious service to the colonial government.[67] Still others, much like elsewhere in India, understood how to leverage for their benefit the conditions of the permanent land settlement. They recognized that the more arable lands of the canal colony combined with their existing capital and connections to the British offered tremendous financial advantages in the Lower Bari Doab. As Scott suggests, 'Those in the colonies who first plumbed the mysteries of the new tenure administration enjoyed unique opportunities.'[68] A significant problem, however, was that those with the deepest understanding of these legal codes were not agriculturalist but merchants or bankers, those urban rather than rural individuals who had had the longest interaction with the British.[69] Thus, in many ways the system rewarded and empowered the wrong people and hindered those who it was designed to benefit.

Peasant farmers, in contrast, faced a much greater dilemma. For some, their Delhi cash awards were too small even to finance the move from the Delhi District to the Lower Bari Doab let alone meet the costs of cultivating a new farm.[70] Others were reluctant to resettle in the Lower Bari Doab because of its distance from the Delhi District. These Indian agriculturalists were deeply concerned about the social impact resettlement would have on their families, particularly when it came to arranging marriages. As Ramji Lal and 33 other dispossessed farmers from the village of Mauza Manglapuri claimed in a memorial to government, '[we] will be socially ruined owing to the fact that we shall be unable to marry our children ... because our relations and brotherhood ... refuse to give their daughters in marriage owing to [the] great distance, and already since the acquirement [of land], the betrothals and engagements of the children ... have been dissolved'.[71] Equating the importance of marriage to other agricultural cycles in South Asia's rural communities, David Ludden suggests, 'Agrarian history unfolds in the seasons of everyday life in agricultural societies. Farming moves to the rhythm of holiday seasons, wedding seasons, rainy seasons, and seasons of fruit.'[72] For Ramji Lal, resettlement in the Karnal District was too far to maintain basic agrarian social structures like marriage, which not only sealed relations between families but also helped ensure supplies of labour and subsequently agricultural productivity in the future. Shifting to the Lower Bari Doab, even farther away, simply was unthinkable.

Indian peasants also were concerned about the economics of resettlement. Some dispossessed Delhi residents, such as Bhola above, may have been willing to take on long-term debt that lasted generations, but most peasant farmers were not willing to take such risks. For example, only 7 out of 48 peasant farmers accepted reserved lands in the canal colony based on one resettlement report from August 1914.[73] Three years later, only 29 out of 160 peasant farmers accepted the offer.[74]

Nonetheless, some Indian farmers showed remarkable acumen during negotiations with the Land Acquisition Office over their compensations. Sensing British concerns about public opinion, dispossessed farmers pressed for and often received larger reservations of canal land. *Ryots* consistently asked for 5–20 rectangles of land (125–500 acres) instead of the one rectangle authorized for peasants. In most cases, Indian farmers who requested larger reserved lands planned to farm part of the acreage and to rent the remainder, essentially making themselves *zamindars*.[75] For well-organized villagers who could draw upon claims of a special relationship with the British, such as the Sikh community of Rikabganj, their bargaining position was incredibly powerful.[76] This community not only received 750 acres of reserved land in the Lower Bari Doab but also saved a Gurdwara, located immediately next to New Delhi's main government buildings, from destruction by British town planners.[77] In memorial after memorial, Sikhs from this village reminded colonial authorities that their fathers and grandfathers had fought alongside the British in 1857.[78] Some Delhi farmers refused resettlement in the Lower Bari Doab when the Land Acquisition Office failed to meet the demand for more canal land.[79] This was something the British clearly dreaded because resettlement was their primary shield against Indian criticism.

A third group of rural Delhi residents went largely unnoticed, 'Cultivator proprietors', as Metcalf has called them.[80] This group consisted of, for example, carpenters, blacksmiths, masons, or sweepers who did not own farmland but relied on part-time agricultural work to supplement their livelihoods in the Delhi District. Because the British only recognized landowners as deserving compensation, no protection was offered to this semi-agricultural group, which made up a considerable portion of the dispossessed population. These cultivator proprietors, often the most impoverished and most dependent of all rural Delhi residents, were set adrift by the process of land acquisition which broke their connections to even the poorest landowners who might offer seasonal work.

Land acquisitions in the Delhi District reflected an interesting tension between the government's desire to balance the district's land revenues and its land needs for the capital. As the local district government lost lands to the building project, it also lost important land revenues. In response to this potential loss of revenue and its disruption to district administration, Reginald H. Craddock, Home

Department Secretary for the Government of India, encouraged the Land Acquisition Office to allow *zamindars* and *ryots* to continue living on lands acquired by the government under the Land Acquisition Act as long as the lands were not immediately required for building purposes.[81] Lands would then be rented to Indian farmers who were now government tenants holding terminable leases.[82] As an incentive the government offered moderate rents and assured residents that they would be given a one-year notice of termination of their government lease.[83] Many residents were thus allowed to stay on their land, to maintain their way of life, and subsequently to continue paying their land revenues to the Delhi District government. The system worked well for the imperial government. Initial land acquisition expenditures were offset by rents and the retention of the land revenue. According to Craddock, 'Under this method it would probably be possible to show that the money expended in buying out rights without interfering with the occupation of the land would yield government a certain 5 or 6 per cent per annum.'[84] As Craddock understood, most agriculturalists, who did not want to be set adrift, fell in line with the policy. Through the process of land acquisition, the Government of India became the largest landholder in the Delhi District, now doubly benefitting by receiving both rent payments and the traditional land revenue. Delhi's murky land tenure structure, which had favoured Indian farmers by making revenue assessments difficult, was made more transparent and measurable.

The process of land acquisition for the building of New Delhi also benefitted the British land revenue system in another important way. Dispossessed Delhi agriculturalists could be used as settlers in the higher revenue-yielding canal colonies of the Punjab. The Punjab government wanted colonists for its newest irrigation project in the Lower Bari Doab and dispossessed Delhi landowners offered a supply of farmers who readily could begin working the land and paying land revenues. It perhaps would be an overstatement to argue that the British government purposely created a landless peasantry to recolonize an area that offered better agricultural output and thus higher revenues than could be obtained in the Delhi area. But the policy does point to the harsh realities of the colonial system's political economy, which shaped British policies concerning lands and revenues. Canal colonies, like railroads, promised high returns but required extremely large capital investments. The quicker the Government of India found settlers for the Lower Bari Doab, the sooner it would start seeing returns on its investment. Britain's political economy in India worked to advance

British and Indian financial interests at the cost of those at the bottom of Indian society.

A capital rises from agricultural ruin

The major land acquisition proceedings lasted until 1919. Though hundreds of Indians were dispossessed of their lands, few sought appeal in the courts. The Government of India was so pleased with the outcome of the land acquisition proceedings that it awarded Addison, the land acquisition officer who oversaw most of the compensations, an accommodation for the 'great accuracy and fairness which [he] has brought to bear on his work'.[85] What made the Government of India particularly happy with Addison was that he carried out the process 'expeditiously' and with what they saw as great moderation in terms of compensation. 'Feelings of soreness which is aroused by wide acquisition of ancestral properties,' claimed William Malcolm Hailey, Chief Commissioner of the Delhi District, 'had been mitigated by the fairness and impartiality of Addison's land acquisition staff'.[86]

On closer inspection, however, the reasons for Addison's success in completing the land acquisition proceedings with minimal litigation had little to do with his personal administrative abilities or the fairness of British colonial rule as represented by the Land Acquisition Act. The harsh bureaucratic machinery of the Act and a long series of droughts were far more important for limiting the complaints of dispossessed landowners. First, Indians could not appeal the loss of their lands under the Land Acquisition Act; they could only appeal the amount of their compensation for these losses once the machinery of the Land Acquisition Act was set in motion. Those who chose to appeal their compensation were also taking considerable financial risk. When a family from the village of Chitli Kabar lost their appeal, they were forced to pay legal fees totalling Rs 3,200, which was deducted from their original compensation of Rs 7,647.[87] Second, a series of droughts throughout northern India had crippled Delhi's agriculturalists. Since the mid-1890s, the district had suffered repeated and severe droughts that devastated the productivity of the district's soil and the economic conditions of its farmers.[88] The situation became so dire, that land revenues actually were suspended twice in the district during the years 1899–1900 and 1907–1908.[89] The area was particularly hard hit during the period between 1905 and 1909 when the monsoon and winter rains either ended early or failed completely.[90] Prolonged drought of this nature had devastating results in a district where over half the agricultural acreage was dependent solely on the monsoon for its water supply.

Famine relief works similar to the poor laws in Britain were started in earnest by the district government in 1897, the primary work being stone breaking and earth work for the Delhi-Agra Chord Railway, the Ghaziabad-Moradabad Railway, and the Municipal Pumping Station which supplied water to Delhi.[91] This relief work, as Mike Davis has shown, often simply prolonged the misery of impoverished Indians who received food rations that were far short of daily caloric requirements.[92] Famine relief based on the building of railways, again as Davis argues, ironically forced Indians to help build infrastructure that allowed British and Indian speculators to more easily transfer food away from rural to commercial centres where crops were stored, and often hoarded to drive up prices, before shipment to other parts of the world.[93] Adding to the morbidity of droughts in India, Indians weakened by malnutrition more easily succumbed to devastating epidemics that often killed more people than starvation from famine.[94]

Many local landowners in the Delhi District chose to take out loans or to sell farmland during the crisis. The Delhi District government gave Land Improvement Loans and Agriculturalist's Loans, which were often used for the purchase of seed, livestock, and farm implements, with 'unstinted freedom' during the droughts.[95] However, cash-strapped farmers, as in other parts of India, were more likely to seek loans from local *banias* than the government since Indians who received government moneys exposed themselves to property assessments that might just lead to higher revenue demands in the future.[96] Figure 8.1 shows that the selling of land was usually an act of desperation as can be clearly seen by the lower number of sales, which never surpassed 500 per year in the four decades examined. The figure also shows that farmers were coming under increasingly greater financial stress and thus selling or more often mortgaging their lands as the droughts persisted. To be clear, the Delhi District's steady agricultural decline was not simply due to drought but the failure of the colonial government to effectively protect district farmers from its consequences. As Mike Davis has argued, drought inexorably led to famine precisely because British infrastructural development had more deeply incorporated Indian agriculture into the global free market.[97] Left with few options in an agricultural system shaped by free market principles, landowners were consistently forced to mortgage smaller and smaller pieces of land to obtain money to purchase their basic needs. In some instances, Indian farmers redeemed their loans. The amount of redeemed land closely paralleled mortgaged land but there was one important difference. When quality lands were mortgaged, they usually stayed that way because Indian farmers suffering from repeated droughts rarely raised enough surplus capital to redeem the most expensive loans on their most productive lands. As Metcalf claims, 'Once in debt a peasant was usually unable to extricate himself.'[98] During moments of rare fluidity, they could redeem certain lands but because their financial situation was so precarious these redemptions often concerned the most inexpensive, lowest quality lands. Because of the long duration of the drought period, around 15 years, many local landowners found themselves under a considerable weight of debt. Thus, many landowners in the Delhi area were more inclined to accept the British government's land compensation and to begin life anew as farmers in the Lower Bari Doab or less commonly in the Karnal and Rohtak Districts. Many landowners refused to leave the district and simply took their cash awards and blended into the old city of Delhi or resettled amongst kin groups in lands to the east of the Yamuna River.[99]

Britain's colonial land and revenue policies impacted Indians differently depending on their position in colonial society. The Land Acquisition Act, shaped by Britain's political economy, continued to reward those Indians who previously had done well under British rule.

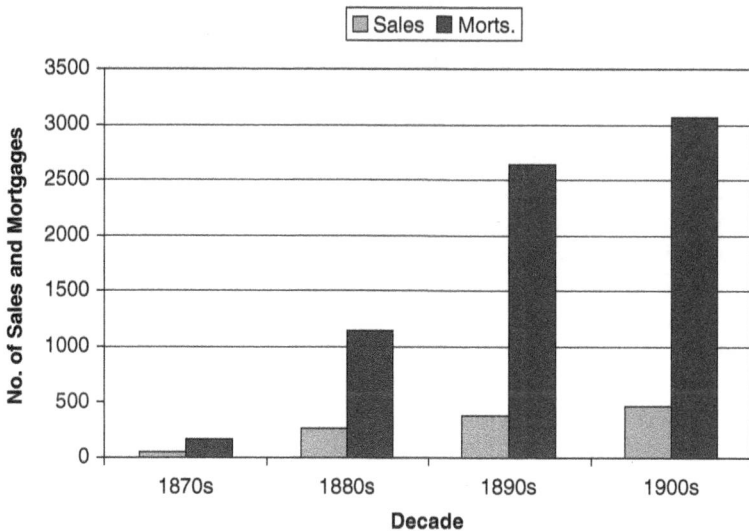

Figure 8.1 Sales and mortgages in the Delhi area[100]

The few large landowners who had their lands acquired for the building of the new capital leveraged their Delhi lands for better canal lands in the Lower Bari Doab. Dispossessed *ryots* who accepted resettlement in the canal colony could also improve their economic and social standing; however, resettlement meant taking on long-term government debt far beyond anything most Delhi farmers had ever known. For many, the colonial government's offer of compensation and resettlement was an empty gesture; they were far too financially ruined by years of drought to contemplate restarting life on lands set aside for resettlement. Lastly, the Land Acquisition Act made no allowances for the rights of Indians who did not own land but who were still intimately tied to the village through a complex agricultural labour system. These landless villagers, such as menials or small craftsmen, were set adrift when the village landowners left. Thus, a colonial Land Act shaped by the hard-edged values of the free market tended to destroy the economically weakest members of rural Delhi society. Without property, they had no rights to compensation and little to no chance of starting a farm, even if they chose to do so, in the Lower Bari Doab.

Though more and more colonial officials, like Hardinge, had become convinced that British colonial policy should encourage Indian involvement in colonial government, they continued to undermine their colonial reforms by holding firm to the political economy that had shaped the colonial system itself. In the case of land acquisitions in the Delhi District, the British argued that they were offering Indians greater agricultural opportunities in the canal colony for poorer Delhi lands. Yet the underlying assumptions, preferences, and discriminations of the Land Acquisition Act created tremendous social dislocation and distress. The Delhi awards, assessed at market value, were typically too low to be used for anything but the most basic resettlement purposes. Resettled Delhi farmers, consequently, became bound to the colonial government even more closely through debt. This indebtedness in turn encouraged farmers to produce cash crops for a global market centred in London, weakening rural India's economic health when world demand for its products declined.

9
Conclusion: The Inauguration of New Delhi, 1931 – A British Empire for the Twentieth Century

The meaning of imperial Delhi reached both its fullest expression as well as its fullest contradiction in February 1931, when the new capital was opened to the world in an inauguration that lasted a week. From the city's earliest beginnings in 1911, the capital was meant to be much more than a place to do the work of the imperial government. It was destined to be a crowning achievement in colonial architecture and colonial town planning, a capital worthy of the British Empire. 'Consummated' on what Edwin Montagu, Undersecretary of State for India, called 'virgin soil', New Delhi's precise location, its structures, its design, its rigorously controlled road grid, its monuments commemorating important imperial persons and events were artfully combined to make the capital a new temple of empire.[1] New Delhi was meant to be the quintessential statement of what British imperial rule had meant and continued to mean for Britain and for India.

The new capital had been heralded as an important step toward Indian responsible government where Indians methodically and slowly gained greater political power under the watchful gaze of British colonial officialdom. This deeply paternalistic vision remained unaltered by the time of the inauguration even though India's political climate had changed a great deal over the last twenty years. Hardinge's government, which reached out to Indians as few had done, and the political reforms promised during the Great War, caused a brief respite in British and Indian antagonisms between 1912 and 1918.[2] However, Indian agitation once again emerged after the war. There were many reasons for strained colonial relations. The economic and social dislocations caused by the Great War and by Britain's greater incorporation of the Indian economy into a much larger global economy caused massive inflation and rural and urban unrest between 1919 and 1922. The shortcomings of the Government of India Act of 1919[3] alongside the continued use of the anti-sedition Rowlatt Acts[4] and the tragic massacre of Indian demonstrators in Jallianwallah Bagh Park in Amritsar[5] in April 1919 further exacerbated the strained relations between Britain and India. M. K. Gandhi's rise to power in the Indian National Congress, his ability to bring together India's masses with its educated elites, and the particular anti-colonial strategies that he brought to bear against British rule were particularly important. The boycotting of British goods, revenues, and other imperial policies damaged the colonial administration's political economy in India, the very reason for having an empire in the first place. Gandhi's elevation of anti-colonialism as a moral and spiritual reawakening created a powerful threat to British rule.

Edwin Montagu had claimed in 1912 that the era of racial difference had come to a close and that Britain need not fear the 'educated Indian'.[6] Yet the British colonial administration had fallen far short of these high principles since Montagu's appeal to the House of Commons. New Delhi's inaugural ceremonies underscored these failings; they served as a precise point where colonial policies that politically empowered Indians intersected long-held British racial and cultural assumptions about Indians and indeed about themselves. While British officials worked hard to resolve British-Indian antagonisms, their deeply ingrained ideas about India's difference continually fractured the very vision they worked so hard to create. In the end, New Delhi failed as a liberal strategy of colonial control, for many Indian nationalists realized that the traditional social and racial hierarchies that sustained the British Empire remained intact underneath this imperial rhetoric of political devolution. Rather than misunderstanding the inauguration's promise of political reform, as some colonial officials assumed, many Indian nationalist leaders understood the message all too well.

The inauguration of New Delhi and dominion status

New Delhi's inauguration in 1931 provided the perfect opportunity to introduce and disseminate Britain's latest promise of political reform in India: dominion status. As with all previous political reforms offered by British officials, the goal was not to give India independence but to secure Britain's Indian Empire in the face of what had now become a determined and organized all-India anti-colonial movement led by Gandhi and the Indian National Congress. In 1927 the British Parliament attempted to weaken the movement by appointing a statutory commission to study and recommend further constitutional reforms for India.[7] However,

Parliament's stunningly imprudent selection of an all-white commission exacerbated rather than assuaged Indian anti-colonial sentiment. The statutory commission (commonly called the Simon Commission after its chairman, John Simon) met well-planned demonstrations and boycotts sponsored by the Indian National Congress as it travelled throughout India in 1928 and 1929.[8] The political chaos caused by the Simon Commission forced Lord Irwin (Viceroy of India, 1926–31) to call for a series of Round Table Conferences to examine the question of political reform.[9] Unlike the earlier Simon Commission – which resisted adding Indians to the commission and only did so belatedly in a failed attempt to end the demonstrations and boycotts that threatened its work – the Round Table Conferences began and ended with a large, albeit selective, Indian representation. Building on the 1919 Government of India Act's bifurcated system of reserved and transferred subjects, the conferences fashioned a federal-like colonial state where Indian provincial legislatures were given more political power over domestic policies while Britain continued to control foreign policy, the military, and the police. The first Round Table Conference, which ended in early 1931, asserted what Lord Irwin had publicly stated in October 1929: the purpose of continued British rule in India was to move the colony toward dominion status.[10] India's elevation to a dominion would make it the newest member of an exclusive imperial club consisting of Australia, Canada, New Zealand, and South Africa, the four great dominions of the British Empire. Many British officials hoped that this major prize would undermine the most radical elements of the Indian nationalist movement and strengthen the hand of those Indian moderates who continued to believe that working within a constitutional process would lead to a stronger India when independence finally arrived.

The inaugural ceremonies attempted to mirror these political changes while at the same time celebrating the Raj's splendour. Imperial pageantry, imperial ritual, and imperial precedence were much on display at the inauguration. There were gun salutes for the viceroy, massed military parades, formal inspections, pennant-draped avenues, and highly formalized seating arrangements for specially invited guests and British officials. Yet compared to the all-India scope of previous imperial ceremonies, such as George V's Durbar in 1911, the inaugural ceremonies were subdued. A variety of minor events were held including a field hockey match held near the Mori Gate in old Delhi, a 'Hog Hunters Ball' at the exclusive Gymkhana Club, banquets, garden parties, evening soirees, a polo tournament, and air displays by the Royal Air Force.[11] But these were relatively superfluous activities designed to connect the three major events: the unveiling of four Dominion Columns, the Peoples' Fete, and the commemoration of the All-India War Memorial.

Interestingly, the most important government structures such as Lutyens' Viceroy's House or Baker's Secretariats received little direct attention. Instead, inaugural planners chose key monuments in new and old Delhi to stage the ceremonies, using Lutyens' and primarily Baker's government buildings as imperial backdrops. Perhaps this was due to the controversy surrounding the cost of the structures, especially the Viceroy's House, which for many seemed overly extravagant and expensive in the context of the present economic difficulties faced by the empire.[12] On the other hand, Britain's new vision for its Indian Empire required carefully balancing the constitutional reforms being debated in London with a reaffirmation of its continued presence and importance in the national life of India. Furthermore, the large government structures' use as backdrops made the proposed constitutional changes seem less threatening to those who feared Indian nationalism. Indeed, the inauguration allowed colonial officials to proclaim that these constitutional reforms were not only encouraged but also made possible by the British Empire, which was still strong and confident enough to adapt to a changing colonial world. Thus, while political transformation was occurring in India, there was still remarkable imperial continuity. Consequently, many of the speeches made by British officials at the various ceremonies portrayed a spirit of continued sacrifice and loyalty, which was in the best interest of both Britain and India.

Appropriately, the inaugural planners used the unveiling of four Dominion Columns to set the stage for the inauguration. The columns were positioned between Baker's north and south Secretariats on either side of the Kingsway and were exceedingly important for expressing Britain's particular conception of constitutional reform in India. While the unveiling ceremony did not elevate India to dominion status, it directly alluded to the Round Table Conference's discussions to do so in the future. Baker approached Lord Chelmsford in March 1920 with the idea of building Dominion Columns between his Secretariats.[13] Initially, the columns were meant to express 'the great historic fact that the four dominions and India fought shoulder to shoulder in the Great War'.[14] Baker modelled the dominion columns after the pillars of Asoka, a Buddhist Mauryan Emperor, who inscribed his laws on stone columns throughout South Asia in the third century BC.[15] The columns were made of a similar red stone material as the government structures and stood 41.5 ft. from base to tip. The base of each column carried the coat of arms of its contributing dominion and an inscription: 'Canada to India, 1930', 'Australia to India, 1930', etc.[16] On top of each column rested a white stone globe with a bronze ship atop heading eastward under full sail. Allegorically, the bronze ship, an East India Merchant Man, signified the centrality of India to Britain's maritime empire. The columns themselves linked the British colonial government with Asoka's reign, which was recognized as a golden era of law-giving akin to Hammurabi's rule of Babylon. By the time of the inauguration, the columns had gone from memorials of wartime sacrifices to allegorical statements writ in stone concerning the social, political, and economic benefits for India if it remained under the aegis of the British Empire as a dominion.

Yet for all the rhetoric about dominion status, the imperial ritual surrounding the unveiling ceremony fell far short of the promise and served simply to remind most Indians of their continued colonial status. Seating arrangements were limited to two distinguished blocs: one for British high-ranking civil and military officers and the other for distinguished guests (a handful of Indian princes or their heirs-apparent and the heads of state for Nepal, Japan, Persia, and Afghanistan). The vast majority of Indians who wanted to see the inauguration were confined to the roofs of Baker's Secretariats.[17] A heavy police cordon secured the processional way and the government forum between the two Secretariats.

In general, the unveiling ceremonies tended to emphasize India's political and cultural difference from Britain.[18] For many British officials, India's particular history – steeped in autocracy and caste – had created social and political conditions that made it far different than the other great dominions. Britain's 'interpretive strategies for knowing India', according to Bernard Cohn, created lasting impressions of India as 'the land of oriental despotism, with its cycles of strong but lawless rules, whose inability to create political order based on anything but unbridled power led inevitably to its own destruction...'.[19] This reading of India as a land of despots and arbitrary rule made Indians 'a people ... thoroughly fitted by habit for a foreign yoke'.[20] If the British were characterized by a deep-seated belief in the rule of law, India was characterized by its absence, for in India law was simply the will of the despot. In contrast, as Arthur Balfour claimed in June 1910 while comparing colonial subjects to the *freeborn* Englishmen, 'Western nations as soon as they emerge into history show the beginnings of those capacities for self-government.'[21] For men like Balfour, the white settler colonies of Canada, Australia, New Zealand, and South Africa had become prosperous, self-governing nations because of hard-working, industrious settlers whose core identities were shaped by the pursuit of liberty and individual freedom, both of which were maintained by the rule of law. India, lacking such a history, had reached a seminal point in its history, as speechwriters at the unveiling made clear. Its political advances toward self-government could easily evaporate or be squandered by premature independence. Unlike the other dominions, India still required British tutelage in responsible government. As Sir John Monash of Australia carefully stated in his unveiling speech, 'While on the one hand, the people of India can be assured of our sympathy for a measure of self-government, my fellow citizens in Australia are equally concerned that nothing may happen to loosen the bonds which bind all subjects of the King Emperor in a common loyalty and that integrity of our great Commonwealth of nations may be preserved inviolate.'[22]

Several months before the inauguration in a published talk, John Simon had made a similar argument concerning the obstacles to India's natural growth toward self-government. Simon metaphorically fused architecture with constitutional reform while simultaneously reaffirming Britain's pedagogical role in India: '[A constitution] is a work of architecture, like a great cathedral, which must stand on solid earth, and be designed to resist all the strains and stresses that will assail it, and to give room and protection not to one section but to all manner of people.'[23] Continued British administration, then, was essential in providing a sound political foundation upon which a self-governing state, which protected the liberties of all its citizens through the rule of law, could be built in India. For Simon, self-government in India – like a plant needing appropriate soil and nutrients – required further tending by the British.

India's difference from the other dominions immediately appeared in the press. 'The function was deliberately designed to show the white-man's superiority', reported the *Lahore Tribune*, 'and to emphasize the fact that India could do well to remain within the British Empire and not to talk of independence'.[24] The same paper continued, 'General opinion expressed that it was too much official and a whiteman's show and that those in charge of arrangements had failed to catch the imagination of the people ... altogether the first ceremony proved to be very cold and frigid from the popular point of view.'[25] And this difference was apparent in England as well. When describing the unveiling ceremonies, *The Times* reported, 'It would be idle to pretend that the ceremony had any popular support. The attendance was confined entirely to those admitted by invitation. All the approaches were plastered with armed police, and little encouragement was given to anyone who desired to offer a demonstration, friendly or otherwise.'[26]

Clearly, as the press in India and Britain pointed out, inaugural planners had missed a tremendous opportunity to shift the political momentum in India. Although British officials had seemed to move in this direction, even calling for it in their speeches, their offer of liberal reform simultaneously reaffirmed the very colonial assumptions that forever marked Indians as culturally, politically and socially different. What India required was further British tutelage in responsible government rather than independence. Thus, the columns were a reminder not only of India's difference but its colonial domination. If the unveiling of the Dominion Columns portended India's future as an integral part of the British Empire, the next major event reminded people of India's past.

While the unveiling ceremonies had been a relatively closed affair, the People's Fete was designed to be a public event. The fete was held the following afternoon in front of old Delhi's Red Fort. Knowing that this event would be the only one attended by the average Indian, British planners used the occasion to send a series of messages to Indians. While it is impossible to know the exact number of Indian onlookers, the fact that the fete was held near one of the most densely populated areas of the old Indian city and that attendance was open to all (and not by invitation as with the other main events) suggests that many Indians were present. To dispel any assumption in the minds of Indians that the elevation to dominion status meant independence, inaugural planners used the People's Fete to remind Indians of their colonial past and their continued colonial status. Not too subtly, the fete was a reminder of Britain's legitimate claim to India by right of conquest.

The fete was advertised as a panorama of Indian history, but it was, in reality, a history of British imperial rule presented through a martial filter of military drill and regimental music. Fete activities included wrestling matches, tent pegging competitions, vaulting displays by the Royal Deccan Horse, bagpipe music by the 42nd Black Watch, and an aerial night performance by the Royal Air Force. The fete closed with a grand finale of fireworks and the singing of 'God Save the King', reminding attendees, once again, that they belonged to the British Empire.

While at the most immediate level the fete reminded Indians of Britain's monopoly of force in India, it also pointed to India's long colonial history under the Mughals and later the British. The Red Fort was central to this message. Built by the Mughal Emperor Shahjahan, no other structure in the Delhi area better symbolized the *end* of the Mughal and the *beginning* of the British Empire. It was here that in 1803 the Mughal Emperor Shah Alam received General Lake who had just defeated a Maratha Army on the east bank of the Yamuna River.[27] Half a century later the Red Fort once again loomed large in British imperial history when the British recaptured the palace at the end of the Indian uprising in 1857.[28] The British put their imperial stamp on the Red Fort by building four story barracks and garrisoning British troops within its confines.[29] What once had been the ultimate symbol of Mughal rule had become a statement of Britain's imperial legitimacy in India, earned and maintained by force of arms.

The People's Fete carried an additional message that was directly related to India's material progress under British rule. The fete's meaning and style encouraged Indians to ask questions about their colonial past and indeed about themselves by juxtaposing India's last two imperial rulers, the Mughals and the British. If foreign empires were seemingly destined to dominate India, as the past 600 years seemed to suggest, then would it not be wiser to support the empire that had brought the greatest benefits? Whereas the Mughals had expanded India's artistic and architectural sensibilities through court poetry and monumental architecture, Britain claimed that it had materially advanced India through economic development. The latter was made explicit by what seems an anomaly amongst the fete's military drill: a parade of decorated cars celebrating the progress made in modern transportation in India. While the Mughals had built magnificent mausoleums, such as Shahjahan's Taj Mahal, the British had busied themselves building steeled roads, modern ports, and telegraph lines. According to Ian Kerr, the British had laid 25,000 miles of railway lines between 1850 and 1900.[30] For inaugural planners, then, British colonial officials may have lacked the artistic temperament of the Mughals, but their reasoned materialism and engineering skills made possible the integration and unification of an extremely diverse subcontinent. This material rather than aesthetic British temperament ensured good government, good business, and in the end good rule. This particular rendering of the colonial past created a specific kind of colonial knowledge. 'Its function', as Ranajit Guha writes, 'was to erect that past as a pedestal on which the triumphs and glories of the colonizers and their instrument, the colonial state, could be displayed to best advantage'.[31] Yet who actually benefitted from Britain's material development of India is a matter of debate. If the seven-anna third class fare allowed long distance travel for millions of Indians, 'joining friends and uniting the anxious', as Niall Ferguson writes, the same trains made it easier for the Government of India and British and Indian capitalists to more effectively reorder India's economy for their economic advantage.

If the first two major inaugural ceremonies represented the benefits of British rule, the last major event, the dedication of the All-India War Memorial, symbolized Britain and India's inseparability. The memorial, a large archway designed by Edwin Lutyens, commemorated Indians who had died in World War I and the Afghan Wars. The archway spanned the Kingsway, the main processional route, that passed between Herbert Baker's Secretariats and his Dominion Columns and ended at Lutyens' Viceroy's House. The memorial's importance is evidenced by its placement as the eastern axial point in the new capital. Lutyens' arch, according to David Crellin, was a 'creative reworking of the Arc de Triomphe'.[32] Lutyens reduced the ornamentation on his memorial arch and made his 'proportions slimmer and more elegant' by making the height of the opening two and half times its width.[33] The names of 13,617 Indian soldiers were inscribed into the memorial.[34] The arch was part of the work of the Imperial War Graves Commission, which received its Royal Charter in 1917, to aid in the erection of headstones and memorials for soldiers who had died in World War I without commemoration.[35] The names of fallen Indian soldiers were on more than 150 memorials from the Middle East to East Africa, and from Gallipoli to the large memorials at Neuve Chapelle in France and the Menin Gate in Belgium.[36]

Lutyens was more than an architect and city planner. He was also one of England's most important war memorial designers. Here, he had strong ideas about how memorials of the Great War should look and what icons should be used.[37] Receiving commissions to build memorials in Europe during the war, he struggled with finding suitable designs that would symbolize the war's profound loss of life.[38] Building on the same building philosophy that shaped his architectural designs, he finally determined that only sparse, classical, universal designs – what Christopher Hussey called Lutyens' 'Elemental Mode' – could adequately convey this message of collective loss.[39] He was also well aware of the religious diversity of the allied forces and was one of the most ardent critics of using any sort of religious iconography on memorials. Instead, he believed that a simple stone or bronze ball captured the 'elemental (universal) responses to the terrible loss of life' in the Great War, as Jay Winter writes.[40]

While showing a deep open-mindedness concerning the commemoration of fallen soldiers from different religious backgrounds, Lutyens was remarkably traditional about the existing colonial order.[41] For Lutyens, the All-India War Memorial symbolized 'duty, discipline, unity, fraternity, loyalty, service, and sacrifice ... encouraging continued partnership in the established order, and celebrating the ideal and fact of British rule over India'.[42] Though building a monument to memorialize Indians who had supposedly died fighting for freedom in France and though certainly in favour of showing religious respect by designing a memorial that approached war time sacrifices in a universal manner, Lutyens continued to ground his memorial in British imperial paternalism.

That paternalism was repeated during the All-India War Memorial's dedication ceremony, which was characterized by much of the same imperial ritual as the unveiling of the Dominion Columns (see Figure 9.1). Attendance at the event was by invitation only though the monument was supposed to express the shared sacrifices of both British and Indians in the Great War. After several speeches, the fire of remembrance was lit to the doleful sound of 'last post'. The viceroy and other high officials, a British soldier, a British airman, and an Indian soldier chosen by lot from the Indian Army then placed wreaths on the memorial.[43] The ceremony ended with attendees departing underneath the archway – the entire procession conducted to the sound of 'A Long Way to Tipperary' played by British and Indian regimental bands.[44]

Figure 9.1   Commemoration of Edwin Lutyens' All-India War Memorial during New Delhi's inaugural ceremonies, February 1931

The speeches made during the commemoration of the All-India War Memorial completed the inauguration's new vision of empire in India. Major-General Fabian Ware of the Imperial War Graves Commission gave the opening address. He spoke of what he believed was an unbreakable bond between Britain and India, a bond forged long ago but tested and made stronger by the fiery crucible of the Great War. According to Ware, both nations had answered the call when the challenge came: 'As I stand here today ... I remember how we looked into their eyes unperturbed by their strange surroundings and said to ourselves, "Thank God the Indians have also come".'[45] For Ware, the great threat of World War I was not simply the annihilation of the British Empire but the destruction of the values it stood for. 'On the day of testing, when the flails of the almighty separated the chaff from the grain,' claimed Ware, 'India was found standing freely shoulder to shoulder with other nations of the Empire on the side of right and freedom'.[46]

The commemoration reaffirmed what Joseph Chamberlain called in 1902 a 'community of sacrifice'.[47] This community empowered, strengthened and, possibly, made the British Empire eternal. But what precisely was this community of sacrifice? John Robert Seeley described it in 1882 as a 'Greater Britain' movement that derived its strength from the larger communities of race, religion, and interests shared by Britain and its four great dominions. The empire endured because Anglo-Saxons, who were spread throughout the world, were willing to make sacrifices for the empire and its ideals. At the heart of this imperial thinking was an obdurate belief in England's unique relationship to democratic reform, particularly in regard to liberty.[48] Hence, whiteness, and especially *Englishness*, became intimately connected with the didactic process of spreading self-government and political reform to the much more numerous non-Anglo-Saxon races of the empire. Colonial rule, as Thomas Metcalf insists, was made possible by the creation of a difference that privileged Britain.[49] Citing their own political heritage consisting of profoundly important democratic moments such as the signing of the *Magna Carta*, the Glorious Revolution, or the three great reform bills of the nineteenth century, British officials could claim that no other people were better qualified to teach Indians responsible government than themselves.

Here was the crux of the problem with India's elevation to dominion status. Politically, it could become a dominion of the empire – an integral member of that 'imperial brotherhood' that officials spoke of during the unveiling of the dominion columns and the commemoration of the war memorial – but how could it possibly be part of Chamberlain or Ware's 'community of sacrifice'? Indians, simply, were the wrong race and largely practised the wrong religions. This inherent, troubling problem both strengthened and weakened Britain's position in India at a critical moment as is made clear by Irwin's speech which followed Ware's.

Where General Ware had narrowed the meaning of the war down to the shared sacrifices made by soldiers of the empire, Irwin used the opportunity to argue that Britain secured the rights of all colonial subjects. Applauding the efforts of Indians in World War I, Irwin stated, 'We are here to recall the four unforgettable years during which nations and peoples and races ... became one in a common impulse of loyalty to the throne and one in the defence unto death of the rights they had won under the protection of that sovereign.'[50] Irwin's speech was a pointed statement directed at the Indian independence movement. Highlighting the tremendous diversity of the British Empire, he drew attention to the unifying power of the British Empire and underscored the tenuousness of the rights and benefits that Indians had gained under British rule. Indeed, warned Irwin, the progress made by India toward independence could be easily lost without Britain's continued help, guidance, and imperial protection.

Thus, ironically, Indian independence had become possible only through continued British domination. While on the surface the inauguration disseminated a message of greater Indian liberty brought about by its elevated dominion status, underneath it continued to reaffirm the traditional colonial order. And just as this ambiguous colonial policy of give and take encouraged rather than weakened Indian nationalist sentiment in the early twentieth century, the inauguration's double message of dominion status alongside continued British domination failed to silence many members of the Indian independence movement. Six months before New Delhi's inaugural ceremonies Indian National Congress leaders had stated in a letter to the government, 'We notice no symptoms of conversion of the English official world view that it is India's men and women who must decide what is best for India.'[51] The inaugural ceremonies gave these nationalists no reason to change their minds. Indeed, the inauguration's reaffirmation of Britain's paternalism in India underscored the connection between constitutional reform and imperial imposition in the national life of India. As one Indian newspaper claimed while covering the inauguration, 'India knows New Delhi. India understands New Delhi. India is not in it.'[52] The imperial vision proposed by New Delhi collapsed under the weight of its own ambiguity and contradictions.

The inauguration of New Delhi serves as an example of the ways in which the British Empire tried to redefine its imperial mission in India in response to a dynamic and remarkably diverse all-India independence movement. This redefinition allowed colonial policy makers to proclaim that Britain's imperial position had not become weakened in India but that its imperial role had merely changed, from one of colonial master to one of liberal educator. Subsequently, it enabled colonial officials to obscure or indefinitely postpone the actual moment of independence since they were the ultimate arbiters of India's growth toward responsible government. This continued use of liberal reform for authoritarian reasons caused New Delhi to fail as a strategy meant to stabilize British-India. The depth of this failure becomes much more striking when New Delhi is recognized as a symbol of a *new* imperial vision for India based on liberal reforms. It failed as an imperial strategy not simply because it was a bold statement of imperial power that needed to be resisted but because it represented a highly ambivalent space where forms of knowledge and language – ways of seeing and understanding the world – were contained, produced, shaped, consumed and, ultimately, contested.[53]

Notes

1 Introduction: Seeing Like a (Colonial) State

1. In 1877, Lord Lytton staged a durbar to commemorate Queen Victoria's ascension as empress of India, a politico-romantic policy which used the perceived majesty of empire to reinvigorate a conservative party led by Benjamin Disraeli. Lord Curzon, one of the most noted colonial officials of the era, held a second imperial durbar for Edward VII in 1903. As some critics quipped, this second durbar was more a celebration of Curzon than a commemoration of Edward's ascension to the throne.

2. Charles Hardinge, *My Indian Years: 1910–1916: The Reminiscences of Lord Hardinge of Penshurst* (London: John Murray, 1948), 18. Sir John Hewitt, the Lt Governor of the United Provinces, chaired the durbar committee, which also included four Ruling Chiefs. Colonel Maxwell, Hardinge's Military Secretary, was appointed to the committee as well to serve as Hardinge's direct representative.

3. Ibid., 18. The original plan was to have the imperial crown travel with the king's entourage, but Hardinge was informed that the crown could not leave England. Consequently, the king proposed to have a special crown made in India, but of course this meant that Indian revenues would have to be used to pay for it. Without Hardinge's knowledge, Walter Lawrence, a confidante of the king, approached the Maharajas of Burdwan and Tagore about raising a subscription among the ruling chiefs to pay for the crown. Hardinge vetoed the idea as soon as he learned about it because of the potential for political disaster if the princes could not collect enough money. Additionally, Hardinge felt that it demeaned the position of the king to have to resort to such methods. Instead, he brought the question to his executive council, which passed a resolution to pay for the crown from Indian revenues. Hardinge demanded that the crown be sent back to England to be kept with the rest of the royal regalia since it was too tempting a prize to keep in India.

4. Ibid., 46–7. Many onlookers failed to recognize the king who had refused to ride the state elephant, the normal practice at these imperial state entrances. He was dressed in normal review uniform and rode a horse like everyone else. Further diminishing his physical presence, the horse he rode was small in stature but easy to handle since it would have been an absolute disaster if the king became unseated in front of his Indian colonial subjects during his royal entry. Hardinge had to ride up and tell him to begin 'salaaming' to the people so that they would register him as their emperor. The king mentioned at the time that he was disappointed that the crowds failed to recognize him.

5. The worst incident of the durbar, which garnered much notoriety, occurred when the Gaekwar of Baroda seemed to insult the royal couple by improperly performing his obeisance, turning his back on the royal couple, and reportedly laughing disrespectfully as he walked away.

6. Just before the announcement, packets containing details of the scheme were handed out to high-ranking members in the crowd and the proclamation was published as a state paper to be read in Parliament.

7. Hardinge, *My Indian Years*, 52.

8. R. E. Frykenberg, 'The Coronation Durbar of 1911: Some Implications', in *Delhi through the Ages: Essays in Urban History, Culture, and Society*, ed. R. E. Frykenberg (Oxford: Oxford University Press, 1986), 240. Frykenberg has written that this secrecy almost caused a constitutional crisis in Britain since Parliament was not asked for advice on such a costly colonial policy.

9. 'Transfer of the Seat of Government from Calcutta to Delhi and the Constitutional Changes in Bengal', Government of India Proceedings, Home Department, Delhi Branch, December 1911, nos. 8-11, part A (National Archives of India).

10. See the reprint of John Robert Seeley, *The Expansion of England: Two Courses of Lectures* (Cambridge: Cambridge University Press, 2010). Seeley's book began as a series of 1881–1882 Cambridge lectures, the goal of which was to convince England's next generation of leaders that empire should not be taken for granted.

11. Anthony King, *Colonial Urban Development: Culture, Social Power and Environment* (London: Routledge & Kegan Paul, 1976), 183.

12. Ibid., 244.

13. See Robert Grant Irving, *Indian Summer: Lutyens, Baker, and Imperial Delhi* (New Haven: Yale University Press, 1981).

14. See Thomas Metcalf, *An Imperial Vision: Indian Architecture and Britain's Raj* (Oxford: Oxford University Press 1989).

15. See Stephen Legg, *Spaces of Colonialism: Delhi's Urban Governmentalities* (Malden: Blackwell, 2007).

16. For an understanding of the development of Antonio Gramsci's thinking about hegemony, society, and revolution, see *Selections from Political Writings, 1921–1926*, ed. Quinton Hoare (London: Lawrence and Wishart, 1978) and *Selections from the Prison Notebooks*, eds. Quinton Hoare and Geoffrey Nowell-Smith (New York: International Publishers, 1971).

17. See F. A. Eustis and Z. H. Zaidi, 'King, Viceroy, and Cabinet: The Modification of the Partition of Bengal, 1911', *History*, vol. 49, issue 166 (1964): 171–84 for an examination of the king's excitement about the role he would play in the reunification of Bengal.

18. James C. Scott, *Seeing Like a State: How Certain Schemes to Improve the Human Condition Have Failed* (New Haven: Yale University Press, 1998), 88.

19. Devolution was a term often used by British colonial officials to refer to the process of granting greater government responsibility to British India's provincial legislatures. Political reforms such as the 1909 Indian Councils Act increased the number of elected Indian officials in these legislatures.

20. Scott, *Seeing Like a State*, 320.

21. Ibid., 321.

22. Herbert Baker, 'The New Delhi: Eastern and Western Architecture: A Problem of Style', *The Times*, 3 October 1912, 7.

23. For nuanced and sympathetic readings of Baker's contributions to the building of New Delhi, see Metcalf's *An Imperial Vision* and 'Architecture and Empire: Sir Herbert Baker and the Building of New Delhi', in Frykenberg (ed.), *Delhi through the Ages*.

24. Metcalf, *An Imperial Vision*, 228.
25. Ibid., 234.
26. Scott, *Seeing Like a State*, 108.
27. The permanent settlement of Bengal was an agreement between the East India Company and Bengali landlords that gave the latter private ownership of lands while fixing the land revenue at high rates. Enlightened ideas about private property, free trade, and social advancement grounded the settlement. While it was intended to empower Indian landowners and especially *ryots* (peasants), it had the effect of placing poor, indebted farmers at the mercy of men with access to capital such as large landowners, merchants and bankers.
28. Of course, it need hardly be said that these principles could be and were used as justification for Britain's economic exploitation of India, what Dadabhai Naoroji called the 'drain'.
29. Engraved in stone, these placards and their message are located on the east facing sides of the two Secretariats, which abut the main government inter-section, so that they can be read by passers-by.
30. Barry Hindess, 'The Liberal Government of Unfreedom', *Alternatives,* vol. 26 (2001): 101.
31. Uday Mehta, 'Liberal Strategies of Exclusion', in *Tensions of Empire: Colonial Cultures in a Bourgeois World*, eds. Frederick Cooper and Ann Laura Stoler (Berkeley: University of California Press, 1997), 59–86.
32. Mehta, *Liberalism and Empire: A Study in Nineteenth-Century British Liberal Thought* (Chicago: University of Chicago Press, 1999), 107.
33. See Thomas Metcalf, *Ideologies of the Raj: The New Cambridge History of India, Volume 3, Part 4* (Cambridge: Cambridge University Press, 1997).
34. See Donald W. Ferrell, 'Delhi, 1911–1922: Society and Politics in the New Imperial Capital of India', PhD dissertation, 1969, Australia National University, Canberra; and Stephen Legg, *Spaces of Colonialism*.
35. See Ranajit Guha, *Dominance without Hegemony: History and Power in Colonial India* (Cambridge, MA: Harvard University Press, 1998).
36. See P. J. Cain and A. G. Hopkins, *British Imperialism: Innovation and Expansion, 1688–1914* and *British Imperialism: Crisis and Deconstruction, 1914–1990* (London: Longman, 1993).
37. They make their argument, partially, by building on John Hobson's and Vladimir I. Lenin's economic critiques of empire, *Imperialism, A Study* (1902) and *Imperialism: The Highest Stage of Capitalism* (1916), respectively. Hobson saw empire as a corrupted form of British capitalism that evolved in response to Britain's endemic domestic under-consumption caused by the poverty of the labouring classes. The lack of consumption at home encouraged those with capital to invest abroad. For Lenin, empire was the result of monopoly capitalists who, after swallowing up all the capital they could find at home, forced their respective nations to expand into Africa, Asia, and Latin America in search of fresh markets and investment opportunities. As such, empire was 'the last stage of capitalism' just before its violent collapse. While Lenin and Hobson differed in their final conclusions, both saw imperial expansion driven by the desires of powerful finance capitalists who were intimately and influentially connected to government policy makers.
38. John Darwin, *The End of the British Empire: The Historical Debate* (Oxford: Basil Blackwell, 1991), 4.

39. Ibid.
40. Hansard's House of Commons Debates, vol. 56, 7 August 1913, 1889.
41. Thomas Metcalf, *The Aftermath of Revolt: India 1857–1870* (Princeton, NJ: Princeton University Press, 1964), 47.
42. Narayani Gupta, *Delhi between Two Empires, 1803–1931: Society, Government and Urban Growth* (Delhi: Oxford University Press, 1981), 140.
43. Metcalf, *The Aftermath of Revolt*, 46.
44. Omar Khalidi, 'Ethnic Group Recruitment in the Indian Army: The Contrasting Cases of Sikhs, Muslims, Gurkhas and Others', *Pacific Affairs*, vol. 74, no. 4 (Winter, 2001–2002): 530. Khalidi argues that British military officials most actively used the martial theory of race for Indian recruitment after the mutiny.
45. Metcalf, *The Aftermath of Revolt*, 47. With the annexation of these last territories on the subcontinent, foreign duty now meant crossing the Bay of Bengal, the Arabian Sea, or the Indian Ocean.
46. E. I. Brodkin, 'Proprietary Mutations and the Mutiny in Rohilkhand', *The Journal of Asian Studies*, vol. 28, no. 4 (August 1969): 667–83.
47. S. B. Chaudhuri, *Civil Rebellion in the Indian Mutinies: 1857–1859* (Calcutta: World Press, 1957) and Thomas Metcalf, *The Aftermath of Revolt*.
48. Metcalf, *The Aftermath of Revolt*, 83.
49. Brodkin, 'Proprietary Mutations', 668.
50. Ira Klein, 'Materialism, Mutiny, and Modernization in British India', *Modern Asian Studies*, vol. 34, no. 3 (2000): 554.
51. Some Sepoys believed this grease came from pigs or cows, and thus handling the cartridges meant disobeying important religious tenets, whether Hindu or Muslim.
52. There have been excellent studies completed on the interconnection of empire and the liberal imperial project. See Theodore Koditschek, *Liberalism, Imperialism, and the Historical Imagination: Nineteenth-Century Visions of Greater Britain* (Cambridge: Cambridge University Press, 2011); Uday Mehta, *Liberalism and Empire: A Study in Nineteenth-Century Liberal Thought* (Chicago: University of Chicago Press, 1999); Jennifer Pitts, *A Turn to Empire: The Rise of Imperial Liberalism in Britain and France* (Princeton, NJ: Princeton University Press, 2005); and Catherine Hall, *Civilising Subjects: Metropole and Colony in the English Imagination, 1830–1867* (Chicago: University of Chicago Press, 2002).
53. See Catherine Hall, *White, Male and Middle Class: Explorations in Feminism and History* (New York: Routledge, Chapman & Hall, 1992) for an examination of changing British attitudes toward the liberal imperial project.
54. Metcalf, 'The Influence of the Mutiny of 1857 on Land Policy in India', *The Historical Journal*, vol. 4, no. 2 (1961): 152–63.
55. Brodkin, 'The Struggle for Succession: Rebels and Loyalists in the Indian Mutiny of 1857', *Modern Asian Studies*, vol. 6, no. 3 (1972): 277–90.
56. Hugh Tinker, '1857 and 1957: The Mutiny and Modern India', *International Affairs (Royal Institute of International Affairs 1944)*, vol. 34, no. 1 (January 1958): 58.
57. Ibid., 60.
58. Don Randall, 'Autumn 1857: The Making of the Indian "Mutiny"', *Victorian Literature and Culture*, vol. 31, no. 1 (2003): 6.
59. See Ranajit Guha, 'The Prose of Counter Insurgency', in *Subaltern Studies II: Writings on South Asian History and Society*, ed. Ranajit Guha (Delhi: Oxford University Press, 1983).

60. Randall, 9.
61. Hardinge, *My Indian Years*, 79.
62. For example, Wilson visited the grave of John Nicholson, one of the great heroes of the mutiny, as well as the ruined Lucknow Residency.
63. Sir Guy Fleetwood Wilson, *Letters to Nobody, 1908–1913* (London: John Murray, 1921), 119. His memoires are filled with exploits that tested his nerve against India's most dangerous animals in some of India's most inhospitable locations.
64. Sir Guy Fleetwood Wilson, *Letters to Somebody: A Retrospect* (London: Cassell and Company, 1922), 56. Because of his father's financial ruin, which left the family living indefinitely in Florence, he spent his entire childhood in Italy. His Italian tutors instilled in him not only love for his adopted country but sensitivity to a people's national aspirations. For the rest of his life, he saw himself as English by birth but Italian by culture.
65. Indeed, he was eighteen when he first saw cricket or football played and claimed that 'I am almost the only Englishman to whom a ball means nothing'. He learned to box because of the many beatings he took as a young man in England.
66. Wilson, *Letters to Nobody*, 12.
67. Ibid., 178. Whenever possible, Wilson attempted to close the distance between western educated Indians and British officials through unofficial activities such as dinner parties. As an example of his positive views of India's educated classes, Wilson claimed, 'I should find it difficult in London ... to get together a set of men more intelligent, more interesting, and of more refined manners than the Indians who dined with me'.
68. Ibid., 62.
69. Wilson, *Letters to Somebody*, 25. His father and mother originally had been supporters of the Austrian Army and were friends with many of its officers. But after watching or learning about the army's repeated offences against Italians, they changed their minds and became ardent supporters of Italian nationalism. Indeed, *The Times* noted in his mother's obituary that because of 'her tactful intercession more than one prominent Italian owed his freedom, if not his life'.
70. Hansard's House of Commons Debates, vol. 41, 30 July 1912, 1983.
71. The political reforms promised by the Montagu-Chelmsford Agreement became deeply flawed under the Government of India Act of 1919. What had begun as an offer of tremendous reform that would move India toward responsible government became a piece of legislation that institutionalized British political paternalism in India. With marked hubris, the constitution created under the Government of India Act was designed to give elected Indian officials experience with British style democratic proceedings. This tutorial in representative forms of government was done under the watchful eye of British officials.
72. Hardinge was born at Dufferin Lodge, Highgate, a residence his father was renting in order to be close to his work as Undersecretary of State at the War Office.
73. His grandfathers were Field Marshalls and one, Sir Henry Hardinge, had been Governor General of India.
74. Of all the men Hardinge battled with during his career, Curzon was undoubtedly his greatest foe. Both men exhibited incredibly different approaches to

how diplomacy should be accomplished and how the interests of Britain could be best advanced. While Curzon was overly aggressive, emotional, pompous and unyielding, Hardinge was sober, diffident and conciliatory when necessary. Of course, their most bitter disagreement was over Hardinge's reversal of Curzon's partition of Bengal. Curzon never forgave Hardinge.

75. Other than being Viceroy of India, Hardinge served as ambassador to Russia and France, the latter being the highest position an officer could hold in the diplomatic service.
76. Hardinge, *My Indian Years*, 1.
77. Ibid.
78. Charles Hardinge, *Old Diplomacy: The Reminiscences of Lord Hardinge of Penshurst* (London: John Murray, 1947), 187.
79. The Anglo-French Peace Treaty, the Egypt Crisis, World War One, and the Paris Peace Conference.
80. Mark Bence-Jones, *The Viceroys of India* (New York: St Martin's Press, 1982), 211.
81. Concerning the tremendous personal losses he suffered while viceroy, Hardinge simply said in his memoires, 'what a mercy it is that the future is a closed book'.
82. Hardinge, *My Indian Years*, 91.
83. Ibid., 140. See David Lockwood, *The Indian Bourgeoisie: A Political History of the Indian Capitalist Class in the Early Twentieth Century* (London: I. B. Tauris, 2012) for an excellent study of the tension between the Government of India, Indian capitalists such as J. R. D. Tata, and Indian nationalists who promoted the swadeshi movement.
84. Leah Reynolds' *A Hindu Education: The Early Years of Banaras Hindu University* (Oxford: Oxford University Press, 2005) wonderfully captures Hardinge's pragmatic imperialism. He supported the university because he hoped it would produce graduates who were loyal to the British Empire.
85. Hardinge, *Old Diplomacy*, 13.
86. Ibid., 41.
87. Hardinge, *My Indian Years*, 34.
88. Ibid., 109.
89. Ibid.
90. Ibid., 89.
91. Ibid., 143.
92. Ibid., 141. In 1930, after the debacle of the Indian Statutory Commission, Irwin publicly announced that dominion status was the official goal of the British Empire in India. The statutory commission had been sent to India to evaluate India's progress toward responsible government and to make recommendations for further colonial reforms. However, the all-white commission, chaired by John Simon, was met with Indian protests and boycotts, forcing Irwin to make the announcement about dominion status. For monographs on this important topic, see Andrew Muldoon, *Empire, Politics, and the Creation of the 1935 Act: Last Act of the Raj* (Farnham: Ashgate, 2009); Sugata Bose and Ayesha Jalal, *Modern South Asia: History, Culture, and Political Economy* (London: Routledge, 2004); Carl Bridge, *Holding India to the Empire: The British Conservative Party and the 1935 Constitution* (New York: Sterling, 1986), and Robin James Moore, *The Crisis of Indian Unity, 1917–1940* (Oxford: Oxford University Press, 1974).

2   The Transfer of Britain's Imperial Capital: 'A Bold Stroke of Statesmanship'

1. Lord Hardinge and his Executive Council to Lord Crewe, Secretary of State for India, 25 August 1911, Home Department, Delhi Branch (National Archives of India). Hardinge, his executive council, and the Secretary of State for India carried on long discussions concerning the importance of Delhi as the traditional seat of empire in India. Also see Stephen Blake, *Shajahanabad: The Sovereign City in Mughal India, 1639–1739* (Cambridge: Cambridge University Press, 1991), 5–13. Blake argues that north Indian rulers had occupied the area around Delhi for nearly a thousand years because of its strategic location. The remains of at least ten Indo-Muslim imperial capitals are present in the Delhi Triangle, a 60 sq. mile area.

2. R. E. Frykenberg, 'The Coronation Durbar of 1911: Some Implications', in *Delhi through the Ages: Essays in Urban History, Culture, and Society*, ed. R. E. Frykenberg (Oxford: Oxford University Press, 1986), 228. Curzon left India shortly after the bill was signed and thus never had to deal with the direct consequences of his decision.

3. Robert Grant Irving, *Indian Summer: Lutyens, Baker and Imperial Delhi* (New Haven: Yale University Press, 1981), 18.

4. Sugata Bose and Ayesha Jalal, *Modern South Asia: History, Culture, Political Economy* (New York: Routledge, 1997), 95. Riseley's comment has been noted repeatedly in studies that address partition because it so clearly underscores the colonial policy's aggressive political calculations.

5. Hardinge to Crewe, 25 August 1911. Hardinge's government realized that the Bengali Hindu majority had a legitimate political grievance against partition due to the recent passage of the Indian Councils Act of 1909 (also known as the Morley-Minto Reforms). The Act expanded the number of elected seats on provincial councils but did little for Bengali Hindus whose majority had been weakened by partition.

6. Hardinge to Crewe, 13 July 1911, in 'Transfer of the Seat of Government of India from Calcutta to Delhi and the Creation of a New Lieut.-Governorship at Patna,' Home Department, Public Branch, no. 448, 1923 (National Archives of India).

7. Charles Hardinge, *My Indian Years: 1910–1916: The Reminiscences of Lord Hardinge of Penshurst* (London: John Murray, 1948), 36.

8. See Nayana Goradia, *Lord Curzon: The Last of the British Moghuls* (Oxford: Oxford University Press, 1997).

9. Hardinge, *My Indian Years*, 20.

10. Ibid., 26.

11. Ibid.

12. Hardinge to Crewe, 6 July 1911, Home Department, Public Branch, no. 448, 1923 (National Archives of India).

13. Sir Guy Fleetwood Wilson, *Letters to Nobody, 1908–1913* (London: John Murray, 1921).

14. Ibid., 8.

15. For more on the Maniktala Bomb Conspiracy, see Peter Heehs, 'The Maniktala Secret Society: An Early Bengali Terrorist Group', *Indian Economic and Social History Review*, no. 29 (1992): 349–70; Ranabir Samaddar, 'Law and Terror

in the Age of Colonial Constitution Making', *Diogenes*, 53, no. 4 (2006): 18–33; and Partha Chatterjee, 'Bombs and Nationalism in Bengal', Centre for Studies in Social Sciences, Calcutta, 1–33, sarr.emory.edu/subalterndocs/Chatterjee.pdf.

16. P. J. Cain and A. G. Hopkins conclude that powerful finance capitalists and financial institutions seeking investment opportunities drove imperial expansion.

17. The percentage is based on the research of Charles Feinstein, 'Britain's Overseas Investments in 1913', *Economic History Review*, 2nd ser., XLIII, 2 (1990): 288–95.

18. Wilson, *Letters to Nobody*, 160.

19. Ibid., 159.

20. It needs to be added that Lancashire continued to have a powerful impact on colonial policy in India even as late as the 1930s. Lancashire's commercial interests pressured Lord Irwin, viceroy of India from 1926 to 1931, to begin negotiations with Gandhi over ending nationalist boycotts of Lancashire textiles. The talks became known as the Gandhi–Irwin Pact.

21. Wilson, *Letters to Nobody*, 160. Of all the newly industrializing nations, Wilson feared Japan the most because of its proximity, comparatively, to India. Mrinalini Sinha, in *Specters of Mother India: The Global Restructuring of an Empire* (Durham, NC: Duke University Press, 2006), also touches on the manner in which foreign competition transformed the culture of empire in India.

22. Wilson, *Letters to Nobody*, 160.

23. Ibid., 159.

24. See John Fisher, *Curzon and British Imperialism in the Middle East, 1916–1919* (London: Routledge, 1999). The Mesopotamian Campaign, which began well but ended badly for British and Indian troops who were forced to surrender at Kut-al-Amara, was another controversy originally tied to Hardinge. After bearing months of pointed accusations about his involvement in the debacle and even pressure to resign from the government, his name eventually was cleared by a parliamentary committee.

25. Hardinge, *My Indian Years*, 36.

26. Ibid.

27. Ibid.

28. 'Note by his Excellency the Viceroy', 20 June 1911, in 'Transfer of the Seat of Government of India from Calcutta to Delhi and the Creation of a New Lieut.-Governorship at Patna', Home Department, Public Branch, no. 448, 1923 (National Archives of India).

29. See Sinha, *Colonial Masculinity: The 'Manly Englishman' and the 'Effeminate Bengali' in the Late Nineteenth Century* (Manchester: Manchester University Press, 1995).

30. The Morley-Minto Reforms expanded the number of elected Indian officials on municipal and provincial legislative councils.

31. Hardinge, *My Indian Years*, 37.

32. Ibid., 2.

33. Ibid., 32.

34. 'Transfer of the Seat of Government of India from Calcutta to Delhi', 5.

35. Ibid., 5.

36. Ibid., 32. *Dacoit* refers to ritualized murder.

37. Hardinge, *My Indian Years*, 36.
38. Hansard's House of Lords Debates, vol. XI, 21 February 1912, 174.
39. 'Transfer of the Seat of Government of India from Calcutta to Delhi', 2.
40. Hardinge, *My Indian Years*, 37.
41. Ibid.
42. Throughout the first three decades of the twentieth century the protection of minorities was commonly used by the British as a justification for British rule in India.
43. 'Transfer of the Seat of Government of India from Calcutta to Delhi', 3.
44. Hardinge, *My Indian Years*, 25.
45. 'Transfer of the Seat of Government of India from Calcutta to Delhi', 3.
46. The transfer of the capital to Delhi brought smaller benefits as well. It was nearer to Simla which would lessen the amount of time and reduce the costs of the annual government migration between the winter and summer capitals. For six months of the year Delhi had a good climate, which would extend the time the government sat in its new capital as well.
47. 'Transfer of the Seat of Government of India from Calcutta to Delhi', 5.
48. Ibid.
49. In his memoires, Hardinge claimed that Carlyle 'was the most difficult member of my council', but he felt that Butler was 'a charming and able man and a very good friend'.
50. John L. Jenkins never got to see the outcome and impact of the scheme he helped create. He died shortly after George V's durbar. Hardinge saw his death as a great loss and claimed he was 'a most able and useful man with whom I always got on extremely well'. He was replaced by Reginald Craddock, who Hardinge thought was very able but very 'sun-baked and reactionary in his ideas'.
51. 'Note by the Hon'ble J.L. Jenkins', 24 June 1911 in 'Transfer of the Seat of Government of India from Calcutta to Delhi'.
52. Lord Lansdowne, who had been viceroy of India from 1888 to 1894, had spoken against having an Indian on the council, but Hardinge claimed that 'I have a very happy remembrance of his (Imam's) invariable personal loyalty to me and of his exceptional usefulness.'
53. 'Note by the Hon'ble Syed Ali Imam', 1 July 1911, in 'Transfer of the Seat of Government of India from Calcutta to Delhi'.
54. Ibid., 18.
55. Bihar would later dominate Orissa in a similar fashion that Bengal had dominated Bihar. By the mid 1920s, the people of Orissa were asking for separation from Bihar along racial and sentimental lines. So compelling were their demands for autonomy that the Simon Commission, first sent to India in 1927 to assess Indian constitutional development, set up an ancillary commission to examine the possibility of dividing Bihar and Orissa.
56. 'Note by the Hon'ble Syed Ali Imam'.
57. Ibid., 17.
58. During a parliamentary debate on 17 June 1912, Crewe defended the Government of India's reapportionment of Bengal against accusations made by the nationalist newspaper *Amrita Bazar Patrika*, which had shown animosity to the transfer. He explained away the paper's criticism by claiming '...there have been a certain number of extreme people on both sides who

have disapproved of the policy because it is not entirely worked out in their favour. What those that agree with the organ (the *Amrita Bazar Patrika*) would have liked would be not merely that Bengal should have been differently partitioned, but that it should have been so partitioned as to include in the new Bengal every village where the Bengali language is spoken.' Crewe concluded, 'the mere fact our policy is objected to from different ends for different reasons, and objected to in parts simply because different races and places find something which they do not consider entirely in their favour, I confess does not give us any serious uneasiness'.

59. Viceroy in Council to Crewe, 25 August 1911, Home Department, Delhi Branch, December 1911, nos. 8-11, Part A (National Archives of India).
60. Ibid.
61. Ibid., 14.
62. This policy was later taken up in the Montagu–Chelmsford Agreement, 1917, which ultimately became the Government of India Act 1919.
63. 'Note by the Hon'ble W.H. Clark', 3 July 1911, in 'Transfer of the Seat of Government of India from Calcutta to Delhi'.
64. Ibid., 21.
65. Ibid.
66. Ibid. Clark was quite right to be concerned about the impact that the transfer would have on the European community in Calcutta. The most immediate and vitriolic outbursts about the transfer came from British commercial interests in Calcutta. The outrage was mollified somewhat when the Government of India guaranteed Calcutta businessmen commercial space in the new capital.
67. The Southern Punjab Railway, The East Indian Railway, the Delhi-Ambala-Kalka Railway, the Rajputana-Malwa Railway, and the Agra-Delhi Chord Railway terminated in the city.
68. 'Note by the Hon'ble Mr. S.H. Butler', 30 June 1911, in 'Transfer of the Seat of Government of India from Calcutta to Delhi'.
69. Ibid., 12.
70. 'Note by the Hon'ble R. W. Carlyle', 29 June 1911, in 'Transfer of the Seat of Government of India from Calcutta to Delhi'.
71. See R. E. Frykenberg, 'The Coronation Durbar of 1911: Some Implications'.
72. Hansard's House of Lords Debates, vol. X, 12 December 1912, 802.
73. 'Note by the Hon'ble Sir Guy Fleetwood Wilson', 22 June 1911, in 'Transfer of the Seat of Government of India from Calcutta to Delhi'.
74. Ibid., 6.
75. Wilson, *Letters to Nobody*, 63.
76. 'Note by the Hon'ble Sir Guy Fleetwood Wilson', 22 June 1911, in 'Transfer of the Seat of Government of India from Calcutta to Delhi', 5.
77. 'Note by the Hon'ble S.H. Butler', 14 August 1911, in 'Transfer of the Seat of the Government of India from Calcutta to Delhi'.
78. Hardinge, *My Indian Years*, 38.
79. Ibid.
80. Ibid., 39.
81. Ibid. See F. A. Eustis II and Z. H. Zaidi, 'King, Viceroy and Cabinet: The Modification of the Partition of Bengal, 1911', *History*, vol. 49, issue 166 (1964): 171–84 for an examination of the king's excitement about the role he would play in the settlement of Bengal.

82. Hardinge, *My Indian Years*, 45. One major problem with keeping the scheme secret was that eventually the Government of India printing office would need to be let in on the secret so that it would have time to print the necessary gazettes and news-sheets for the durbar. Hardinge dealt with the problem by simply creating an isolated Press Camp, which was given three days' worth of food and accommodation. The camp was then surrounded by a cordon of police and soldiers, and no one was allowed in or out until the actual durbar ceremony.

83. Hardinge, *My Indian Years*, 39.

84. Ibid.

85. Ibid., 40.

86. Bernard S. Cohn, 'Representing Authority in Victorian England', in *The Invention of Tradition*, eds. Eric Hobsbawm and Terence Ranger (New York: Cambridge University Press, 1987), 169.

87. Ibid., 168–9.

88. 'Grant of Remission of Sentences to Prisoners on the Occasion of the Delhi Durbar', Home Department, Judicial Branch, January 1912, nos. 50–69 (National Archives of India).

89. Hansard's House of Lords Debates, vol. X, 12 December 1911, 801. My emphasis. Lord Morley repeated the king's announcement to the House of Lords on the day of the imperial durbar.

90. Viceroy in Council to Crewe, 25 August 1911.

91. Crewe to Viceroy in Council, Home Department, Delhi Branch, December 1911, nos. 8–11, Part A. (National Archives of India).

92. Ibid.

93. Ibid.

94. Viceroy in Council to Crewe, 25 August 1911.

95. John Darwin, *The End of the British Empire: The Historical Debate* (Oxford: Oxford University Press, 1991), 4.

3   New Delhi's New Vision for a New Raj: An 'Altar of Humanity'

1. David A. Johnson, 'A British Empire for the Twentieth Century: The Inauguration of New Delhi, 1931', *Urban History*, 35, no. 3 (2008): 462–84.

2. Charles Hardinge, *My Indian Years: 1910–1916: The Reminiscences of Lord Hardinge of Penshurst* (London: John Murray, 1948), 52–3.

3. Ibid., p. 53. H. M. G. was a play on letters in that the paper had been using the initials to refer to the king and his entourage (His Majesty's Government) in its coverage of the recent royal visit. Now, the paper was using the same acronym to attack Hardinge.

4. Siraj-ud-daulah was a Nawab of Bengal. When the East India Company refused his command to destroy the fortifications being built at Fort William (Calcutta), Siraj-ud-daulah ordered his army in June 1756 to capture the fort. A story emerged that he threw officers of the East India Company into an extremely small cell where a supposed 146 of them died of exhaustion. The episode, largely written about by Englishmen, became known as the Black Hole of Calcutta.

5. The story came from a foreign correspondent who said, with a nautical bent, that 'the viceroy's flag was struck' as Hardinge departed. He meant that the flag was lowered when the viceroy left, a common practice, but Calcutta's European press used the story to suggest that an eyewitness had seen lightning strike the flag.
6. Ibid., 68.
7. Hardinge, *My Indian Years*, 53.
8. 'Transfer of the Seat of Government from Calcutta to Delhi and the Constitutional Changes in Bengal', Home Department, Delhi Branch, 1911, nos. 8-11, Part A. The paragraph also can be found in Curzon's first major attack on the transfer of the capital in February 1912. See Hansard's House of Lords Debates, vol. XI, 21 February 1912, 164.
9. See John G. Darwin, 'Imperialism in Decline? Tendencies in British Imperial Policy between the Wars', *The Historical Journal*, 23, no. 3 (1980): 678, and Darwin, *Britain, Egypt and the Middle East: Imperial Policy in the Aftermath of War, 1918–1922* (New York: St Martin's Press, 1981) for an extended study of Britain's interwar colonial policy in Egypt and the Middle East.
10. For a recent historiography of the rise of the British Empire primarily from an economic standpoint, see Anthony Webster, *The Debate on the Rise of the British Empire* (Manchester: Manchester University Press, 2006).
11. Hansard's House of Lords Debates, vol. XI, 232.
12. Ibid., 228.
13. Ibid., 232.
14. Ibid., 209.
15. Ibid.
16. Ibid.
17. Ibid., 213.
18. Ibid.
19. Ibid., 219.
20. Ibid.
21. Hansard's House of Lords Debates, vol. XII, 17 June 1912, 104.
22. Hansard's House of Lords Debates, vol. XI, 205.
23. Ibid., 198.
24. Ibid., 203.
25. Ibid., 221.
26. The constitutional question and its resolution have been covered by R. E. Frykenberg, 'The Coronation Durbar of 1911: Some Implications', in *Delhi through the Ages: Selected Essays in Urban History, Culture, and Society*, ed. R. E. Frykenberg (Oxford: Oxford University Press, 1993), 240.
27. As an advocate of the arts and crafts movement in England and the empire, King feared the official town planning committee, which consisted of Captain George Swinton, John Brodie, and Edwin Lutyens, would design a *western* city devoid of Indian building sentiments.
28. Robert Carlyle, a member of the viceroy's executive council, had voiced similar concerns during the secret debates to transfer the capital. These discussions are examined in Chapter 2.
29. Hansard's House of Lords Debates, vol. XI, 242–3.
30. Ibid.
31. Ibid., 138.

32. Ibid., 150.
33. Ibid., 146.
34. Hansard's House of Lords Debates, vol. XII, 86.
35. See Lovat Fraser, *India under Curzon and After* (London: William Heinemann, 1911).
36. Fraser was so upset that he met with Hardinge to issue a personal grievance. The meeting took place in Bombay shortly after Hardinge said goodbye to the king and queen.
37. Hansard's House of Lords Debates, vol. XI, 152.
38. Ibid., 162.
39. Ibid., 193.
40. Ibid., 195.
41. Ibid., 190.
42. Ibid., 194.
43. Ibid., 216.
44. Ibid.
45. Ibid., 225–6.
46. Ibid., 226. My emphasis.
47. Ibid.
48. Hansard's House of Commons Debates, vol. 41, 30 July 1912, 1906.
49. Hansard's House of Commons Debates, vol. 56, 7 August 1913, 1790.
50. Hansard's House of Commons Debates, vol. 41, 1906–1907.
51. Ibid., 1907.
52. Hansard's House of Commons Debates, vol. 56, 1803.
53. Hansard's House of Commons Debates, vol. 41, 1907–1908.
54. Sir Guy Fleetwood Wilson, *Letters to Nobody, 1908–1913* (London: John Murray, 1921), 58.
55. Ibid., 58–9.
56. Ibid., 59.
57. Ibid., 62.
58. Ibid.
59. Ibid., 189.
60. Rees had been a member of the Indian Civil Service from 1875–1901 where he served as Undersecretary to the Madras Government, District Magistrate, Collector, Civil Sessions Judge, Department Registrar, British Resident in Travancore and Cochin. Later, he was an additional member of the Governor-General's Council from 1895–1897 and 1898–1900. He served as government translator in Persian, Tamil, Telugu, and Hindustani. He also spoke Arabic and Russian. Rees wrote several books on India including *Notes of a Journey from Kasveen to Hamadan across the Karaghan Country* (1885); *Narratives of Tours in India Made by His Excellency Lord Connemara, Governor of Madras, 1886–1890* (1891); *The Mahomedans* (1894), *The Real India* (1910), and *Current Political Problems: With Pros and Cons* (1912).
61. Hansard's House of Commons Debates, vol. 41, 1985. Along with Lord Ronaldshay, Rees was one of the most outspoken supporters in parliament of the opium trade in India. Brushing aside questions about the morality of government-sponsored drug trafficking, Rees believed that British and Indian business interests were rightfully meeting a consumptive demand for the drug.
62. Hansard's House of Commons Debates, vol. 56, 1849.

63. One has to wonder about the consequences of Jenkins' untimely death from fever shortly after George V's durbar. Hardinge, who tremendously valued Jenkins' counsel, claimed his passing was a significant loss to the Government of India.
64. 'Note by the Hon'ble J.L. Jenkins', 24 June 1911, in 'Transfer of the Seat of Government of India from Calcutta to Delhi', 9.
65. Hansard's House of Lords Debates, vol. XII, 143.
66. Hansard's House of Lords Debates, vol. XI, 165.
67. Ibid., 240.
68. Ibid.
69. Ibid.
70. Ibid., 165.
71. Ibid.
72. Hansard's House of Lords Debates, vol. XI, 165.
73. Ibid.
74. Ibid., 244.
75. Hansard's House of Lords Debates, vol. XII, 152.
76. Ibid., 144. Also see *The Rt. Hon. Mr. E. S. Montagu on Indian Affairs*, 1917, pp. 295–312, Speech of Montagu, 22 April 1912.
77. Ibid.
78. Ibid.
79. Ibid., 145.
80. Ibid.
81. Hansard's House of Commons Debates, vol. 41, 1911.
82. Ibid., 1949. Lord Ronaldshay had served as aide-de-camp to Lord Curzon when Viceroy of India, had been a chairman of the Central Asian Society, and wrote several books on India including *Sport and Politics under an Eastern Sky* (1902), *On the Outskirts of Empire in Asia* (1904), *A Wandering Student in the Far East* (1908), and *An Eastern Miscellany* (1911). Later, he wrote biographies of Lords Curzon (1928) and Cromer (1932).
83. Hansard's House of Lords Debates, vol. XII, 113.
84. Ibid., 155.
85. Ibid., 153–4.
86. Ibid., 154.
87. Ibid., 153–4.
88. Ibid., 155.
89. Ibid.
90. Ibid., 156.
91. Ibid., 156–7.
92. Ibid.
93. Hansard's House of Commons Debates, vol. 41, 1877.
94. Ibid.
95. Ibid.
96. Ibid., 1907–8.
97. Ibid.
98. Ibid.
99. Ibid.
100. See Thomas Babington Macaulay, 'Minute of 2 February 1835 on Indian Education'.

101. Wilson, *Letters to Nobody,* 189–90.
102. Ibid., 205.
103. Ibid., 206.
104. Ibid., 207.
105. Hansard's House of Commons Debates, vol. 41, 1901.
106. Ibid.
107. Ibid., 1885.
108. Wilson, *Letters to Nobody,* 201.
109. Ibid., 200–1.
110. Ibid., 58.
111. Ibid., 202.
112. Ibid.
113. Ibid., 201.
114. Ibid.
115. Hansard's House of Commons Debates, vol. 56, 1803.
116. Ibid., 1807.
117. Ibid.
118. Ibid., 1803.
119. Ibid., 1804.
120. Ibid.
121. A Public Services Commission, chaired by Lord Islington (John Dickson-Poynder), had been formed in September 1912 to investigate all levels of the Indian Civil Service with the point of redressing systemic problems. Lord Islington's committee, which published its report in 1917 (World War One caused delays), dealt with many of Montagu's concerns. See H. H. Dodwell, *The Cambridge History of the British Empire,* Volume 4, 1929, 377.
122. Hansard's House of Commons Debates, vol. 56, 1805.
123. See Andrew Muldoon, *Empire, Politics, and the Creation of the 1935 Act: Last Act of the Raj* (Farnham: Ashgate, 2009). Building upon Christopher Bayly's *Empire and Information: Intelligence Gathering and Social Communications in India, 1780–1870* (Cambridge: Cambridge University Press, 1996), Muldoon cogently shows that there were systemic problems in the Government of India's information-gathering network. Formulaic reporting, according to Muldoon, plagued the Raj's massive bureaucracy and its reporting system, which often reflected shallow cultural assumptions and imperial stereotypes rather than solid evidence. This ultimately led to Britain overestimating the strength of their position in India and, conversely, to misreading the actual strength of the Indian National Congress. Worse, district officers – typically junior in rank and mired in this massive colonial bureaucracy – systematically produced flawed reports that, for reasons of self-interest, made districts appear more peaceful than they really were.
124. Hansard's House of Commons Debates, vol. 56, 1805.
125. Ibid.
126. Ibid., 1806.
127. Wilson, *Letters to Nobody,* 63–4.
128. Ibid., 64.
129. Ibid., 194.
130. Ibid., 190–1.
131. Ibid., 194.

132. Ibid., 202.
133. Darwin, 'Imperialism in Decline?' 678.
134. For an excellent study of the way in which class and social status shaped British and Indian interactions in Britain, See Martin Wainwright, *'The Better Class' of Indians: Social Rank, Imperial Identity, and South Asians in Britain, 1858–1914* (Manchester: Manchester University Press, 2012).

4   Colonial Finance and the Building of New Delhi: The High Cost of Reform

1. Hansard's House of Commons Debates, vol. 39, 13 June 1912, 1199.
2. As the main proponent of the Victoria Memorial in Calcutta, Curzon had a relatively good appreciation for the cost of large building projects in India. In the end, the final cost to build the new capital was closer to £16,000,000.
3. Hansard's House of Lords Debates, vol. XII, 17 June 1912, 107–8.
4. Ibid. The metaphor of a millstone weighing down not only the Government of India but Indians as well became a common refrain during these financial debates.
5. Ibid., 108.
6. Ibid., 90.
7. Ibid.
8. Ibid., 91–2.
9. Ibid., 92.
10. Ibid., 148.
11. Ibid.
12. Once one of India's greatest cities, Delhi had been in a state of decline for well over a century. The Indian uprising in 1857 and its aftermath, which included massive demolitions around the Red Fort, further diminished Delhi's Mughal splendour. See Narayani Gupta, *Delhi between Two Empires* (Oxford: Oxford University Press, 1981) for an examination of Britain's reoccupation of Delhi after 1857.
13. Gupta has shown that Delhi became an important manufacturing centre in the latter decades of the nineteenth century. By 1901, of the approximately 75,000 male Indian workers in Delhi, about 50 per cent were engaged in manufacturing with 25 per cent in commerce. Much of this industrial growth occurred in the Delhi suburbs of Sadr Bazaar and Sabzi Mandi to the west and north-west of the old city. The growth of the textile industry in particular can be seen in the increased number of factories in the district: 5,000 in 1891, 11,000 in 1901, and 23,000 in 1911.
14. Hansard's House of Lords Debates, vol. XI, 21 February 1912, 161.
15. Peter J. Cain and Antony G. Hopkins argue, in *British Imperialism: Innovation and Expansion, 1688–1914* and *British Imperialism: Crisis and Deconstruction, 1914–1990* (London: Longman Group, 1993), that London-based financiers had deep historical connections to Britain's landed elites, the traditional leaders of English society. Because England's aristocracy saw finance capitalism as a respectable way to spend one's time and money, many members of London's financial community were either drawn from England's landed elites or shared similar public school educations and other cultural affinities.

Thus, London's masters of finance were deeply intertwined with a powerful *rentier* class who often offered up its male scions to England's political class. Industrial capitalists from provincial cities such as Manchester were important economic forces, but their lack of shared cultural experience with England's traditional elite meant that their political influence was limited.

16. Hansard's House of Lords Debates, vol. XI, 161.
17. Ibid.
18. Ibid.
19. Bengal and especially Calcutta were what John Darwin calls a 'bridgehead' of imperial expansion. Peter Marshall, *Bengal: The British Bridgehead: Eastern India, 1740–1828* (Cambridge: Cambridge University Press, 2006), used the notion of a bridgehead in his own study of India. Likewise, Christopher Bayly, *Indian Society and the Making of the British Empire* (Cambridge: Cambridge University Press, 1990), focused on the importance of Bengal for imperial expansion.
20. Hansard's House of Lords Debates, vol. XI, 145.
21. Ibid., 161.
22. Ibid., 171.
23. Hansard's House of Lords Debates, vol. XII, 87.
24. Hansard's House of Lords Debates, vol. XI, 237.
25. Ibid.
26. Hansard's House of Lords Debates, vol. XII, 124–5.
27. Hansard's House of Lords Debates, vol. XI, 191.
28. See Chapter 2 of this study for an examination of Clark's concerns about the transfer and building of a new capital at Delhi.
29. Hansard's House of Commons Debates, vol. 56, 7 August 1913, 1876.
30. Ibid.
31. Ibid., 1877.
32. Ibid.
33. Ibid., 1878.
34. Ibid.
35. House of Lords Debates, vol. XI, 175–6.
36. Ibid., 217.
37. Ibid.
38. In an effort to appease the Calcutta commercial community, the Government of India included a commercial district, Connaught Place, in the new capital. While many Calcutta firms sent requests for commercial space in this district, it paled in comparison to the commercial presence, both British and Indian, in Calcutta.
39. Hansard's House of Commons Debates, vol. 41, 30 July 1912, 1912.
40. Hansard's House of Commons Debates, vol. 45, 20 December 1912, 1923. Rees served in the Indian Civil Service from 1875–1901 where he held a variety of high offices particularly in the Madras Presidency. In private life, he was chairman of the British Central Africa Company and director of the South Indian Railway Company. He also was involved in the Bengal Dooars Railway Company, Consolidated Tea and Lands Company, and the Mysore Gold Mining Company. Lastly, he was member of council for the East Indian Association and a fellow of the University of Madras.
41. Hansard's House of Commons Debates, vol. 41, 1983.

42. Ibid.
43. Hansard's House of Commons Debates, vol. 56, 1835.
44. See R. K. Newman, 'India and the Anglo-Chinese Opium Agreements, 1907–1914', *Modern Asian Studies*, vol. 23, no. 3 (1989): 525–60.
45. Hansard's House of Commons Debates, vol. 41, 1939.
46. See Mrinalini Sinha, *Colonial Masculinity: The 'Manly Englishman' and the 'Effeminate Bengali' in the Late Nineteenth Century* (Manchester: Manchester University Press, 1995), for an examination of the Ilbert controversy and its negative impact on British and Indian relations.
47. Sir Guy Fleetwood Wilson, *Letters to Nobody, 1908–1913* (London: John Murray 1921), 17. Wilson was one of the oldest British Finance Ministers to ever hold the office. The work was so incredibly hard for him that at one point he wrote in his diary, 'I now know what a jellyfish feels when he melts away on the sand in the sun.'
48. Hansard's House of Commons Debates, vol. 41, 1939.
49. Ibid., 1940.
50. Such was the animosity shown toward Wilson that he never received a K. C. S. I. (Knight Commander of the Most Exalted Order of the Star of India). This honour was relatively typical for officers who had served on the viceroy's executive council.
51. The bill received three readings in the House of Lords, once in February and twice in June 1912.
52. Hansard's House of Lords Debates, vol. XII, 94.
53. Ibid., 90.
54. Cain and Hopkins argue, in *British Imperialism,* that guaranteed returns on capital investments were one of the driving forces behind imperial expansion. London finance capitalists were constantly looking for investment opportunities abroad.
55. Cain and Hopkins use the phrase 'gentlemanly capitalism' to describe the impetus behind and the reasons for Britain's imperial expansion beginning in 1688.
56. Hansard's House of Lords Debates, vol. XII, 106. For an interesting look at Midleton's political life and the events he lived through and perhaps helped shape, see his memoire *Records and Reactions, 1856–1939* (New York: E. P. Dutton and Company Inc., 1939).
57. Ibid.
58. Ibid.
59. Hansard's House of Commons Debates, vol. 41, 1973.
60. Ibid.
61. Ibid., 1982.
62. Ibid., 1914.
63. Ibid., 1915.
64. Ibid.
65. Ibid.
66. Ibid.
67. Ibid.
68. Ibid., 1915–1916. My emphasis.
69. Hansard's House of Commons Debates, vol. 56, 1878.
70. Ibid., 1879.

71. Hansard's House of Commons Debates, vol. 41, 1954.
72. Ibid., 1968.
73. Ibid.
74. Hansard's House of Lords Debates, vol. XII, 94.
75. Ibid.
76. Ibid., 99.
77. Ibid.
78. Ibid., 107.
79. Ibid.
80. Ibid., 120.
81. Ibid.
82. Ibid., 120–1.
83. Crewe, 17 June 1912, 122.
84. Hansard's House of Commons Debates, vol. 56, 1900.
85. Ibid., 1784.
86. Charles Hardinge, *My Indian Years: 1910–1916: The Reminiscences of Lord Hardinge of Penshurst* (London: John Murray, 1948), 3–4.
87. Wilson, *Letters to Nobody*, 162.
88. Ibid., 163.
89. Ibid.
90. Ibid., 164.
91. Ibid.
92. Ibid., 165.
93. Ibid., 166.
94. Ibid., 167.
95. Ibid.
96. See Michael Mandelbaum, *Democracy's Good Name: The Rise and Risks of the World's Most Popular Form of Government* (New York: Public Affairs, 2008). Mandelbaum has approached this very question in detail. He argues that the spreading of the free market to undeveloped or developing parts of the world is the first step toward their democratization since the give and take of the market place, where prices are established by finding a consensus between willing sellers and willing buyers, makes for an excellent democratic model. Lawmakers do something very similar when they come together in legislative bodies to debate and resolve their different political interests. The values that make the free market work, again according to Mandelbaum, are precisely the same values that make democracy function at its best. Mandelbaum finds India a particularly interesting test case for his theory, arguing that Britain's long inculcation of free market thinking during the colonial period created a remarkably stable democracy in independent India. What strikingly is missing in his analysis is a detailed study of Pakistan, which was also part of Britain's Indian Empire but has followed a considerably different political trajectory than India. Mandelbaum also fails to examine the negative social impact British free market policy had on local Indian communities whose economic priorities became determined by markets not at home but in London.
97. Wilson, *Letters to Nobody*, 169.
98. See John Robert Seeley, *The Expansion of England: Two Courses of Lectures* (London: Macmillan and Co., 1883).

99. For Seeley, the failure to escape from a mercantilist rendering of empire and its subsequent system of colonial exploitation had caused England's first empire to collapse at the end of the eighteenth century when the American colonies broke away. Greater Britain, however, represented an expanded imperial state consisting of equal partners tied together by shared communities of race, religion, and interests.

5 Competing Visions of Empire in the Colonial Built Environment

1. The laying of the foundation stones occurred on 15 December 1911, four days after George's imperial durbar.
2. Home Department, Delhi Branch, April, 1912, nos. 103–39 (National Archives of India).
3. Part of the grandness of the planning had to do with the economic health of British-India between 1911 and 1913, the exact years when the city was being planned and laid out. During his 1913 presentation of the East Indian Budget to the House of Commons, Edwin Montagu claimed in reference to the building project and its related reforms, 'The financial prosperity of India is so wonderful that I think we are entitled to take a little bigger risk than we can in a country like this [England].'
4. Home Department, Delhi Branch, April 1912, nos. 103–39.
5. Hardinge Official Correspondence, Lord Crewe, Secretary of State for India, to Lord Hardinge, Viceroy of India, 1 February 1912 (Nehru Memorial Library). Crewe learned of his name through the Local Government Board. Brodie responded that he was interested in being part of the imperial Delhi town planning committee but that the Liverpool Corporation would agree only to a three-month absence.
6. Hardinge Official Correspondence, Crewe to Hardinge, 25 January 1912.
7. See S. D. Adshead, 'City Improvement', *Town Planning Review*, Vol. 1, no. 3, 1910; *New Towns for Old* (London: JM Dent & Sons, 1943); *Town Planning and Town Development* (London: Methuen & Co., 1923); *A New England* (London: F. Muller Ltd, 1941); *Modern Methods of Building* (London: P. S. King, 1937); and *York: A Plan for Progress and Preservation* (York, 1948). He also made studies on West Essex, South Essex, Teignmouth, and Oxfordshire.
8. See Hardinge Official Correspondence, Cyril Jackson, London City Council, to Crewe, 5 February 1912. Captain Swinton to Cyril Jackson, 5 February 1912. Captain Swinton to Thomas Holderness, 15 February 1912.
9. Ibid., Cyril Jackson to Crewe, 5 February 1912.
10. Ibid., Swinton to Cyril Jackson, 5 February 1912.
11. Ibid., Crewe to Hardinge, 16 February 1912.
12. Ibid.
13. Ibid.
14. Hamilton also had been an aide-de-camp to Lord Lansdowne in Canada
15. Ibid., Frederic Hamilton to Lord Lansdowne, 3 February 1912.
16. Ibid.
17. Ibid.
18. Ibid., Crewe to Hardinge, 16 February 1912.

19. Ibid., Richmond Ritchie to Hardinge, 2 February 1912.
20. Ibid., Thomas Holderness, 'Memorandum', 5 February 1912. Cain and Hopkins argue that amateurism was an important part of a gentleman's identity. This amateurism could involve animal husbandry, as Harriet Ritvo has shown in *The Animal Estate*, to astronomy, the natural sciences, the arts, and, of course, politics.
21. Hardinge Official Correspondence, Hardinge to Crewe, 3 March 1912.
22. The city is often referred to as 'Lutyens' Delhi' even today.
23. Hardinge Official Correspondence, Hardinge to Ritchie, 30 December 1911 and Hardinge to Crewe, 27 January 1912.
24. Ibid., Hardinge to Ritchie, 6 January 1912.
25. See Linda B. Fritzinger, *Diplomat without Portfolio: Valentine Chirol, his Life and 'The Times'* (London: I. B. Tauris, 2006). Chirol was foreign editor from 1899 to 1912.
26. Hardinge Official Correspondence, Reginald Barratt to Valentine Chirol, 4 February 1912.
27. Ibid.
28. Ibid.
29. Ibid.
30. Ibid., Crewe to Hardinge, 12 March 1912. All three members had similar terms of engagement in terms of allowances, housing and expenses. The only difference was in their fees with Brodie receiving 1,750 guineas, Lutyens 1,500 guineas, and Swinton 500.
31. A discussion of New Delhi's Architectural Board consisting of Lutyens, Baker, and Swinton until his resignation is discussed in the following chapter.
32. See Jane Ridley, *The Architect and his Wife* (London: Chatto and Windus, 2002).
33. Hardinge Official Correspondence, Swinton to Thomas Holderness, 15 February 1912.
34. Ibid.
35. Ibid., Hardinge to Crewe, 31 May 1912.
36. Special Town Planning Committee, 'Final Report of the Town Planning Committee for the New Imperial Capital', Home Department, Public Branch, July 1913, nos. 62–63, Part A (National Archives of India).
37. Hardinge Official Correspondence, Communiqué, 12 March 1913.
38. 'Information to Be Collected and Work to Be Carried Out in the Absence of the Town Planning Committee', Home Department, Delhi Branch, 1912, no. 18, Part B (National Archives of India). P. H. Clutterbuck had been the director of the municipal gardens at Agra.
39. 'Project Estimate for Works', vol. 1, 1913, Reports and Abstracts of Expenditures, Home Department, 1913. Ward and deMontmorency admitted that this first budget was based on rudimentary information and that it was impossible to make estimates for a project that might takes decades to complete. They headed their budget report with the words, 'It is a practicable impossibility to make an estimate to cover the total and ultimate cost of building the new capital for the reasons that it has never been laid down by any authority what works and operations are covered by the term "new capital," that the growth of a new capital must be gradual, and that it is not possible to frame an estimate now to cover works to be commenced a decade or more hence.'
40. Ibid.

41. Between 1912 and 1927 the Government of India met in the civil lines in what was called the 'temporary works'. For an excellent study of these works, see Narayani Gupta's *Delhi between Two Empires* (Delhi: Oxford University Press, 1981).
42. Special Town Planning Committee, 'Final Report of the Town Planning Committee'.
43. One of the most important aspects of Victoria's proclamation was that it declared Indians to be full British subjects with all the privileges and duties that British citizenship entailed. This stated ideal was easier to proclaim than to live by.
44. Sir Bradford Leslie, 'Delhi: The Metropolis of India', *Journal of the Royal Society of Arts*, vol. 61, no. 3136, 27 December 1912, 133–48. See also 'Royal Society of Arts: Award of Medals', *The Times*, 3 July 1913, 4.
45. Though Leslie was not a member of Parliament, he belonged to associations that included parliamentary critics of the building project. For example, J. D. Rees and Leslie belonged to the East India Association and the British Central Africa Company. Rees, one of the most vocal critics of the new capital, actually chaired the Royal Society of Arts meeting where Leslie presented his paper. Leslie also had close ties to men who owned property in Delhi's civil lines, and these men were powerful proponents of Leslie's scheme. The new capital would certainly cause some disruption, but these men, if they played their cards right, hoped to gain far more in return. Their great fear was being isolated from the Government of India. This was precisely what the official town planning committee was proposing with the selection of the south site. A new capital built on the southern site ran the risk of transforming the civil lines into a second-class European community in the Delhi District. As such, property values in the civil lines were sure to decline.
46. He painted the Duke of Wellington to celebrate the queen's coronation.
47. 'Obituary: Sir Bradford Leslie: A Great Builder of Bridges', *The Times*, 22 March 1926, 19.
48. Ibid.
49. 'The Railway Congress at Brussels', *The Times*, 20 August 1885, 6.
50. 'Jubilee Honours for India', *The Times*, 16 February 1887, 12. The bridge received its name in honour of Queen Victoria's Jubilee. Leslie became a Knight Commander to the Most Eminent Order of the Indian Empire.
51. Leslie often was listed as a notable attendee in *The Times*' coverage of London's special events.
52. 'Classified Advertising: Miscellaneous Companies', *The Times*, 11 December 1905, 19.
53. Two points are clear when looking at his advice to both government and private investors. First, Indian railway companies should seek to better connect Indian communities to a larger global market. This meant building railway lines that shortened the time travel between India's productive hinterland – most notably the Punjab's newly built canal colonies – to port cities such as Calcutta, Bombay, and Karachi. Second, companies and government should develop cost-saving strategies whenever possible when building infrastructure such as railways, a lesson that he had learned as an apprentice with Brunel. One of Leslie's fondest memories had to do with innovations he developed in using second-hand material from older Indian railways to build

new railway lines. His basic impulse was to economize at every opportunity and in the process to save government money and to increase the profits of private investors.

54. He was an officer and member of the Council of the Institution of Civil Engineers and was an Officer of Public Instruction. He was a member of the East India Association and the British Farmers Association. He was a trustee for debenture holders for the Ramnad Raj Sterling Loan and the Ramnad Zemindary Sterling Debenture Loan. Along with the above-mentioned East India Railway, he was involved in the British Central Africa Company and the Oudh and Rohilkund Railway Company.

55. After leaving Delhi, the most important rail centre in upper India, the new railway passed through the towns of Rohtuck, Jhind, Tohansh, Bhatinda, Sherghar, Abokar, Minchinabad, and Bhawalpore. The benefits of the new line were marketed as reducing the distance between Delhi and Karachi by 227 miles, which brought Indian goods 'one day nearer Europe than Bombay'. The line also opened up populated, well-irrigated lands in the Punjab's Lower Bari Doab where the government was expanding canal colonies. These canal colonies were in addition to the Punjab's Upper Bari Doab canal colonies, which were fed by the Indus, Jhelum, Chenab, Ravi, Beas, and Sutlej rivers. The government planned to extend these canals into the Lower Bari Doab over the next decade, precisely where the Southern would eventually run.

56. The Secretary of State promised the payment of interest at the rate of £3 10s on the Southern's share and debenture capital during construction and gave favourable rates for carrying the building materials necessary to build the new railway. While the Government of India did not offer government-guaranteed interest on investments in the new railway, it did approve a rebate, if necessary, drawn from the Northwestern State Railway towards ensuring 3½ per cent interest on the Southern's capital account in India. The rebate was a subsidy offered by government in case the new railway company failed to meet its offered subscription of 3½ per cent.

57. The railway began with a share capital of £966,000 in 96,600 shares worth £10 each earning 3½ per cent interest. The company's debenture stock – trusteed by the Marquis of Tweeddale and the Rt Hon. Herbert J. Gladstone – was worth £500,000 also earning 3½ per cent, not redeemable until 1919. The London Joint Stock Bank and the Royal Bank of Scotland received subscriptions from investors between 1 and 2 August 1895, an extremely short period of time suggesting that Leslie already had his investors lined up.

58. The Government of India allowed the Southern to use without charge lands that its line crossed, and the Secretary of State, Lord George Hamilton, promised to use his influence to win similar concessions from Indian states where the line passed through. The Government of India, using the resources of the older Northwestern State Railway, would work and maintain the line after its completion and supply all the rolling stock (engines and railcars) for the new railway. When and if the Secretary of State for India decided to purchase the railway, the amount could not be less than the total capital expenditure or more than 20 per cent of the original capital expenditure.

59. Leslie used examples to show that the area of his town plan equalled or was greater than the government areas of London and Paris. According

to Leslie, one square mile was enough to include 'Westminster Abbey, the Houses of Parliament, Buckingham Palace, nearly all the government offices, Belgravia, Clubland, Hotel land, theatres, shops, etc.' In reference to Paris, he argued that 'from the Arc de Triomphe to and including the *Ecole Militaire* thence to *Place de la Bastille* and back to the *Arc de Triomphe* is a triangle of 2½ square miles'.

60. Leslie, 'Delhi: The Metropolis of India', 139.
61. Ibid., 135.
62. Ibid.
63. Hardinge Official Correspondence, Major General Beresford Lovett to Hardinge, 23 December 1911.
64. Leslie, 'Delhi: The Metropolis of India', 138. A secondary road would run behind the shops for the purpose of moving trade goods. Leslie did not want to recreate problems such as were seen in London where delivery carts often congested the streets.
65. Ibid., 139. Furthermore, Leslie's town plan maintained the connections and relations that the civil lines and the old city had established earlier and used many of the durbar-improved conveniences already present in the area such as the Delhi Railway Station, the post office, and an enlarged water filtration system. While building in the civil lines meant some disruptions for Delhi's European community, in general it would remain relatively intact. Local businesses potentially benefitted from having more government officials and private citizens in their city, and residents could enjoy the new beauty of their surroundings on a daily basis.
66. Hansard's House of Lords Debates, vol. XI, 22 February 1912, 238–9.
67. Leslie, 'Delhi: The Metropolis of India', 133–48.
68. Ibid.
69. Ibid. Finlay was deeply involved in Indian commerce and trade and had written a study on the subject, *History of Provincial Financial Arrangements* (1887).
70. Ibid.
71. Ibid.
72. Ibid., 147.
73. Wilmot Corfield, 'Delhi: The Metropolis of India', *Journal of the Royal Society of Arts*, vol. 61, no. 3137, 3 January 1913, 180.
74. Ibid.
75. Hardinge Official Correspondence, Hardinge to Crewe, 20 January 1913.
76. 'Publication of the Report of Site for New Capital,' Home Department, Public, July 1913 nos. 68–80 Part B (National Archives of India).
77. Hansard's House of Lords Debates, vol. XII, 17 June 1912, 95. Curzon was relatively familiar with the Delhi area since he was interested in its architecture. He even had authorized stabilization work on some of the area's ancient ruins such as the Qtub Minar.
78. Hardinge Official Correspondence, 'Report of the Committee Appointed under the Orders of his Excellency the Viceroy to Report upon the Comparative Healthiness of the Proposed Northern and Southern Sites for the New Imperial City of Delhi', 4 March 1913. Also see Hardinge Official Correspondence, Hardinge to Crewe, 20 January 1913.
79. Ibid., Hardinge to Wilson, 12 February 1913.

80. Ibid., Hardinge to Holderness, 6 February 1913. Most of the civil lines, they argued, would have to be purchased and substantially reworked to make the site suitable as the capital. This would include purchasing 120 expensive bungalows, because Hardinge wanted rent revenue to flow back into the Government of India rather than to private individuals as it did in Simla and Calcutta. This had been a major concern of Sir William H. Clark, Member for Commerce and Industry in the Government of India during the original discussions with the viceroy in his executive council in 1911. Further harming business interests, it would be necessary to remove the important manufacturing suburb of Sabzi Mandi, which would disadvantage the manufacturing community of Delhi.
81. Special Town Planning Committee, 'Possibility of Building the Imperial Capital on the North Site', 11 March 1913 (National Archives of India).
82. Hardinge Official Correspondence, 'Report of the Committee ... to Report upon the Comparative Healthiness ...'.
83. Hardinge Official Correspondence, Lutyens to Hardinge, 20 September 1912.
84. Ibid., Memorandum, Hardinge to Executive Council, 4 March 1913.
85. Ibid., Swinton to Hardinge, 4 March 1913.
86. Ibid.
87. Ibid.
88. Ibid., Swinton to Hardinge, 23 February 1913.
89. Ibid.
90. Ibid., E. Cotes, 'The Case of the Northern Site'; and Swinton, 'A Reply to Mr. Cotes' Brief Summary by Captain Swinton', 10 March 1913.
91. Ibid.
92. *The India List and India Office List, 1905* (London: Harrison and Sons, 1905).
93. Hardinge Official Correspondence, 'Report of the Committee...to Report upon the Comparative Healthiness...'.
94. 'Report of a Committee Ordered to Assemble by G.O.C.C.', 16 September 1845. Chief Commissioner's Office, Education Department, no. 8, 1916 (Reprinted) (Delhi State Archives).
95. Ibid.
96. Hardinge Official Correspondence, 'Report of the Committee...to Report upon the Comparative Healthiness...'.
97. Ibid.
98. Ibid.
99. Ibid.
100. C. P. Lukis, 'Anti-Mosquito Measures in India', *The British Medical Journal*, vol. 1, no. 2662 (6 January 1912), 23–5. Lately, he had been involved in developing medical education classes in Amritsar that focused on combatting malaria and its spread.
101. Hardinge Official Correspondence, Memorandum, Hardinge to Executive Council, 4 March 1913.
102. Bahadur Shah, a highly cultured man who far preferred art to war, was forced to go along with the uprising due to the large presence of sepoys in the city.
103. Dalrymple, 165.
104. 'Report of the Delhi Town Planning Committee on the Choice of a Site for the New Imperial Capital'. Home Department, Delhi Branch, July 1912,

nos. 1–2, 8. See Jay Winter, *Sites of Memory, Sites of Mourning: The Great War in European Cultural History* (Cambridge: Cambridge University Press, 1998).

105. 'Report of the Delhi Town Planning Committee on the Choice of a Site for the New Imperial Capital'. Home Department, Delhi Branch, July 1912, nos. 1–2, 7 (National Archives of India). This was a preliminary site report that compared and contrasted various locations in the Delhi District as per their suitability for housing the new capital.

106. Hardinge Official Correspondence, Du Boulay to Roberts, 29 January 1913.

107. Gupta, 125.

108. Ibid.

109. Ibid., 30.

110. According to Gupta, fearful memories of the uprising were reignited in Delhi not by any aggressive Indian actions since 1857 but by a growing détente between Delhi's Hindu and Muslim communities in the late nineteenth century. This cooperation occurred during a time of tremendous social pressure and economic change in Delhi. A series of devastating droughts caused thousands of famine victims to flood into Delhi to escape the ravages of dearth and disease in northern India. Additionally, rapid industrial and railroad development made Delhi one of the Punjab's largest industrial centres by the end of the nineteenth century, changing the physical look of Delhi and its suburbs. These urbanizing pressures brought together rather than drove apart the Hindu and Muslim communities. As Gupta suggests, the growing association between Delhi's Hindu and Muslim populations reminded Delhi's European residents of the potential dangers of Indian communal unity.

111. Leslie envisioned a private ferry company to taxi Indian government workers from their homes on the east bank to their places of work on the west bank. The ferry service was a perfect example of Leslie's desire to use the building of a new capital to benefit commerce in the imperial world. His town plan called for important civic needs, such as transportation and lighting, to be turned over to the private sector, theoretically lowering the cost of government while encouraging private investment in municipal services.

112. John Darwin, *The End of the British Empire: The Historical Debate* (Oxford: Basil Blackwell, 1991), 4.

113. Paragraph three stated in clear terms the Government of India's plan to begin devolving political responsibility, when possible, to loyal Indians. This was a trend that had already begun, but paragraph three gave it a stamp of approval.

114. Lord Hardinge Official Correspondence, Hardinge to Baker, 30 August 1913.

115. Ibid., Hardinge to Curzon, 30 October 1912.

116. Ibid., Hardinge to Lutyens, 28 March 1913.

117. Hansard's House of Commons Debates, East India Revenue Accounts (Indian Budget), vol. 41, 30 July 1912.

118. Sir Guy Fleetwood Wilson, *Letters to Nobody, 1908–1913* (London: John Murray, 1921), 193.

119. Ibid., 195.

120. See Robert Grant Irving, *Indian Summer: Lutyens, Baker, and Imperial Delhi* (New Haven: Yale University Press, 1981).

121. Governor General in Council, 'Transfer of the Seat of Government of India from Calcutta to Delhi' (National Archives of India).
122. Herbert Baker, 'Architectural Design: Symbolism in Stone and Marble', *The Times,* 18 February 1930.
123. Ibid.
124. Ibid.

6 Hardinge's Imperial Delhi Committee and his Architectural Board: The Perfect Building Establishment for the Perfect Colonial Capital

1. See James C. Scott, *Seeing Like a State: How Certain Schemes to Improve the Human Condition Have Failed* (New Haven: Yale University Press, 1998).
2. Hardinge Official Correspondence, Hardinge in Council to Crewe, 27 February 1913.
3. Ibid.
4. Ibid.
5. See Charles Hardinge, *Old Diplomacy: The Reminiscences of Lord Hardinge of Penshurst* (London: John Murray, 1947). Hardinge met with the king almost weekly before he became viceroy. The sessions were meant to keep the king abreast of foreign affairs and happenings in the Foreign Office.
6. Official Hardinge Correspondence, Wilson to Hardinge, 26 December 1911.
7. Ibid.
8. See Ruth Johnson Cunningham, *Contributions to Administration and Constitutional Development in India and the British Colonies in Africa* (Columbia: University of South Carolina Press, 1976), 15.
9. The same was true for Indian clerks. In 1908, a committee chaired by M. S. Meston drafted a report – 'Committee to Investigate the Complaints of the Clerk in the Government of India Secretariats and in Certain Other Offices of the Imperial Departments, In Regard to Insufficiency of Pay and Prospects, 1908 – Report' – that investigated the complaints of clerks in regard to their pay and lack of career advancement.
10. Hardinge Official Correspondence, W. B. Gordon, 'Administration of New Delhi during the Construction Stage', 23 July 1912. It is interesting to note that Gordon's use of the name 'New Delhi' is one of the first times this title was used. Typically, during these early days the city was referred to as the 'new imperial capital' or the 'the new Delhi'. The title, 'New Delhi', was not given until 1926 when Baker's Secretariats began to be used by government officials and clerks.
11. Ibid.
12. Ibid.
13. Ibid.
14. Ibid.
15. Ibid.
16. Ibid.
17. Ibid.
18. Ibid.
19. Ibid., R. H. Craddock to Hardinge, 25 July 1912.

20. Ibid.
21. Ibid.
22. H. C. Beadon, *Final Report of the Third Regular Settlement of the Delhi District, 1906–1910* (Civil and Military Gazette Press, 1910).
23. Hardinge Official Correspondence, R. H. Craddock to Hardinge, 25 July 1912.
24. Ibid., Hardinge to Craddock, 31 July 1912.
25. Ibid., R. H. Craddock to Hardinge, 25 July 1912.
26. Gordon and Craddock's belief that membership on the committee would bring personal rewards and advance was proven true by the subsequent careers of Hailey and deMontmorency. Hailey became one of the most respected officers in the Indian Civil Service and held a series of high offices, including Finance and Home Secretary from 1919 to 1924, Governor of the Punjab from 1924 to 1928, and Governor of the United Provinces from 1928 to 1930. An anonymous official wrote to Hailey shortly after he had been appointed as head of the Imperial Delhi Committee. The writer, who claimed to have been promised the position by an unknown official close to the building project, congratulated Hailey but also told him how painful it was to be passed over since he knew being on the committee was a major stepping stone to high officialdom in the Indian Civil Service. DeMontmorency's selection as Hailey's Personal Assistant and Secretary to the Imperial Delhi Committee also opened doors that might possibly have been closed to him. He twice became Governor of the Punjab in 1928–32 and then again in 1932–33. Promotion in the colonial service also meant social advancement via highly sought after titles, and men and women avidly scanned the New Year's list, which listed these awards. The importance of these awards can be seen in the habit of the Government of India to elevate an official's title to meet what it believed was the office's civil rank. For example, Hailey was given a C.I.E. for serving on the central committee that managed the 1911 durbar and a G.C.I.E. when he became the Governor of the United Provinces. Hardinge himself took his older brother's official title, Hardinge of Penshurst, when he became Viceroy of India.
27. Hardinge Official Correspondence, Hardinge in Council to Crewe, 27 February 1913.
28. Ibid., Gordon to DuBoulay, 18 January 1913.
29. Ibid.
30. Ibid.
31. Ibid.
32. Ibid.
33. Ibid.
34. Ibid.
35. Ibid., Hardinge in Council to Crewe, 27 February 1913.
36. Ibid.
37. Other members included H. T. Keeling, previously Superintending Engineer, Madras Public Works Department, who served as Chief Engineer for the building project. Mr H. G. Stokes, Deputy Secretary to the Government of India in the Financial Department served as Finance Member. He was later replaced by G. Rainy. W. H. Nichols, previously Consulting Architect to the Government of Madras after service in the Archaeological Department of the Government of

India served as Architect Member. The Director General of the Indian Medical Service, the Electrical Advisor to the Government of India, the Sanitary Commissioner with the Government of India, and representatives from the Army Department and Railway Department served as consulting members.

38. Hardinge Official Correspondence, Crewe to Hardinge, 11 March 1913.
39. Chelmsford Official Correspondence, Lord Chelmsford to Austen Chamberlain, 21 July 1916.
40. Ibid., Chelmsford to Hardinge, 18 August 1916.
41. Throughout 1912 and into 1913, Joseph King, a member of the House of Commons, repeatedly stood to question whether or not the Government of India planned to hold a competition to select an architect.
42. Hardinge Official Correspondence, Leonard A. Stokes to Richmond Ritchie, 11 June 1912.
43. Ibid.
44. Ibid.
45. 'The Future Delhi', *The Times*, 19 October 1912, 7.
46. Hardinge Official Correspondence, Hardinge to Crewe, 16 July 1912; and Hardinge to Lutyens, 18 July 1912.
47. Ibid.
48. See Thomas Metcalf, *An Imperial Vision: Indian Architecture and Britain's Raj* (Oxford: Oxford University Press 1989).
49. Ibid., 234.
50. Hardinge Official Correspondence, Hardinge to Ritchie, 11 July 1912.
51. Ibid., Memorandum from Hardinge, 1 January 1913. Thomas Metcalf, in *An Imperial Vision*, nicely describes Hardinge and Lutyens' long argument over the use of the rounded western arch or the Indian pointed arch. Hardinge argued that pointed rather than rounded arches should be used in the new capital's government structures since the latter held no meaning for Indians. Urging Lutyens to find a way to blend the pointed arch with western building traditions, Hardinge claimed, 'it is no use fighting against tradition and symbolism of centuries. To do so spells failure, while to adopt them and blend them with English traditions spells success.'
52. Ibid., Hardinge to Lutyens, 27 August 1912.
53. Ibid., Hardinge to Lutyens, 27 August 1912.
54. Ibid., Hardinge to Lutyens, 27 August 1912. Pathan referred to the earliest Moslem architecture in India.
55. Ibid., Lutyens to Hardinge, 13 September 1912.
56. Of course, one of the great ironies of New Delhi's architectural style is that, in the end, Lutyens did successfully fuse Indian and western building traditions in his famous, and indeed beautiful, Government House, later called the Viceroy's House. The structure and its famous dome stand as one of the great examples of architectural fusion in the modern world.
57. Herbert Baker, 'The New Delhi: Eastern and Western Architecture: A Problem of Style', *The Times*, 3 October 1912, 7.
58. Hardinge Official Correspondence, Swinton to Hardinge, 10 October 1912.
59. Ibid., Swinton to Hardinge, 3 October 1912.
60. See Thomas Metcalf, 'Architecture and Empire: Sir Herbert Baker and the Building of New Delhi', in *Delhi through the Ages: Essays in Urban History, Culture, and Society*, ed. R. E. Frykenberg (Oxford: Oxford University Press, 1986).

61. In his response to Baker's letter, Curzon repeated the sentiment that Indian architecture by itself was inherently incapable of meeting the needs of Lord Hardinge. He too called for a western classical approach, specifically 'a colonial adaptation of the Palladian style'. The best example of this type of architecture, he claimed, was the Government House at Calcutta, which, interestingly, was based on Kedleston Hall, Curzon's own estate in Derbyshire, England.

62. Bradford Leslie, 'Delhi: The Metropolis of India', *Journal of the Royal Society of Arts*, vol. 61, no. 3136 (27 December 1912): 133–48.

63. Hardinge Official Correspondence, Swinton to Hardinge, 10 October 1912.

64. 'The New Delhi: Eastern and Western Architecture', *The Times*, 3 October 1912, 7.

65. Ibid.

66. Leslie, 'Delhi: The Metropolis of India', 145–46.

67. Wilmot Corfield, 'Delhi: The Metropolis of India', 180. Corfield spent time in India and was the editor of *The Philatelic Journal of India*, an officer of the Philatelic Society of India, and the curator of the Indian National Stamp Collection at the Victoria Museum in Calcutta. Corfield went on to say that 'It will be time enough to entrust the designs for the new capital to Indian artists when they have turned out a few postage stamps inconspicuous for crudity of expression.'

68. E. B. Havell, 'The Architecture of the New Delhi', *The Times*, 8 October 1912, 5.

69. Ibid. Roger Eliot Fry was an artist, an influential art critic, and a member of London's famous Bloomsbury Group.

70. Ibid.

71. Ibid.

72. Hansard's House of Commons Debates, vol. 45, 20 December 1912, 1949.

73. Leslie, 'Delhi: The Metropolis of India', 147.

74. Ibid.

75. Ibid.

76. Ibid.

77. Ibid.

78. Ibid.

79. Ibid.

80. 'The New Delhi', *The Times*, 3 October 1912, 7.

81. Ibid.

82. Ibid.

83. Ibid. The hubris here is evident and especially ironic in that *The Times* had no further to look than neighbouring Shahjahanabad for an example of a richly designed, complex city that was designed to house commercial, royal, and residential units. See Stephen Blake's *Shahjahanabad: The Sovereign City in Mughal India, 1639–1739* (Cambridge: Cambridge University Press, 2002) and his 'Cityscape of an Imperial Capital: Shahjahanabad in 1739', in *Delhi through the Ages*. Also see Hamida Khatoon Naqvi, 'Shahjahanabad: The Mughal Delhi, 1638–1803', in *Delhi through the Ages*.

84. Corfield, 'Delhi: The Metropolis of India', 180.

85. Ibid.

86. 'The New Delhi', *The Times*, 3 October 1912, 7.

87. Ibid.

88. Ibid.
89. Ibid.
90. Ibid.
91. Ibid.
92. Ibid.
93. Leslie, 'Delhi: The Metropolis of India', 145.
94. Hardinge Official Correspondence, F. H. Lucas to DuBoulay, 18 October 1912.
95. Ibid.
96. Ibid., Reginald Barratt to Hardinge, 10 November 1912.
97. Ibid.
98. Ibid., Lutyens to Hardinge, 1 November 1912.
99. Ibid., Hardinge to Crewe, 5 January 1913.
100. Ibid., Barratt to Hardinge, 10 January 1913.
101. Ibid.
102. Thomas G. Jackson, 'The New Delhi: The Principles of Architecture', *The Times*, 11 October 1912, 5.
103. Ibid.
104. Ibid.
105. Ibid.
106. Ibid.
107. Ibid.
108. Hardinge Official Correspondence, Baker to Hardinge, 21 March 1913.
109. Ibid., Baker to Hardinge, 25 July 1913. Baker's stress.
110. Ibid., Baker to Hardinge, 21 March 1913.
111. Ibid.
112. Ibid.
113. Ibid., Baker to Hardinge, 25 July 1913.
114. Both communities shared a western tradition that eased the search for South Africa's colonial architectural style for Baker.
115. Hardinge Official Correspondence, Baker to Hardinge, 21 March 1913.
116. Ibid.
117. Ibid., Baker to Hardinge, 6 August 1913.
118. Baker's search for an architectural style for modern India did benefit the Government of India, and Hardinge in particular, in one important way. Baker's correspondence, often expressed in deeply philosophic tones, gave Hardinge's government the language it needed to articulate the capital's new vision to the world. The Government of India, in dispatches to the India Office or in statements to the press, often repeated the ideas and wording used by Baker when discussing his search for an architectural style for a new India.
119. Hardinge Official Correspondence, Press Release, 1914.
120. Ibid.
121. Ibid.
122. Ibid.
123. Ibid., Hailey to Hardinge, 13 August 1913.
124. Ibid., Hailey to DuBoulay, 3 September 1913.
125. Ibid.
126. Ibid., Hardinge to Swinton, 12 September 1912.

127. Ibid., Hardinge to Lutyens, 19 August 1912.
128. Reasons vary for why Swinton departed. He claimed that it stemmed from the extreme controversy surrounding the building of New Delhi and that he was not equal to the task. Hardinge, for his part, believed he did so out of frustration with Lutyens who had become obsessed with the Viceroy's House, losing sight of the overall town plan in the process.

7 'A New Jewel in an Old Setting': The Cultural Politics of Colonial Space

1. See James C. Scott, *Seeing Like a State: How Certain Schemes to Improve the Human Condition Have Failed* (New Haven: Yale University Press, 1998). Scott examines Brasilia as an example of high modernism. It was the brainchild of Juscelino Kubitschek, the president of Brazil from 1956 to 1961, Oscar Niemeyer, the chief architect for public buildings, and Lucio Costa, the winning architect.
2. Ibid., 104.
3. See Andrew Legg, *Spaces of Colonialism: Delhi's Urban Governmentalities* (Malden: Blackwell, 2007) for the most recent monograph on the relationship between the new and older Delhis. Legg uses three cases studies – including the spatial layout of New Delhi, its policing, and its slum clearances – to show how the British liberal colonial project became strikingly illiberal in the colonial context.
4. Of course, the corruption that town planners saw in old Delhi had its own internal logic that emerged from the street level, as the author and urban activist Jan Jacobs would say, rather than the rarefied atmosphere of the master planner. See Jan Jacobs, *The Death and Life of Great American Cities* (New York: Vintage Books, 1961). As Scott suggests when discussing old cities that have been shaped by multiple generations of humans, 'The fact that the layout of the city, having developed without any overall design, lacks a consistent geometric logic does not mean that it was at all confusing to its inhabitants.'
5. J. P. Hewitt to J. L. Jenkins, 30 December 1911, Home Department, Delhi Branch, April 1912, nos. 103–39, Part A (National Archives of India).
6. Robert Grant Irving, *Indian Summer: Lutyens, Baker, and Imperial Delhi* (New Haven: Yale University Press, 1981), 89–90.
7. Hardinge Official Correspondence, Note by His Excellency the Viceroy, 17 July 1912.
8. Hardinge Official Correspondence, Extract from a Letter from His Excellency the Viceroy to Reginald Craddock, 30 July 1912.
9. Hardinge Official Correspondence, Note by His Excellency, no. 310, 31 July 1912. It should not be surprising that Lutyens showed an interest in placing Indian palaces at the centre of the earliest town plan. According to F. A. Eustis II and Z. H. Zaidi, George V's original interest in transferring the capital from Calcutta to Delhi stemmed from his desire to bring the Government of India into a closer relationship with the Indian princes. See Eustis and Zaidi, 'King, Viceroy and Cabinet: The Modification of the Partition of Bengal, 1911', *History*, vol. 49, issue 166 (1964): 171–84.
10. Hardinge Official Correspondence, Note by His Excellency, no. 310, 31 July 1912.

11. Ibid., Note by His Excellency the Viceroy, 17 July 1912.
12. Ibid.
13. Ibid., Note By His Excellency the Viceroy, no. 16, 14 August 1912.
14. Ibid.
15. Ibid., Note by His Excellency the Viceroy, 17 July 1912.
16. Ibid., Sir Louis Dane to Hardinge, 25 July 1912.
17. Ibid., Note by His Excellency, no. 310, 31 July 1912.
18. Ibid.
19. Ibid.
20. Ibid.
21. Ibid., Hardinge to William Malcolm Hailey, 28 July 1913.
22. Lanchester's contributions to the field include *Zanzibar: A Study in Tropical Town Planning* (1923), *Town Planning in Madras and Zanzibar* (1923), *Talks on Town Planning* (1924), and *The Art of Town Planning* (1925).
23. Hardinge Official Correspondence, Hardinge to Richmond Ritchie, 11 July 1912.
24. Ibid., Note by His Excellency, no. 310, 31 July 1912.
25. Ibid., 'Extract from a letter from His Excellency the Viceroy to Reginald Craddock', 30 July 1912.
26. Ibid., H. V. Lanchester, 'Fifth Report of Mr. H. V. Lanchester'.
27. Ibid.
28. Ibid.
29. Ibid., Lutyens to Hardinge, 9 August 1912.
30. Ibid., deMontmorency to DuBoulay, 7 September 1912.
31. Ibid., Hardinge to Swinton, 23 September 1912.
32. Ibid.
33. Ibid., Swinton to Hardinge, 18 October 1912.
34. Ibid., Joint Note by Mr M. Nethersole Secretary to the Government of India, Public Works Department, and Mr C. E. V. Goument, Chief Engineer, Buildings and Roads Branch, United Provinces, on the Proposed Layout of New Delhi, 14 August 1912. Nethersole and Goument believed that covering garden areas with three feet of soil and effectively treating natural depressions and spoil pockets would allow for enough trees and shrubs to beautify the area.
35. Ibid., Note By His Excellency the Viceroy, no. 16, 14 August 1912.
36. Ibid.
37. Ibid., Lutyens to Hardinge, 20 September 1912.
38. Ibid.
39. Ibid.
40. Ibid., Swinton to Hardinge, 20 September 1912.
41. Ibid.
42. Ibid., Swinton to Hardinge, 19 December 1912.
43. Ibid., Swinton to Hardinge, 20 September 1912.
44. Ibid.
45. Ibid., Swinton to Hardinge, 3 October 1912.
46. Ibid., Swinton to Hardinge, 19 December 1912.
47. Ibid., Hardinge to Swinton, 22 October 1912.
48. Ibid., Hardinge to Swinton, 8 September 1912.
49. Ibid., Swinton to Hardinge, 19 December 1912.
50. Ibid., Hardinge to Lutyens, 17 September 1912.

51. Ibid., Swinton to Hardinge, 14 January 1913.
52. Hardinge Official Correspondence, 'Memorandum to Executive Council from Lord Hardinge', 4 March 1913.
53. Chief Commissioner of Delhi, 'Report on the Administration of Delhi Province, 1913–1914'.
54. Delhi Town Planning Committee, 'Report of the Delhi Town Planning Committee on the Choice of Site for the New Imperial Capital, Home Department, Delhi Branch, July 1912, nos. 1–2 (National Archives of India).
55. Ibid.
56. Ibid.
57. 'Delhi: New and Old: The Future Capital: New Jewel in an Old Setting', *The Times*, 18 February 1930, 50.
58. Hardinge Official Correspondence, Baker to Hardinge, 21 March 1913.
59. Ibid.
60. Ibid., Hailey to Hardinge, 21 May 1913.
61. Ibid.
62. Ibid., Hailey to Hardinge, 2 December 1914.
63. Ibid., Hardinge to Hailey, 4 December 1914.
64. Ibid.
65. Ibid.
66. Ibid., Hardinge to Hailey, 10 December 1914.
67. Ibid., Baker to deMontmorency, 18 December 1913.
68. Ibid., Hardinge to Holderness, 16 June 1914.
69. To be fair, Lutyens' desire was not simply a reflection of colonial hubris. As one of England's pre-eminent landscape architects, he had a deep understanding of how to use the land's natural characteristics to emphasize architecture.
70. Lord Hardinge Official Correspondence, 'Proceedings of the One Hundred and First Meeting of the Imperial Delhi Committee Held at Raisina on 18 February 1916'.
71. Ibid., Hardinge to Hailey, 13 March 1916.
72. 'Delhi, New and Old', *The Times*, 18 February 1930, 50.
73. The Chamber of Princes was a body that formalized interactions between the various heads of Indian states and the Government of India.
74. Ibid., Hardinge to Swinton, 14 October 1912.
75. Hansard's House of Commons Debates, vol. 56, 7 August 1912, 3311.
76. Ibid., 3312.
77. Ibid.
78. To be sure, the viceroy still retained significant powers over the legislation passed in these houses.
79. Herbert Baker, 'Architectural Design: Symbolism in Stone and Marble', *The Times*, 18 February 1930, 50.
80. Ibid.
81. As described at the beginning of the present study, paragraph three of the official report to transfer the capital dealt with India's political evolution. The paragraph argued that the transfer was a central part of this political reform.
82. 'Area Required for Various Purposes in New Imperial Capital', Home, Delhi Branch, October 1912, no. 10, Deposit (National Archives of India).
83. Ibid.

84. Ibid.
85. Ibid.
86. Ibid.
87. Ibid.
88. Much as scholars such as Anne Stoler have written on imperial codes of behaviour, it was absolutely essential that British residences be kept in good order to maintain Britain's imperial respectability.
89. 'Area Required for Various Purposes in New Imperial Capital'.
90. Except in a few rare instances, most department officers were British while Indians and Anglo-Indians filled the clerical establishment. This department information was subsequently used to lay out the residential areas of the town plan. The largest residential compound, 200 sq. acres, belonged to Government House, which included the viceroy's house, a private garden, and residences for the viceroy's staff. The Commander-in-Chief's compound, located just south of the viceroy's, was also relatively large, over 63 acres. Members of the Viceroy's Council were given 6-acre compounds. Generals, Secretaries, and Heads of Departments were allotted 5 acres each. Colonels, Deputy Secretaries, Additional Secretaries, and heads of minor departments were given 4 acres. Undersecretaries were allotted 3 acres, and Registrars and Superintendents were given 1.75 acres.
91. 'Area Required for Various Purposes in New Imperial Capital'.
92. Ibid.
93. Ibid.
94. Ibid.
95. Ibid.
96. Hardinge Official Correspondence, 'The Humble Memorial of Chandra Narayan Mathur, a Member of the Ministerial Establishment of the Home Department', 28 August 1915.
97. Ibid.
98. 'Information to Be Collected and Work to Be Carried Out in the Absence of the Town Planning Committee', Home Department, Delhi Branch, December 1912, no. 18, Part B (National Archives of India).
99. The flaw of this thinking is clear for any current New Delhi resident, many of whom actively pursue membership in various clubs such as the India International Centre.
100. Rebecca Brown, 'The Cemeteries and the Suburbs: Patna's Challenges to the Colonial City in South Asia', *Journal of Urban History*, vol. 29, no. 2 (January 2003): 151–3.
101. Hardinge Official Correspondence, Extract from a Letter from His Excellency the Viceroy to Reginald Craddock, 30 July 1912.
102. As will be seen in the following chapter, there was a legal process that detailed how private property could become public property and Hardinge's Land Acquisition Office followed the rules to the letter (unfortunately, as it turned out, for many Indian landowners).
103. Ibid., Note By His Excellency the Viceroy, no. 310, 31 July 1912. Also see Hardinge Official Correspondence, Hardinge to Crewe, 11 August 1912 for similar information.
104. Ibid.

105. See Ann Laura Stoler, 'Making Empire Respectable: The Politics of Race and Sexual Morality in 20th Century Colonial Cultures', *American Ethnologist*, vol. 16, no. 4 (November 1989): 634–60, for an analysis of the relationship between empire and respectability.
106. R. H. Craddock, Home Department, Public Branch, July 1913, nos. 62–63, Part A (National Archives of India).
107. Scott, *Seeing Like a State*, 310.
108. Ibid.

8 Land Acquisition, Landlessness, and the Building of New Delhi

1. See Amartya Sen's forward to the 1996 republication of Ranajit Guha's *A Rule of Property for Bengal: An Essay on the Idea of Permanent Settlement* (Durham, NC: Duke University Press, 1996), ix–x.
2. Guha, *A Rule of Property for Bengal*, 9.
3. Francis was a member of the Governor General's Council and an outspoken critic of Warren Hastings.
4. Thomas Metcalf, 'The British and the Moneylender in Nineteenth-Century India', *The Journal of Modern History*, vol. 34, no. 4 (December 1962), 390–7. British district collectors often complained that endemic rural debt stemmed from the poor economic choices made by Indian farmers. According to these officials, Indian famers too often lavished moneys on non-revenue yielding expenses such as weddings, births, and burials or on religious rites when they should have been using their moneys to improve their farms or to pay off old debts. Thus they placed family, community and religion over sound economic planning. Of course, it was these very social and cultural practices and many others that held together local communities. Metcalf has published considerably on the topic of land tenure, land revenue, and the mutiny. Along with the above, see 'The Struggle over Land Tenure in India, 1860–1868', *The Journal of Asian Studies*, vol. 21, no. 3 (May 1962); 'The Influence of the Mutiny of 1857 on Land Policy in India', *The Historical Journal*, vol. 4, no. 2 (1961); and 'Landlords without Land: The U.P. Zamindars Today', *Pacific Affairs*, vol. 40, no. 1/2 (Spring-Summer, 1976).
5. Ibid.
6. Ibid., 396.
7. James C. Scott, *Seeing Like a Secret: How Certain Schemes to Improve the Human Condition Have Failed* (New Haven: Yale University Press, 1998), 81.
8. Ibid., 36.
9. Ibid., 81.
10. Ibid., 47.
11. Thomas Metcalf, *Land, Landlords, and the British Raj: Northern India in the Nineteenth-Century* (Berkeley: University of California Press, 1979), 55.
12. Scott, *Seeing Like a Secret*, 35.
13. Ibid., 35.
14. Niall Ferguson, *Empire: The Rise and Demise of the British World Order and the Lessons for Global Power* (New York: Basic Books, 2003).

15. Michael Mandelbaum, *Democracy's Good Name: The Rise and Risks of the World's Most Popular Form of Government* (Philadelphia: Public Affairs, 2007).
16. Ibid., 63–5.
17. John Gray, *False Dawn: The Delusions of Global Capitalism* (New York: The New Press, 1998), 17.
18. Ibid. Gray points to three major transformations in Britain in the mid-nineteenth century that led to the rise of the free-market as an economic system in Britain. First, the proponents of mercantilism, after a long drawn out war, lost to the proponents of free trade. Second, Britain transformed its poor laws in such a way as to make it extremely difficult and onerous on families to receive poor relief, thus forcing the poor to take whatever work was available even if the pay was below subsistence levels. And third, government removed the remaining controls on wages, which allowed workers' labour to be bought and sold freely on the market. Created during the 1830s, Britain's free market-oriented political economy became the model, he argues, for later 'neo-liberal policies'.
19. Ibid. A more natural, and thus sustainable, economic system is one that encourages social cohesion and security for citizens, according to Gray.
20. *Punjab District Gazetteer*, Volume V, Part A, Delhi District, 1912 (National Archives of India).
21. H. C. Beadon, 'Final Report of the Third Regular Settlement of the Delhi District, 1906–1910' (National Archives of India). The reports provided a baseline for determining appropriate land revenues by (re)classifying land quality and land ownership.
22. Metcalf, *Land, Landlords, and the British Raj.*
23. Report by Geoffrey F. deMontmorency, 18 March 1912, Home Department (National Archives of India).
24. Beadon, 'Final Report of the Third Regular Settlement', 103. The British divided the cultivated area into 'irrigable' and 'unirrigable' tracts. Of the irrigable tracts, the land was further divided into 'land irrigable from wells' (*chahi*), 'land irrigable by canals' (*nahri*), and 'land irrigable from other sources' (*abi*).
25. David Ludden, *An Agrarian History of South Asia: The New Cambridge History of India, Volume 4, Part 4* (Cambridge: Cambridge University Press, 1999), 22.
26. Beadon, 'Final Report of the Third Regular Settlement', 128.
27. Beadon, *Delhi District Gazetteer, 1911*, 129 (National Archives of India).
28. Ibid., 123.
29. Beadon, 'Final Report of the Third Regular Settlement'.
30. Ludden, 24.
31. Ibid.
32. Beadon, *Delhi District Gazetteer*, 109 (National Archives of India).
33. Metcalf, *Land, Landlords, and the British Raj.*
34. Beadon, 'Final Report of the Third Regular Settlement', 135–6.
35. Ibid., 132.
36. Chief Commissioner of the Delhi District, 'Report on the Administration of Delhi Province, 1913–1914', 17–20 (Delhi State Archives).
37. P. J. Marshall, *Bengal, The British Bridgehead: Eastern India, 1740–1828* (Cambridge: Cambridge University Press, 1987), 149–50.
38. Ibid.
39. Scott, 33.
40. Ibid.

41. Beadon, 'Final Report of the Third Regular Settlement'.
42. Ludden, 24.
43. Scott, 24.
44. *Punjab Gazette*, Notification, no. 775, 21 December 1911 (National Archives of India).
45. Scott, 48.
46. J. Addison, 'Report on Land Acquisitions at Delhi by Mr. J. Addison, The Special Land Acquisition Officer', Home Department, Public, August 1915, no. 8, Public A (National Archives of India).
47. Ibid.
48. Ibid.
49. Ibid.
50. Report by deMontmorency, 14 March 1912. Home Department, May 1912, no. 15, Proceedings (National Archives of India).
51. See Metcalf, *Land, Landlords, and the British Raj*; Marshall, *Bengal: The British Bridgehead*; and Guha, *A Rule of Property for Bengal*.
52. DeMontmorency, 'Grant of Compensation in Land to Expropriated Landowners in the Delhi Area', 27 June 1912, Home Department, Delhi Branch, August 1912, nos. 72–73, Proceedings (National Archives of India). See also A. M. Stow, Senior Secretary to the Financial Commissioner, Punjab, 'Proposed Grant of Land Elsewhere as Compensation to the Hereditary Landowners and Tenants of Villages in the Neighborhood of Delhi', 1 June 1912, Home Department, Delhi Branch, Proceedings, May 1912, no. 15, Part A (National Archives of India). The Karnal District had 3,281 acres in the following *birs*: Bir Inindari, Kandra Kheri, Theh Nahri, Bir Pipli, and Bir Sojra. In the Rohtak District there was 1,683 acres in Bir Chuchukwas and Bir Sunarwala.
53. The British improved and expanded the Mughal canal systems of the Punjab using the rivers Jehlam, Chenab, Ravi, Beas, and Sutlej, which flowed northeast to south-west. The Government of India then auctioned these canal lands. The term 'Bari' comes from combining Beas and Ravi. These irrigation works required large capital investments but often paid high returns even in bad years.
54. F. C. Bourne, 'Final Settlement Report of the Lower Bari Doab Canal Colony, 1927–1935' (National Archives of India).
55. H. J. Maynard, 'A Note', 4 February 1914, Chief Commissioner's Office, Delhi District, 108/1914 (National Archives of India).
56. Ibid.
57. The scale was as follows: half to one acre in Delhi was equal to five acres in the canal; one to five acres was equal to ten acres; five to ten acres was equal to fifteen acres; ten to fifteen acres was equal to twenty acres; etc.
58. DeMontmorency, 'Grant of Compensation in Land to Expropriated Landowners', 27 June 1912 (National Archives of India).
59. H. B. Holmes, 'Grant of Compensation in Land to Expropriated Landowners in the Delhi Area', 16 July 1912 (National Archives of India).
60. Ibid.
61. Ibid.
62. Metcalf, *Ideologies of the Raj* and Cohn, *Colonialism and its Forms of Knowledge*.
63. Hon'ble Mr H. Wheeler to Secretary of the Government of the Punjab, 19 August 1912, Notification 803, Chief Commissioner's Office, Delhi District, Revenue and Agriculture, 108/1914 (National Archives of India).

64. Special Land Acquisition Officer to Imperial Delhi Committee, 26 August 1914, no. 386-L.A. (Delhi State Archives).
65. The canal colony was divided into squares or rectangles of 25 acres. At times colony officers would let land at half a rectangle but preferred letting one rectangle.
66. Wheeler, 19 August 1912.
67. Many of these *muafis* and *jagirs* were given to Delhi residents who aided or remained loyal to the British during the mutiny in 1857.
68. Scott, *Seeing Like a Secret*, 48.
69. Metcalf, 'The British and the Moneylender'.
70. Official correspondence between William Hailey, Chief Commissioner of Delhi, and Michael O'Dwyer, Lt Governor of the Punjab, 26 January 1914 and 19 February 1914, Chief Commissioner's Office, Revenue and Agriculture, 108/1914 (Delhi State Archives). See also note by H. J. Maynard, 2 February 1914.
71. 'Memorial of Ramji Lal and 33 Others, Expropriated Landholders of Mauza Manglapuri, District Delhi, Praying for the Grant of Sunarwali Bir in the Jhajjar Tahsil of the Rohtak District, Punjab', 13 April 1914, Proceedings of the Department of Revenue and Agriculture, 1914, August–December (National Archives of India).
72. Ludden, *An Ararian History of South Asia*, 19–20.
73 'Abstract Showing the Statement of the People, Whose Lands are Acquired for Imperial City and Required to Settle and Cultivate the Lands on Lower Bari Doab', Chief Commissioner's Office, Delhi District, Revenue and Agriculture, 108/1914 (Delhi State Archives).
74. DeMontmorency to Hailey, 14 May 1917, Chief Commissioner, Delhi District, no. 15, 1912, Revenue and Agriculture (Delhi State Archives).
75. Ibid.
76. Rikabganj may have had the greatest leverage of any village in the Delhi District since it lay on Raisina, the site of the central forum and the main government structures.
77. Addison to Hailey, Chief Commissioner Delhi District, 20 December 1913, Chief Commissioner's Officer, Delhi District, Revenue and Agriculture, 108/1914 (Delhi State Archives).
78. The Gurdwara is adjacent to the main government structures at New Delhi and remains an important and thriving religious and communal centre for Sikhs. This land acquisition case generated dozens of memorials written by Sikhs demanding protection of the Rikabganj Gurdwara from town planners who removed a wall to make room for a new road. The British eventually rebuilt the wall and moved the road due to the Sikh community's concerted efforts.
79. 'Abstract Showing the Statement of the People'.
80. Metcalf, *Land, Landlords, and the British Raj*.
81. Reginald H. Craddock to Beadon, 19 June 1912, Home Department, Delhi Branch, June 1912 no. 15 Deposit (National Archives of India).
82. Ibid.
83. Ibid.
84. Ibid.
85. Secretary of Imperial Delhi Committee to Secretary Government of India, 15 May 1915, Department of Revenue and Agriculture, Delhi, Home Department, Public Branch, August 1915, no. 8, Proceedings, Part A (National Archives of India).

86. Ibid.
87. Court of the Divisional Judge, Delhi. Compensation Case no. 39 of 1913. Mohd Amir Khan, Azmat Ullah Khan, and Naimat Ulah Khan, residents of Chitli Kabar, Delhi versus The Secretary of State for India in Council (Delhi State Archives).
88. Mike Davis, *Late Victorian Holocausts: El Nino Famines and the Making of the Third World* (New York: Verso, 2001). Davis argues that late nineteenth-century famines were caused by the incorporation of the tropical zone into a global capitalist market centred on London.
89. Beadon, *Delhi District Gazetteer, 1911.*
90. Ibid.
91. Ibid. Much like poor relief in England, the purpose of famine relief in India was to make it an extremely unattractive choice for Indians.
92. Davis, *Late Victorian Holocausts*, 33–41.
93. Ibid., 111–12.
94. Davis estimates, using figures provided by six different sources, that 12.2–29.3 million people died in India due to famine between 1876 and 1902.
95. Beadon, *Delhi District Gazetteer, 1911*, 117.
96. Marshall, *Bengal: The British Bridgehead.*
97. Davis, *Late Victorian Holocausts.*
98. Metcalf, 'The British and the Moneylender', 392.
99. Memoriam to Chief Commissioner, Delhi, from Shamsher Parkash, 29 January 1917, Delhi, 1917, no. 15, Revenue and Agriculture (National Archives of India).
100. Chief Commissioner, Delhi District, 'Report on the Administration of the Delhi Province', 1913 (National Archives of India).

9   Conclusion: The Inauguration of New Delhi, 1931 – A British Empire for the Twentieth Century

1. Hansard's House of Commons Debates, East India Revenue Accounts (Indian Budget), vol. 41, 30 July 1912, 1883.
2. The 1917 Montagu-Chelmsford Agreement promised India a new constitution that would give Indians greater responsibility in the colonial government. This constitution was passed as the Government of India Act of 1919.
3. The Government of India Act of 1919 enacted a system of government called diarchy, which transferred non-essential political questions to the provinces of British-India. Due to the earlier 1909 Indian Councils Act, which expanded the number of elected officials on provincial and municipal councils, the provincial legislatures now had large numbers of elected Indian representatives. The Government of India, however, reserved control over those political subjects that ensured British rule. These subjects included the military, police, and foreign policy.
4. The Rowlatt Acts, passed in 1919, were a permanent extension of the wartime Defense of India Act, which was enacted to help the Government of India police anti-sedition activities during World War I. Much like the earlier Act, the Rowlatt Acts denied important civil liberties such as the right to a trial by jury or imprisonment without trial.

5. On 13 April 1919, General Dyer ordered troops to open fire on largely Sikh Indian men, women, and children who were peacefully demonstrating against the Rowlatt Acts. Many Indians saw these Acts as a denial of the political reforms promised in the 1917 Montagu-Chelmsford Reforms, which were drafted to encourage continued Indian support of the war effort. According to a statutory commission sent to India in the late 1920s, Sikhs constituted almost 50 per cent of Indian recruits during the war. Thus, Sikhs who had sacrificed so much for the British war effort were extremely upset by the Rowlatt Acts' denial of civil liberties.

6. Hansard's House of Commons Debates, East India Revenue Accounts (Indian Budget), vol. 41, 30 July 1912, 1803.

7. *Report of the Indian Statutory Commission, Volume I – Survey*, Command Paper 3568 (1930), xiii. The commission was authorized under the Government of India Act of 1919, which called for the parliamentary appointment of such bodies every ten years to study India's political growth. Parliament formed this first and only commission after eight rather than the prescribed ten years due to nationalist pressure. The following members of Parliament were nominated to serve: From the Liberal Party, John Allsebrook Simon (Chair); from the Conservative Party, Harry Lawson Webster (Viscount Burnham), Donald Sterling Palmer Howard (Baron Strathcona), Edward Cecil George Cadogan, and George Richard Lane Fox; and from Labour, Clement Attlee and Vernon Hartshorn.

8. For more on the troubled history of the Simon Commission and its political impact, see Andrew Muldoon, *Empire, Politics, and the Creation of the 1935 Act: Last Act of the Raj* (Farnham: Ashgate, 2009), Carl Bridge, *Holding India to the Empire: The British Conservative Party and the 1935 Constitution* (New York: Sterling Publishers, 1986), and Robin James Moore, *The Crisis of Indian Unity, 1917–1940* (Oxford: Oxford University Press, 1974). For India's perspective on the commission, see S. R. Bakshi, *The Simon Commission and Indian Nationalism* (New Delhi: South Asia Books, 1977). For first-hand accounts see Edward O. Cadogan, *The Indian We Saw* (London: John Murray, 1931). Cadogan was appointed to the Simon Commission as a conservative member. His biography, published almost immediately after his service on the commission, provides accounts of the many angry responses shown by Indians to the work of the Simon Commission.

9. Between 1931 and 1935, Britain held three roundtable conferences that culminated in a new Indian constitution under the Government of India Act of 1935. The Indian National Congress boycotted the first conference but more moderate Indian nationalists as well as a delegation from the Indian states attended the meetings in London. See Ian Copland, *The Princes of India in the Endgame of Empire, 1917–1947* (Cambridge: Cambridge University Press, 1997) for a detailed analysis of the role Indian princes played in Britain's attempt to create a federal system in India.

10. Carl Bridge, in *Holding India to the Empire*, shows that considerable government effort went into winning the Simon Commission's approval of Irwin's declaration of dominion status for India. The commission remained deeply sceptical of the offer, causing Edward Cadogan to disparagingly claim that 'India was worth a phrase' in his own biographical account.

11. Foreign and Political Department, No. 131-H, 1930, 'Invitation to ruling chiefs to attend the inauguration events' (National Archives of India).

12. Throughout the building project, the Viceroy's House seems to have been the focus of many of New Delhi's detractors. As Jane Ridley has shown, in *The Architect and his Wife: A Life of Sir Edwin Lutyens* (London: Chatto & Windus, 2002), Parliament members and others who disagreed with the policy of transferring the capital used Lutyens' well-known extravagance to attack the entire building project.
13. Lord Chelmsford Papers, Secretary of State to Chelmsford, 7 April 1920 (Nehru Memorial Library).
14. Ibid., Secretary of State to Chelmsford, 8 September 1920.
15. Romilla Thapar, *A History of India* (New York: Penguin Books, 1966), 73–5. Later imperial rulers would often move the pillars to different locations. There are two in Delhi, one placed in Kotla Firoz Shah just south of the Red Fort and the other on the ridge above the civil lines near the Mutiny Memorial. The pillar at Kotla Firoz Shah is still standing and, according to Percival Spear, was originally erected near Ambala, a city north of Delhi, in 250 BC. The Tughlak Emperor Firoz Shah moved it to Delhi in the fourteenth century.
16. *Times of India*, 'The Dominion Columns: Modeled after the Style of Asoka's Pillars', 10 February 1931.
17. Robert Grant Irving's *Indian Summer: Lutyens, Baker and Imperial Delhi* (New Haven: Yale University Press, 1981) has photos that capture Indians standing on the roof of at least one Secretariat.
18. For studies of the exclusionary practices of liberal reform in the colonial context, see Thomas Metcalf, *Ideologies of the Raj, The New Cambridge History of India, III, 4* (Cambridge: Cambridge University Press, 1995); Bernard Cohn, *Colonialism and its Forms of Knowledge* (Princeton: Princeton University Press, 1996); Uday Mehta, *Liberalism and Empire: A Study in Nineteenth-Century British Liberal Thought* (Chicago: University of Chicago Press, 1999), and Barry Hindess, 'The Liberal Government of Unfreedom', *Alternatives*, vol. 26 (2001). For general studies of the history of the progressive project in India, see Theodore Koditschek, *Liberalism, Imperialism, and the Historical Imagination: Nineteenth-Century Visions of Greater Britain* (Cambridge: Cambridge University Press, 2011), Jennifer Pitts, *A Turn to Empire: The Rise of Imperial Liberalism in Britain and France* (Princeton: Princeton University Press, 2005), and Catherine Hall, *Civilising Subjects: Metropole and Colony in the English Imagination, 1830–1867* (Chicago: University of Chicago Press, 2002).
19. Cohn, *Colonialism and its Forms of Knowledge*, 79.
20. Metcalf, *Ideologies of the Raj*, 105.
21. A. P. Thornton, *The Imperial Idea and its Enemies: A Study in British Power* (London: Macmillan & Co. Ltd., 1963), 359.
22. *Lahore Tribune*, 'Inauguration of New Delhi: Dominions' Sympathy for India', Wednesday, 11 February 1931.
23. John Simon, *India and the Simon Report: A Talk by the Rt. Hon. Sir John Simon* (London: Coward-MacCann, 1930), 36–7.
24. *Lahore Tribune*, 'Inauguration of New Delhi: Lacks Popular Fervour, Demonstration of Whiteman's Superiority', 13 February 1931.
25. Ibid.
26. *The Times*, 'The Inaugural Ceremony: Dominions' Gift, Four Pillars of Fellowship', 11 February 1931, 12.

27. Percival Spear, *Twilight of the Mughals* (Cambridge: Cambridge University Press, 1951), 35. Lake's defeat of the Marathas left the East India Company the paramount power in India.
28. William Dalrymple, *The Last Mughal: The Fall of a Dynasty: Delhi, 1857* (New York: Vintage, 2007), 320–62.
29. For good descriptions of old Delhi's post-1857 transformations, see Anthony King, *Colonial Urban Development: Culture, Social Power and Environment* (London: Routledge & Paul, 1976), Narayani Gupta, *Delhi between Two Empire: Society, Government and Urban Growth* (Oxford: Oxford University Press, 1981), and Stephen Legg, *Spaces of Colonialism: Delhi's Urban Governmentalities* (Malden: Blackwell, 2007).
30. See Ian J. Kerr, *Building the Railways of the Raj, 1850–1900* (Oxford: Oxford University Press, 1995).
31. Ranajit Guha, *Dominance without Hegemony: History and Power in Colonial India* (Harvard: Harvard University Press, 1998), 3.
32. David Crellin, ' "Some Corner of a Foreign Field": Lutyens, Empire and the Sites of Remembrance', in *Lutyens Abroad: The Work of Sir Edwin Lutyens Outside the British Isles* (British School at Rome, 2002), 103.
33. Ibid.
34. Home Department, File No. 66, Public, 1931 (National Archives of India).
35. Jay Winter, *Sites of Memory, Sites of Mourning: The Great War in European Cultural History* (Cambridge: Cambridge University Press, 1995), 23 and Crellin, 101.
36. *Lahore Tribune*, 'Indian War Memorial Opened: General Ware Dwells on Memories of Great War', 14 February 1931.
37. Lutyens designed small memorials for families as well as large ones such as the Cenotaph in London.
38. Some of Lutyens' deepest thoughts about commemorating death are found in a collection of letters, *The Letters of Edwin Lutyens to his Wife Emily*, Clayre Percy and Jane Ridley, eds. (London: Harper Collins Publishers, 1985).
39. Crellin, 'Some Corner of a Foreign Field', 101.
40. Winter, *Sites of Memory, Sites of Mourning*, 107. See also Crellin, 'Some Corner of a Foreign Field', 108.
41. See Jane Ridley, *The Architect and his Wife* (London: Chatto & Windus, 2002); Metcalf, *An Imperial Vision*; and Clayre Percy and Jane Ridley's edited volume, *The Letters of Edwin Lutyens to his Wife Emily* (London: Collins, 1985), for examples of his well-documented chauvinism.
42. Irving, *Indian Summer*, 259.
43. Home Department, File No. 66, Public, 1931 (National Archives of India). These included India's Commander in Chief, the Chancellor of the Chamber of Princes on behalf of the ruling princes and chiefs, the representatives of the dominions, and the Adjutant General on behalf of the Ex-Services Association of India and Burma.
44. Ibid.
45. *Lahore Tribune*, 14 February 1931. For a detailed examination of the relationship between the British Raj and the Indian Army, see C. A. Bayly's *Indian Society and the Making of the British Empire* (Cambridge: Cambridge University Press, 1990).
46. *Lahore Tribune*, 14 February 1931.

47. Ferguson, *Empire*, 251.
48. See Hindess, 'The Liberal Government of Unfreedom', and Mehta, *Liberalism and Empire.*
49. Metcalf, *Ideologies of the Raj.*
50. *Lahore Tribune,* 14 February 1931.
51. Willingdon Collection, MSS EUR E 240 75, 'The Indian Liberal's Appeal for Co-operation' (British Library).
52. *Bombay Chronicle,* 'New Delhi Autocracy', 13 February 1931.
53. See Stephen Legg, *Spaces of Colonialism: Delhi's Urban Governmentalities.*

Bibliography

Unpublished Official Documents

United Kingdom:

British Library, India Office Records:
Brown Collection
Chelmsford Collection
Hailey Collection
Hardinge Collection
Reading Collection
Reid Collection
Seton Collection
Stopford Papers
Storrs Fox Collection
Templewood Collection
Willingdon Collection
Chief Commissioner of Delhi Reports
Government of India, Finance Department
Proceedings of the Home Department, Delhi, 1912–1916.
Proceedings of the Department of Revenue and Agriculture, 1913–1915.
Proceedings of the Chief Commissioner of Delhi, 1912–1930.
Proceedings of the Chief Commissioner, Imperial Delhi Branch, 1917–1918.

Royal Institute of British Architects
Sir Edwin Lutyens Papers
Sir Herbert Baker Papers

Centre of South Asian Studies at Cambridge
Medd Papers
Shoosmith Papers

National Archives of Britain
British High Commission in India Records
British High Commission in Pakistan Records

India:

Nehru Memorial Museum and Library
Lord Hardinge Papers
Lord Chelmsford Papers

Delhi State Archives
Office of the Chief Commissioner, Delhi Province
Office of the Deputy Commissioner, Delhi Province

National Archives of India, India Office Records
Government of India, Home Department: Delhi Branch
Government of India, Home Department: Judicial Branch
Government of India, Home Department: Police Branch
Government of India, Home Department: Political Branch
Government of India, Home Department: Public Branch
Government of India, Central Public Works Department
– Public Works Department Annual Progress Report for the New Capital Project
   at Delhi, 1915–1932
Government of India, Foreign and Political Department
Fortnightly Reports on the Internal Political Situation in India
Proceedings of the Imperial Delhi Committee, 1913–1916
Report on the Administration of the Delhi Province, 1913–1932
Project Estimates for Works, New Imperial Capital Delhi, Volume I, Reports and
   Abstracts of Expenditure, 1913

Published Official Documents

Town Planning Reports:

'First Report of the Delhi Town Planning Committee on the Choice of a Site
   for the New Imperial Capital, With Two Maps', vol. 20 (East India: Reports of
   Commissioners), Cd. 6885, 1913.
'Final Report of the Delhi Town Planning Committee Regarding the Selected Site,
   With Plan and Two Maps', vol. 20 (East India: Reports of Commissioners), Cd.
   6889, 1913.
'Second Report of the Delhi Town Planning Committee Regarding the North
   Site, with Medical Report and Two Maps', vol. 20 (East India: Reports of
   Commissioners), Cd. 6888, 1913.

Settlement Reports:

F. C. Bourne, Esquire, I. C. S., *Final Settlement Report of the Lower Bari Doab Canal
   Colony, 1927–1935* (Lahore: Printed by the Superintendent, Government
   Printing Office, 1935).
R. C. Bolster, Settlement Officer, *Fourth Regular Settlement of the Lahore District,
   1912–1916* (Lahore: Printed by the Superintendent, Government Printing,
   Punjab, 1916).
The Settlement Report of the Rohtak District in the Hissar Division (Delhi:
   Superintendent Government Printing, India).
Oswald Wood, Esq., 1872–1877 and Completed by R. Maconachie, Esq., 1878–1882,
   Final Report on the Settlement of Land Revenue in the Delhi District, 1882. (Lahore:
   Victoria Press, Said Rajab Ali Shah, 1882).
Major H. C. Beadon, Settlement Officer, *Final Report of the Third Regular Settlement of
   the Delhi District, 1906–1910* (Delhi: Superintendent Government Printing, India).

Gazetteers:

Delhi District Gazetteer, 1911, Vol. V, Part A (Delhi: Superintendent Government Printing, India).

Punjab District Gazetteer, Volume III, Part B, Rohtak District, Statistical Tables, 1912 (Lahore: Printed at the Mufid-I-Ram Press, 1913).

Punjab District Gazetteer, Volume V, Part A, Delhi District, 1912 (Delhi: Superintendent Government Printing, India, 1913).

Punjab District Gazetteer, Volume VI, Part A, Karnal District, 1918 (Lahore: Superintendent of Printing, Punjab, 1919).

Gazetteer of the Karnal District, Part B-Statistics, 1912 (Lahore: Civil and Military Gazette Press, 1912).

Major H. C. Beadon, Settlement Officer, *Code of Tribal Customs in the Delhi District* (Delhi: Superintendent Government Printing, India).

Parliamentary Debates:

Hansards Parliamentary Debates, House of Commons, 5th Series, vols. 32–260, 1911–1931.

Hansards Parliamentary Debates, House of Lords, 5th Series, vols. 10-81, 1911–1931.

Land Acquisition Act:

Walter Russell Donogh, M.A, *The Law of Land Acquisition and Compensation Being The Land Acquisition Acts I of 1894 and XVIII of 1885 as Amended by Acts IV and X of 1914 and Cognate Measures with a Concise Commentary* (Calcutta: Thacker, Spink & Co., 1916).

J. W. Meares, *Land Acquisition Act of 1894* (Calcutta: Office of the Superintendent of Government Printing, India, 1907).

Miscellaneous:

British Sessional Papers, 1919, Command Paper 103, Volume XVI, 739. East India Constitutional Reforms: Lord Southborough's Committees in the House of Commons.

India in 1919–1931: Reports Prepared for Presentation in Parliament in Accordance with the Requirements of the 26th Section of the Government of India Act (Delhi: Anmol Publications, 1919–1931).

Report of the Indian Statutory Commission, Volume I and II (Calcutta: Government of India Central Publication Branch, 1930).

– *Report of the Indian Central Committee, 1928–1929*

– *A Review of the Growth of Education in British India*

Balfour, Andrew, *Note on Housing in the Tropics*, Government of India, Public Works Department, Technical Publication no. 37 (Calcutta: Superintendent, Government Printing, India, 1921).

The Historical Record of the Imperial Visit to India, 1911, Compiled from the Official Records under the Orders of the Viceroy and the Governor-General of India (London: John Murray, 1914).

Nehru, *et al.*, 'Report of the Committee Appointed by the Conference to Determine the Principles of the Constitution of India' (1928).

Newspapers

The Times, London, 1911–1947
Times of India, 1911–1947
Lahore Tribune, 1911–1931
Bombay Chronicle, 1911–1931
Amrita Bazar Patrika, 1905–1911

Secondary Sources

Abu-Lughod, Janet, 'Tales of Two Cities: The Origins of Modern Cairo', *Studies in Society and History*, vol. 7, no. 4 (1965): 429–57.

Adshead, S. D., 'City Improvement', *Town Planning Review*, vol. 1, no. 3, 1910.

—— *Town Planning and Town Development* (London: Methuen & Co., 1923).

—— *Modern Methods of Building* (London: P. S. King, 1937).

—— *A New England* (London: F. Muller Ltd, 1941).

—— *New Towns for Old* (London: JM Dent & Sons, 1943).

—— *York: A Plan for Progress and Preservation* (York, 1948).

Ahmad, Waheed, ed., *Jinnah-Irwin Correspondence (1927–1930)* (Lahore: Research Society of Pakistan, University of the Panjab, 1969).

Allen, Charles, ed., *Plain Tales from the Raj: Images of British India in the Twentieth Century* (London: Abacus, 2011).

—— *Raj: A Scrapbook of British India, 1877–1947* (Harmondsworth: Penguin, 1979).

Alley, Kelly D., 'Gandhiji on the Central Vista: A Postcolonial Refiguring', *Modern Asian Studies*, vol. 31, issue 4 (1997): 967–94.

AlSayyad, Nezar, ed., *Forms of Dominance: On the Architecture and Urbanism of the Colonial Enterprise* (Aldershot: Avebury, 1992).

Amin, Shahid, *Event, Metaphor, Memory: Chauri Chaura, 1922–1992* (Berkeley: University of California Press, 1995).

Anderson, David M. and David Killingray, eds., *Policing the Empire: Government, Authority and Control* (Manchester: Manchester University Press, 1991).

Andrews, Charles Freer, *India and the Simon Report* (London: George Allen & Unwin Ltd, 1930).

Arnold, David, *Police Power and Colonial Rule: Madras 1859–1947* (Delhi and Oxford: Oxford University Press, 1986).

Baker, Herbert, *Architecture and Personalities* (London: Country Life Limited, 1944).

Bakshi, S. R., *The Simon Commission and Indian Nationalism* (New Delhi: Munshiram Manoharlal Publishers, 1977).

—— *Cecil Rhodes, By His Architect, Herbert Baker* (New York: Books for Libraries Press, 1969).

—— 'The New Delhi', *Journal of the Royal Society of Arts*, vol. 74, no. 3841 (July 1926): 773–93.

Banerjea, Sir Surendranath, *A Nation in the Making: Being the Reminiscences of Fifty Years of Public Life* (Oxford: Oxford University Press, 1925).

Barnow, Finn, *Notes on the Urban History of India* (Copenhagen: School of Architecture, 1977).

Basham, Arthur Llewellyn, ed., *A Cultural History of India* (Oxford: Oxford University Press, Clarendon Press, 1975).

Bayly, C. A., *Recovering Liberties: Indian Thought in the Age of Liberalism and Empire* (Cambridge: Cambridge University Press, 2011)

────── *Empire and Information: Intelligence Gathering and Social Communications in India, 1780–1870* (Cambridge: Cambridge University Press, 1996).

────── *Origins of Nationality in South Asia: Patriotism and Ethical Government in the Making of Modern India* (Oxford: Oxford University Press, 1999).

────── *Indian Society and the Making of the British Empire* (Cambridge: Cambridge University Press, 1990).

────── *The Birth of the Modern World, 1780–1914* (Oxford: Blackwell Publishing, 2004).

────── *Imperial Meridian: The British Empire and the World, 1780–1830* (London: Routledge, 1989).

────── *Rulers, Townsmen and Bazaars: North Indian Society in the Age of British Expansion* (Cambridge: Cambridge University Press, 1988).

Beloff, Max, *Imperialist Sunset: Britain's Liberal Empire, 1897–1921* (London: Methuen, 1969).

Bence-Jones, Mark, *Palaces of the Raj: Magnificence and Misery of the Lord Sahibs* (London: George Allen and Unwin, 1973).

────── *The Viceroys of India* (New York: St Martin's Press, 1982).

Bhabha, Homi, *The Location of Culture* (London: Routledge, 1994).

────── *Nation and Narration* (London: Routledge, 1990).

Blake, Stephen P., *Shahjahanabad: The Sovereign City in Mughal India, 1639–1739* (Cambridge: Cambridge University Press, 1991).

Blomfield, Sir Reginald, *Memoirs of an Architect* (London: Macmillan, 1932).

Bogle, J. M. Linton, *Town Planning in India* (Oxford: Oxford University Press, 1929).

Bopegamage, A., *Delhi: A Study in Urban Sociology* (Bombay: University of Bombay, 1957).

Bose, Sugata and Ayesha Jalal, *Nationalism, Democracy, and Development: State and Politics in India* (Delhi and Oxford, Oxford University Press, 1998).

────── *Modern South Asia: History, Culture, and Political Economy* (London: Routledge, 2004).

Breese, Gerald, *Urban and Regional Planning for the Delhi-New Delhi Area: Capital for Conquerors and Country* (Princeton: Princeton University Press, 1974).

Bridge, Carl, *Holding India to the Empire: The British Conservative Party and the 1935 Constitution* (New York: Sterling Publishers, 1986).

Brodkin, E. I., 'The Struggle for Succession: Rebels and Loyalists in the Indian Mutiny of 1857', *Modern Asian Studies*, vol. 6, no. 3 (1972): 277–90.

────── 'Proprietary Mutations and the Mutiny in Rohilkhand', *The Journal of Asian Studies*, vol. 28, no. 4 (August 1969): 667–83.

Bodrick, John, Earl Midleton, *Records and Reactions, 1856–1939* (New York: E. P. Dutton and Company, 1939).

Brown, Frank E., *Roman Architecture* (New York: George Braziller, 1961).

Brown, Judith M., *The Oxford History of the British Empire: Volume IV: The Twentieth Century* (Oxford: Oxford University Press, 2001).

────── *Gandhi and Civil Disobedience: The Mahatma in Indian Politics, 1928–34* (Cambridge: Cambridge University Press, 1977).

Brown, Percy, *Indian Architecture: Buddhist and Hindu Periods*, 5th ed. (Bombay: D. B. Taraporevala, 1965).

—— *Indian Architecture: Islamic Period*, 5th ed. Bombay: D. B. Taraporevala, 1968).

Brown, Rebecca, 'The Cemeteries and the Suburbs: Patna's Challenges to the Colonial City in South Asia', *Journal of Urban History*, vol. 29, no. 2 (January 2003): 151–72.

Buckler, F. W., 'The Political Theory of the Indian Mutiny', *Transactions of the Royal Historical Society*, fourth series, vol. 5 (1922): 71–100.

Burchard, John Ely and Albert Bush-Brown, *The Architecture of America: A Social and Cultural History* (Boston: Little, Brown, 1961).

Butler, Arthur Stanley George, *The Architecture of Sir Edwin Lutyens (With the Collaboration of George Stewart & Christopher Hussey)* (London: Country Life, Charles Scribner's Sons, 1950).

Byron, Robert, 'New Delhi: The First Impression', *The Architectural Review*, 49, January 1931.

—— 'New Delhi: The Individual Buildings', *The Architectural Review*, 49, January 1931.

Cadogan, Edward O., *The India We Saw* (New York: John Murray, 1931).

Cain, P. J. and A. G. Hopkins, *British Imperialism: Innovation and Expansion, 1688–1914* and *British Imperialism: Crisis and Deconstruction, 1914–1990* (London: Longman, 1993).

—— 'Gentlemanly Capitalism and British Expansion Overseas I: The Old Colonial System, 1688–1850', *Economic History Review*, vol. 39, 1986.

—— 'Gentlemanly Capitalism and British Expansion Overseas II: New Imperialism, 1850–1945', *Economic History Review*, vol. 40, 1987.

Cannadine, David, *Ornamentalism: How the British Saw their Empire* (London: Penguin, 2002).

Chakravarty, Gautam, *The Indian Mutiny and the British Imagination* (Cambridge: Cambridge University Press, 2005).

Chatterjee, Partha, *The Nation and its Fragments: Colonial and Postcolonial Histories* (Princeton: Princeton University Press, 1993).

—— 'Bombs and Nationalism in Bengal', Centre for Studies in Social Sciences, Calcutta, 1–33, sarr.emory.edu/subalterndocs/Chatterjee.pdf.

Chaudhuri, S. B., *Civil Rebellion in the Indian Mutinies: 1857–1859* (Calcutta: World Press, 1957).

Chelmsford, Frederic John Napier Thesiger, First Viscount, *Speeches by Lord Chelmsford, Viceroy and Governor-General of India* (Simla: Government Monotype Press, 1919–21).

Christensen, E. A., 'Government Architecture and British Imperialism: Patronage and Imperial Policy in London, Pretoria and New Delhi', PhD dissertation, 1995, Northwestern University, Illinois.

Coatman, John, *Years of Destiny: India, 1926–1932* (London: Jonathan Cape, 1932).

Cohn, Bernard, *Colonialism and its Forms of Knowledge* (Princeton: Princeton University Press, 1996).

Copland, Ian, *The Princes of India in the Endgame of Empire, 1917–1947* (Cambridge: Cambridge University Press, 1997)

Crellin, David, '"Some Corner of a Foreign Field": Lutyens, Empire and the Sites of Remembrance', in *Lutyens Abroad: The Work of Sir Edwin Lutyens Outside the British Isles* (London: British School at Rome, 2002).

Crinson, Mark, *Empire Building: Orientalism and Victorian Architecture* (New York: Routledge, 1996).

——— *Modern Architecture and the End of Empire* (Aldershot: Ashgate, 2003).

Cronin, Richard, *British Policy and Administration in Bengal, 1905–1912* (Calcutta: Firma KLM, 1977).

Cruikshank, Dan, 'Variations and Traditions', *The Architectural Review*, 182, 1086, August 1987.

Cullen, Gordon, *The Ninth Delhi* (New Delhi: Government of India Press, 1961).

Cunningham, Ruth Johnson, *Contributions to Administration and Constitutional Development in India and the British Colonies in Africa* (Columbia: University of South Carolina Press, 1976).

Curtis, William J. R., *Modern Architecture since 1900* (London: Phaidon, 1997).

——— 'Modernism and the Search for Indian Identity', *The Architectural Review*, 182, 1086, August, 1987.

Curzon, George Nathaniel, First Marquess, *Speeches by Lord Curzon of Kedleston, Viceroy and Governor-General of India* (Calcutta: Office of the Superintendent of Government of Printing, India, 1900–6).

Dalrymple, William, *City of Djinns* (New York: Penguin Books, 1993).

——— *The Last Mughal: The Fall of a Dynasty: Delhi, 1857* (New York: Vintage, 2007).

Darwin, John G., *Britain, Egypt and the Middle East: Imperial Policy in the Aftermath of War, 1918–1922* (New York: St Martin's Press, 1981).

——— *The End of the British Empire: The Historical Debate* (Oxford: Basil Blackwell, 1991).

——— *The Empire Project: The Rise and Fall of the British World System, 1830–1970* (Cambridge: Cambridge University Press, 2009).

——— 'Imperialism in Decline? Tendencies in British Imperial Policy Between the Wars', *The Historical Journal*, vol. 23, no. 3 (1980): 657–79.

——— 'The Fear of Falling: British Politics and Imperial Decline Since 1900', *Transactions of the Royal Geographic Society*, fifth series, no. 36 (1986): 27–43.

——— 'Imperialism and the Victorians: The Dynamics of Territorial Expansion', *English Historical Review*, vol. 112, no. 447 (1997): 614–42.

Daunton, M. J., '"Gentlemanly Capitalism" and British Industry, 1820–1914', *Past & Present*, no. 122 (February 1989): 119–58.

——— '"Gentlemanly Capitalism" and British Industry, 1820–1914: Reply', *Past & Present*, no. 132 (August 1991): 170–87.

Davis, Mike, *Late Victorian Holocausts: El Nino Famines and the Making of the Third World* (New York: Verso, 2001).

Davies, Philip, *Splendours of the Raj* (London: John Murray, 1985).

Dean, M., 'Liberal Government and Authoritarianism', *Economy and Society*, vol. 31 (2002): 37–61.

Desai, Philly, 'Colonial and Indigenous Urban Morphologies in India', *South Asia Research*, vol. 15, no. 1 (Spring, 1995).

Dewar, Douglas and H. L. Garrett, 'A Reply to Mr. F. W. Buckler's "The Political Theory of the Indian Mutiny"', *Transactions of the Royal Historical Society*, fourth series, vol. 7 (1924): 131–65.

Dodwell, H. H., *The Cambridge History of the British Empire*, Volume 4, 1929, 377.

Duncan, James S., *The City as Text: The Politics of Landscape Interpretation in the Kandyan Kingdom* (Cambridge: Cambridge University Press, 2005).

Dupont, Veronique, Emma Tarlo and Denis Vidal, *Delhi: Urban Space and Human Destinies* (Delhi: Manohar, 2000).

Dyos, H. J., ed. *The Study of Urban History* (New York: St Martin's Press, 1968).

Engels, D. and S. Marks, *Contesting Colonial Hegemony: State and Society in Africa and India* (London: British Academic Press, 1994).

Etherington, Norman, 'Reconsidering Theories of Imperialism', *History and Theory*, vol. 21, no. 1 (February 1982): 1–36.

Eustis, F. A. and Z. H. Zaidi, 'King, Viceroy, and Cabinet: The Modification of the Partition of Bengal, 1911', *History*, vol. 49, issue 166 (1964): 171–84.

Evenson, Norma, *The Indian Metropolis: A View toward the West* (New Haven: Yale University Press, 1989).

Fanshawe, Herbert Charles, *Sha Jehan's Delhi – Past & Present* (Delhi: Sumit Publications, 1979, reprint).

Fawaz, Leila, C. A. Bayly and Robert Ilbert, *Modernity and Culture from the Mediterranean to the Indian Ocean, 1890–1920* (New York: Columbia University Press, 2002).

Feinstein, Charles, 'Britain's Overseas Investments in 1913', *Economic History Review*, 2nd series, XLIII, 2 (1990): 288–95.

Ferguson, Niall, *Empire: The Rise and Demise of the British World Order and the Lessons for Global Power* (New York: Basic Books, 2003).

Fergusson, James, *History of Indian and Eastern Architecture* (London: John Murray, 1910).

Ferrell, Donald W., 'Delhi, 1911–1922: Society and Politics in the New Imperial Capital of India', PhD dissertation, 1969, Australia National University, Canberra.

Fieldhouse, D. K., 'Imperialism': An Historiographical Revision', *The Economic History Review*, new series, vol. 14, no. 2 (1961): 187–209.

Fisher, John, *Curzon and British Imperialism in the Middle East, 1916–1919* (London: Routledge, 1999).

Fisher, Michael H., 'The Resident in Ritual Court, 1764–1858', *Modern Asian Studies*, vol. 24, issue 3 (1990): 419–58.

Fisher-Tine, Harold and Michael Mann, *Colonialism as Civilizing Mission: Cultural Ideology in British India* (London: Anthem Press, 2004).

Fraser, Lovat, *India under Curzon and After* (London: William Heinemann, 1911).

—— *At Delhi* (Bombay: Times of India Press, Thacker, 1903).

Fritzinger, Linda B., *Diplomat without Portfolio: Valentine Chirol, his Life and 'The Times'* (London: I. B. Tauris, 2006).

Frykenberg, R. E., ed., *Delhi through the Ages: Selected Essays in Urban History, Culture and Society* (Oxford: Oxford University Press, 1986).

Gallagher, John, Ronald Robinson and Alice Denny, *Africa and the Victorians: The Official Mind of Imperialism* (London: Palgrave Macmillan, 1982).

Gallagher, John and Ronald Robinson, 'The Imperialism of Free Trade', *The Economic History Review*, new series, vol. 6, no. 1 (1953): 1–15.

Goradia, Nayana, *Lord Curzon: The Last of the British Moghuls* (Oxford: Oxford University Press, 1997).

Ghosh, Arun, 'Delhi, The Imperial City', *Economic and Political Weekly*, vol. 24, no. 32 (August 1989): 1809–10.

Goswami, Manu, *Producing India: From Colonial Economy to National Space* (Chicago: Chicago University Press, 2004).

Gradidge, Roderick, *Edwin Lutyens: Architect Laureate* (London: Allen & Unwin, 1981).

Gramsci, Antonio, *Selections from Political Writings, 1921–1926*, ed. Quinton Hoare (London: Lawrence and Wishart, 1978).

—— *Selections from the Prison Notebooks*, eds. Quinton Hoare and Geoffrey Nowell-Smith (New York: International Publishers, 1971).

Gray, John, *False Dawn: The Delusions of Global Capitalism* (New York: The New Press, 1998).

Greig, Doreen E., *Herbert Baker in South Africa* (New York: Purnell, 1970).

Guha, Ranajit, *Dominance without Hegemony: History and Power in Colonial India* (Cambridge, MA: Harvard University Press, 1998).

—— 'The Prose of Counter Insurgency', in *Subaltern Studies II: Writings on South Asian History and Society*, ed. Ranajit Guha (Delhi: Oxford University Press, 1983).

—— *A Rule of Property for Bengal: An Essay on the Idea of Permanent Settlement* (Durham, NC: Duke University Press, 1996).

Gupta, Narayani, *Delhi between Two Empires, 1803–1931: Society, Government and Urban Growth* (Oxford: Oxford University Press, 1981).

Gupta, N. and Dilip Bobb, *Delhi: Then and Now* (Delhi: Roli Books, 2008).

Gupta, N. and Jim Masselos, *Beato's Delhi: 1857, 1997* (Delhi: Ravi Dayal Publisher, 2000).

Hall, Catherine, *Civilising Subjects: Metropole and Colony in the English Imagination, 1830–1867* (Chicago: University of Chicago Press, 2002).

—— *White, Male and Middle Class: Explorations in Feminism and History* (New York: Routledge, Chapman and Hall, 1992).

Halstead, John P., *The Second British Empire: Trade, Philanthropy, and Good Government, 1820–1890* (Westport: Greenwood Press, 1983).

Hardinge, Charles, *My Indian Years, 1910–1916: The Reminiscences of Lord Hardinge of Penshurst* (London: John Murray, 1948).

—— *Old Diplomacy: The Reminiscences of Lord Hardinge of Penshurst* (London: John Murray, 1947).

Harris, Jose, *Civil Society in British History: Ideas, Identities, Institutions* (Oxford: Oxford University Press, 2003).

Hasan, Mushiral, *Nationalism and Communal Politics in India, 1885–1930* (Delhi: Manohar Publishers, 1994).

Havell, Ernest Binfield, *Indian Architecture: Its Psychology, Structure, and History from the First Muhammadan Invasion to Present Day* (New Delhi: S. Chand & Co., 1913).

Haynes, Edward S., 'Rajput Ceremonial Interactions as a Mirror of a Dying Indian State System, 1820–1947', *Modern Asian Studies*, vol. 24, issue 3 (1990): 459–92.

Haynes, Douglas, 'Imperial Ritual in a Local Setting: The Ceremonial Order in Surat, 1890–1939', *Modern Asian Studies*, vol. 24, issue 3 (1990): 493–527.

Heehs, Peter, 'The Maniktala Secret Society: An Early Bengali Terrorist Group', *Indian Economic and Social History Review*, no. 29, (1992): 349–70.

Hindess, Barry, 'The Liberal Government of Unfreedom', *Alternatives: Global, Local, Political*, vol. 26, no. 2 (2001): 93–111.

Hobson, John A., *Imperialism: A Study* (1902) (London: George Allen and Unwin, 1938, reprint).

Hobsbawm, Eric and Terence Ranger, eds., *The Invention of Tradition* (Cambridge: Cambridge University Press, 1987).

Hopkins, Andrew and Gavin Stamp, *Lutyens Abroad: The Work of Sir Edwin Lutyens Outside the British Isles* (London: The British School at Rome, 2002).

Howard, Ebenezer, *Garden Cities of To-Morrow*. Edited with a preface by Frederick J. Osborn, and with an introductory essay by Lewis Mumford, 1902 (Cambridge, MA: MIT Press, 1965, reprint).

Hussey, Christopher, *The Life of Sir Edwin Lutyens* (London: Country Life, 1950).

Hynes, William G., *The Economics of Empire: Britain, Africa and the New Imperialism* (London: Longman, 1979).

Inskip, Peter, *Edwin Lutyens* (New York: St Martin's Press, 1986).

Irving, Robert Grant, *Indian Summer: Lutyens, Baker, and Imperial Delhi* (New Haven: Yale University Press, 1981).

Jacobs, Jan, *The Death and Life of Great American Cities* (New York: Vintage Books, 1961).

Jain, A. K., *The Making of a Metropolis: Planning and Growth of Delhi* (New Delhi: National Book Organisation, 1990).

Johnson, David A., 'A British Empire for the Twentieth Century: The Inauguration of New Delhi, 1931', *Urban History*, 35, no. 3 (2008): 462–84.

Joyce, Patrick, *The Rule of Freedom: Liberalism and the Modern City* (London: Verso, 2003).

Kalia, Ravi, *Chandigarh: The Making of an Indian City* (Oxford: Oxford University Press, 1999).

—— 'Bhubaneswar: Contrasting Visions in Traditional Indian and Modern European Architecture', *Journal of Urban History*, 23, January 1997.

—— *Bhubaneswar: From a Temple Town to a Capital City* (Carbondale: Southern Illinois University Press, 1994).

Kanwar, Pamela, *Imperial Simla: The Political Culture of the Raj* (Oxford: Oxford University Press, 2003).

Karan, P. P., 'The Pattern of Indian Towns: A Study in Urban Morphology', *Journal of the American Institute of Planners*, 23 (1957): 70–5.

Khalidi, Omar, 'Ethnic Group Recruitment in the Indian Army: The Contrasting Cases of Sikhs, Muslims, Gurkhas and Others', *Pacific Affairs*, vol. 74, no. 4 (Winter, 2001–2): 529–52.

Kerr, Ian J., *Building the Railways of the Raj, 1850–1900* (Oxford: Oxford University Press, 1995).

Kincaid, Dennis, *British Social Life in India, 1608–1937* (London: Routledge and Kegan Paul, 1973).

King, Anthony, *Colonial Urban Development: Culture, Social Power and Environment* (London: Routledge & Kegan Paul, 1976).

—— *Buildings and Society: Essays on the Social Development of the Built Environment* (Routledge & Kegan Paul, 1980).

—— 'Rethinking Colonialism', *Forms of Dominance*, ed. Nezar AlSayyad (Aldershot: Avebury, 1992).

Klein, Ira, 'Materialism, Mutiny, and Modernization in British India', *Modern Asian Studies*, vol. 34, issue 3 (2000): 545–80.

Koditschek, Theodore, *Liberalism, Imperialism, and the Historical Imagination: Nineteenth-Century Visions of Greater Britain* (Cambridge: Cambridge University Press, 2011).

Kumar, Sunil, *The Present in Delhi's Past* (New Delhi: Three Days Press, 2002).

Laclau, Ernesto and Chantal Mouffe, *Hegemony and Socialist Strategy: Towards a Radical Democratic Politics* (London: Verso, 2001).

Lanchester, Henry V., 'Architecture and Architects in India', *The Journal of the Royal Institute of British Architects*, 30, 10, March 1923.

—— *Zanzibar: A Study in Tropical Town Planning* (1923).

—— *Town Planning in Madras and Zanzibar* (1923).

—— *Talks on Town Planning* (1924).

—— *The Art of Town Planning* (1925).

Legg, Stephen, *Spaces of Colonialism: Delhi's Urban Governmentalities* (Malden: Blackwell, 2007).

—— 'Gendered Politics and Nationalised Homes: Women and the Anti-Colonial Struggle in Delhi, 1930–47', *Gender, Place and Culture*, vol. 10, no. 1 (2003): 7–27.

—— 'Governing Prostitution in Colonial Delhi: From Cantonment Regulations to International Hygiene (1864–1939)', *Social History*, vol. 34, no. 4 (2009): 447–67.

—— 'Memory and Nostalgia', *Cultural Geographies*, 11 (2004): 99–107.

—— 'Ambivalent Improvements: Biography, Biopolitics, and Colonial Delhi', *Environment and Planning*, vol. 40 (1) (2008): 37–56.

—— 'Governmentality, Congestion and Calculation in Colonial Delhi', *Social and Cultural Geography*, vol. 7, no. 5 (2006): 709–29.

—— 'Postcolonial Developmentalities: From Delhi Improvement Trust to the Delhi Development Authority', in *Colonial and Post-Colonial Geographies of India*, eds. Saraswati Raju, Satish Kumar and Stuart Corbridge (London: Sage Publications, 2006).

—— 'Sites of Counter Memory: The Refusal to Forget and the National Struggle in Colonial Delhi', *Historical Geography*, vol. 33 (2005): 180–201.

—— 'Beyond the European Province: Foucault and Postcolonialism', in *Space, Knowledge, and Power: Foucault and Geography*, eds. Jeremy Crampton and Stuart Elden (Farnham: Ashgate, 2007).

Lenin, V. I., *Imperialism: The Highest Stage of Capitalism* (London: Penguin Books, 2010, reprint).

Leslie, Sir Bradford, 'Delhi: The Metropolis of India', *Journal of the Royal Society of Arts*, vol. 61, no. 3136 (27 December 1912): 133–48.

Llewellyn-Jones, Rosie, *A Fatal Friendship: The Nawabs, the British and the City of Lucknow* (Oxford: Oxford University Press, 1985).

Lockwood, David, *The Indian Bourgeoisie: A Political History of the Indian Capitalist Class in the Early Twentieth Century* (London: I. B. Tauris, 2012).

Low, D. A., *Britain and Indian Nationalism: Imprint of Ambiguity, 1929–1942* (Cambridge: Cambridge University Press, 1997).

Ludden, David, *Contesting the Nation: Religion, Community, and the Politics of Democracy in India* (Philadelphia: University of Pennsylvania Press, 1996).

—— *An Agrarian History of South Asia: The New Cambridge History of India, Volume 4, Part 4* (Cambridge: Cambridge University Press, 1999).

Lukis, C. P., 'Anti-Mosquito Measures in India', *The British Medical Journal*, vol. 1, no. 2662, (6 January 1912): 23–5.

MacDonagh, Oliver, 'The Anti-Imperialism of Free Trade', *The Economic History Review*, new series, vol. 14, no. 3 (1962): 489–501.

Malik, Salahuddin, 'The Panjab and the Indian "Mutiny": A Reassessment', *Islamic Studies*, vol. 15, no. 2 (summer 1976): 81–110.

Mandelbaum, Michael, *Democracy's Good Name: The Rise and Risks of the World's Most Popular Form of Government* (New York: Public Affairs, 2008).

Mann, Michael and Samiksha Sehrawat, 'A City with a View: The Afforestation of the Delhi Ridge, 1883–1913', *Modern Asian Studies*, vol. 43, issue 2 (May 2009): 543–70.

Marks, Robert B., *The Origins of the Modern World: A Global and Ecological Narrative from the Fifteenth to the Twenty-first Century* (New York: Rowman & Littlefield Publishers, 2006).

Marriott, John, *The Other Empire: Metropolis, India, and Progress in the Colonial Imagination* (Manchester: Manchester University Press, 2003).

Marshall, Peter, *Bengal: The British Bridgehead: Eastern India, 1740–1828* (Cambridge: Cambridge University Press, 2006).

Meade, Martin, 'Europe in India', *The Architectural Review*, 182, 1086, August 1987.

Mehta, Uday, *Liberalism and Empire: A Study in Nineteenth-Century Liberal Thought* (Chicago: University of Chicago Press, 1999).

―――― 'Liberal Strategies of Exclusion', in *Tensions of Empire: Colonial Cultures in a Bourgeois World*, eds. Frederick Cooper and Ann Laura Stoler (Berkeley: University of California Press, 1997).

Metcalf, Thomas, *An Imperial Vision: Indian Architecture and Britain's Raj* (Berkeley: University of California Press, 1989).

―――― *The Aftermath of Revolt: India 1857–1870* (Princeton: Princeton University Press, 1964)

―――― *Land, Landlords, and the British Raj: Northern India in the Nineteenth-Century* (Berkeley: University of California Press, 1979).

―――― *Modern India: An Interpretive Anthology* (New Delhi: Sterling Publishers Private Limited, 1992).

―――― *Ideologies of the Raj* (Cambridge: Cambridge University Press, 1994).

―――― 'Architecture and the Representation of Empire: India, 1860–1910', *Representations* 6 (Spring 1984): 37–65.

―――― 'The Influence of the Mutiny of 1857 on Land Policy in India', *The Historical Journal*, vol. 4, no. 2 (1961): 152–63.

―――― 'The British and the Moneylender in Nineteenth-Century India', *The Journal of Modern History*, vol. 34, no. 4 (December 1962): 390–7.

―――― 'The Struggle over Land Tenure in India, 1860–1868', *The Journal of Asian Studies*, vol. 21, no. 3 (May 1962): 295–307.

―――― 'Landlords without Land: The U. P. Zamindars Today', *Pacific Affairs*, vol. 40, no. 1/2 (Spring–Summer, 1976): 5–18.

Mitra, Asok, *Delhi: Capital City* (New Delhi: Thomson Press, 1970).

Montagu, Edwin S., *An Indian Diary* (London: William Heinemann, 1930).

Moore, Robin J., *The Crisis of Indian Unity, 1917–1940* (Oxford: Oxford University Press, 1974).

Morris, Jan, *Stones of Empire: The Buildings of the Raj* (Oxford: Oxford University Press, 1983).

Muldoon, Andrew, *Empire, Politics, and the Creation of the 1935 Act: Last Act of the Raj* (Farnham: Ashgate, 2009).

Mumford, Lewis. *The Culture of Cities* (New York: Harcourt, Brace and Co., 1938).

252   *Bibliography*

────── *The City in History: Its Origins, its Transformations, and its Prospects* (New York: Harcourt, Brace and Co., 1961).

Murphy, Rhoads, 'City and Countryside as Ideological Issues: India and China', *Comparative Studies in Society and History*, vol. 14, issue 3 (1972): 250–67.

Nath, V., 'Planning for Delhi', *GeoJournal*, vol. 29, no. 2 (February 1993): 171–80.

Nehru, Jawaharlal *The Discovery of India* (New York: John Day, 1946).

Newman, R. K., 'India and the Anglo-Chinese Opium Agreements, 1907–1914', *Modern Asian Studies*, vol. 23, issue 3 (1989): 525–60.

Nilsson, Sten, *European Architecture in India, 1750–1850* (London: Faber & Faber, 1968).

────── *The New Capitals of India, Pakistan and Bangladesh* (Sweden: Studentlitteratur Lund, 1973).

Nuckolls, Charles W., 'The Durbar Incident', *Modern Asian Studies*, vol. 24, issue 3 (1990): 529–59.

O'Neill, Daniel, *Sir Edwin Lutyens: Country Houses* (London: Lund Humphries, 1980).

Onley, James, *The Arabian Frontier of the British Raj: Merchants, Rulers, and the British in the Nineteenth Century Gulf* (Oxford: Oxford University Press, 2007).

Percy, Clayre and Jane Ridley, eds., *The Letters of Edwin Lutyens to his Wife Lady Emily* (London: Collins, 1985).

Pethe, Prakash, 'Indian Architecture – Quest for Identity', *Architects Trade Journal*, 17, 5–6, May/June, 1987.

Petter, Hugh, *Lutyens in Italy: The Building of the British School at Rome* (London: British School at Rome, 2002).

Pitts, Jennifer, *A Turn to Empire: The Rise of Imperial Liberalism in Britain and France* (Princeton: Princeton University Press, 2005).

Platt, D. C. M., 'The Imperialism of Free Trade: Some Reservations', *The Economic History Review*, new series, vol. 21, no. 2 (1968): 296–306.

────── 'Further Objections to an "Imperialism of Free Trade", 1830–1860', *The Economic History Review*, vol. 26, no. 1 (1973): 77–91.

Pomeranz, Kenneth, *The Great Divergence: China, Europe, and the Making of the Modern World Economy* (Princeton: Princeton University Press, 2001).

Porter, Andrew, *The Oxford History of the British Empire: Volume III: The Nineteenth Century* (Oxford: Oxford University Press, 2001).

Prasad, Ritika, 'Time-Sense: Railways and Temporality in Colonial India', *Modern Asian Studies*, vol. 47, no. 4 (July 2013): 1252–82.

Rabinow, Paul, *French Modern: Norms and Forms of the Social Environment* Cambridge, MA: MIT Press, 1989).

Randall, Don, 'Autumn 1857: The Making of the Indian "Mutiny"', *Victorian Literature and Culture*, vol. 31, issue 1 (2003): 3–17.

Rees, J. D., *Notes of a Journey from Kasveen to Hamadan across the Karaghan Country* (1885).

────── *Narratives of Tours in India Made by His Excellency Lord Connemara, Governor of Madras, 1886–1890* (1891).

────── *The Mahomedans* (1894).

────── *The Real India* (1910).

────── *Current Political Problems: With Pros and Cons* (1912).

Reilly, Charles Herbert, *Representative British Architects of the Present Day* (London: B. T. Bratsford Ltd, 1931).

Reynolds, Leah, *A Hindu Education: The Early Years of Banaras Hindu University* (Oxford: Oxford University Press, 2005).

Ridley, Jane, *The Architect and his Wife: A Life of Edwin* (London: Chatto & Windus, 2002).

Ronaldshay, L. J. L., Lord Zetland, *Sport and Politics under an Eastern Sky* (Edinburgh and London: William Blackwood, 1902).

—— *A Wandering Student in the Far East* (Edinburgh and London: Blackwood, 1908).

—— *India: An Eastern Miscellany* (Edinburgh and London: William Blackwood, 1911).

—— *The Heart of Aryavarta: A Study of the Psychology of India Unrest* (London: Constable & Co., 1925).

—— *Steps towards Indian Home Rule* (London: Hutchinson, 1935).

Rubenstein, W. D., *Capitalism, Culture, and Decline in Britain, 1750–1990* (London: Routledge, 1993).

—— '"Gentlemanly Capitalism" and British Industry, 1820–1914', *Past & Present*, no. 132 (August 1991): 150–70.

Ryland, Shane, 'Edwin Montagu in India, 1917–1918: Politics of the Montagu-Chelmsford Report', *South Asia: Journal of South Asian Studies*, series 1, 3:1 (1973): 79–92.

Said, Edward, *Orientalism* (New York: Vintage Books, 1979).

—— *Culture and Imperialism* (New York: Vintage Books, 1994).

Samaddar, Ranabir, 'Law and Terror in the Age of Colonial Constitution Making', *Diogenes*, vol. 53, no. 4 (2006): 18–33.

Sarkar, Sumit, *The Swadeshi Movement in Bengal, 1903–8* (Delhi and Oxford: Oxford University Press, 1973).

Scott, James C., *Seeing Like a State: How Certain Schemes to Improve the Human Condition Have Failed* (New Haven: Yale University Press, 1998).

Seal, Anil, *The Emergence of Indian Nationalism: Competition and Collaboration in the Late Nineteenth-Century* (Cambridge: Cambridge University Press, 1968).

Seeley, John Robert, *The Expansion of England: Two Courses of Lectures* (Cambridge: Cambridge University Press, 2010).

Semmel, Bernard, *The Rise of Free Trade Imperialism: Classical Political Economy and the Empire of Free Trade and Imperialism, 1750–1850* (New York: Cambridge University Press, 1970).

Sharma, Jyoti, 'The British Treatment of Historic Gardens in the Indian Subcontinent: The Transformation of Delhi's Nawab Safdarjung's Tomb Complex from a Funerary Garden into a Public Park', *Garden History*, vol. 35, no. 2 (winter 2007): 210–28.

Shaw, A. G. L., *Great Britain and the Colonies, 1815–1865* (London: Methuen & Co. Ltd, 1970).

Simon, John, *India and the Simon Report: A Talk by the Rt. Hon. Sir John Simon* (New York: Coward-McMann, 1930).

Singh, Khushwant, *Delhi: A Portrait* (Oxford: Oxford University Press, 1984).

Sinha, Mrinalini, *Spectres of Mother India: The Global Restructuring of an Empire* (Durham, NC: Duke University Press, 2006).

—— *Colonial Masculinity: The 'Manly Englishman' and the 'Effeminate Bengali' in the Late Nineteenth Century* (Manchester: Manchester University Press, 1995).

Southall, Aidan William, *The City in Time and Space* (Cambridge: Cambridge University Press, 1998).

Spear, Percival, *Delhi: A Historical Sketch* (Oxford: Oxford University Press, 1937).
————— *Delhi: Its Monuments and History* (Bombay: Humphrey and Milford, 1945).
————— *Twilight of the Mughals: Studies in Late Mughal Delhi* (Cambridge: Cambridge University Press, 1951).
Spodek, Howard, 'From "Parasitic" to "Generative": The Transformation of Post-Colonial Cities in India', *Journal of Interdisciplinary History*, vol. 5, (1975): 413–43.
Stamp, Gavin, 'Indian Summer', *The Architectural Review*, 159, 952, June 1976.
————— 'British Architecture in India, 1857–1947', *Journal of the Royal Society of Arts*, vol. 129, no. 5298 (May 1981): 357–79.
Stoler, Ann Laura, 'Imperial Debris: Reflections on Ruins and Ruination', *Cultural Anthropology, vol. 23,* no. 2 (2008): 191–219.
————— 'Making Empire Respectable: The Politics of Race and Sexual Morality in 20th Century Colonial Cultures', *American Ethnologist*, vol. 16, no. 4 (November 1989): 634–60.
Thakore, M. P., 'Aspects of the Urban Geography of New Delhi', PhD dissertation, 1962, University College, London.
Thapar, Romilla, *A History of India, Volume I* (London: Penguin Books, 1966).
Thompson, Andrew S., *Imperial Britain: The Empire in British Politics, 1880–1932* (London: Routledge, 2000).
————— *The Empire Strikes Back? The Impact of Imperialism on Britain from the Mid-Nineteenth Century* (London: Routledge, 2005).
Thornton, A. P., *The Imperial Idea and its Enemies: A Study in British Power* (London: Macmillan & Co., 1963).
Tillotson, G. H. R., *The Tradition of Indian Architecture: Continuity, Controversy and Change Since 1850* (New Haven: Yale University Press, 1989).
————— *Paradigms of Indian Architecture: Space and Time in Representation and Design* (Surrey: Curzon, 1998).
Tinker, Hugh, '1857 and 1957: The Mutiny and Modern India', *International Affairs (Royal Institute of International Affairs 1944)*, vol. 34, no. 1 (January 1958): 57–65.
Trevithick, Alan, 'Some Structural and Sequential Aspects of the British Imperial Assemblages at Delhi: 1877–1911', *Modern Asian Studies*, vol. 24, issue 3 (1990): 561–78.
Vale, Lawrence J., *Architecture, Power, and National Identity* (New Haven: Yale University Press, 1992).
Volwahsen, Andreas, *Imperial Delhi: The British Capital of the Indian Empire* (London: Prestel, 2002).
Wainwright, Martin, *'The Better Class' of Indians: Social Rank, Imperial Identity, and South Asians in Britain, 1858–1914* (Manchester: Manchester University Press, 2012).
Watkins, David, *Morality and Architecture Revisited* (Chicago: University of Chicago Press, 2001).
Weaver, Lawrence, *Houses and Gardens by E.L. Lutyens* (London: Country Life, 1914).
Webster, Anthony, *The Debate on the Rise of the British Empire* (Manchester: Manchester University Press, 2006).
————— 'The Development of British Commercial and Political Networks in the Straits Settlements 1800 to 1868: The Rise of a Colonial and Regional Economic Identity', *Modern Asian Studies*, vol. 45, issue 4 (July 2011): 899–929.

—— 'The Strategies and Limits of Gentlemanly Capitalism: The London East India Agency Houses, Provincial Commercial Interests, and the Evolution of British Economic Policy in South and South East Asia, 1800–50', *The Economic History Review*, new series, vol. 59, no. 4 (November 2006): 743–64.

—— 'The Political Economy of Trade Liberalisation: The East India Company Charter Act of 1813', *The Economic History Review*, new series, vol. 43, no. 3 (August 1990): 404–19.

—— 'Business and Empire: A Reassessment of the British Conquest of Burma in 1885', *The Historical Journal*, vol. 43, no. 4 (December 2000): 1003–25.

Wilhide, Elizabeth, *Sir Edwin Lutyens: Building in the English Tradition* (New York: Harry N. Abrams, 2000).

Wilson, Guy Fleetwood, *Letters to Nobody, 1908–1913* (London: John Murray, 1921).

—— *Letters to Somebody: A Retrospect* (London: Cassell and Company, 1922).

Winter, Jay, *Sites of Memory, Sites of Mourning: The Great War in European Cultural History* (Cambridge: Cambridge University Press, 1998).

Wood, Edward Frederick Lindley, Viscount Halifax, *The Indian Problem* (Oxford: Oxford University Press, 1942).

Index

Addison, J., 170–1, 179
Adshead, Stanley, 88–9
Lord Ampthill, Oliver Villiers Russell, 44–7
Amritsar Massacre (1919), 184
anti-colonialism, 21–42, 49, 107, 184
 see also Indian national aspirations;
 Indian National Congress;
 Indian nationalism
Anushilan Samiti, 23
architectural board for imperial
 capital, 8, 90–102, 110–23,
 129–34
 see also Baker, Herbert; Lutyens,
 Edwin; Swinton, George
architectural competitions, 120–1
architectural traditions
 Indo-Saracenic, 126–32
 Mughal, 125–7, 190
 Pathan, 127
 western neo-classical, 5, 8, 120–6, 151
Assam, 28–36, 56, 70

Baker, Herbert
 advisor to imperial town planning
 committee, 102, 108, 123
 architectural board member,
 imperial capital, 5–9, 21, 90,
 107–9, 123–34
 Council House, 149–52
 Dominion Columns, 186–9, 191–3
 Secretariats, 9, 121, 124, 129–30,
 137 40, 144–52, 154, 186–91
 see also Bakerloo; Kingsway; Union
 Buildings, Pretoria South Africa
Bakerloo, 145–8
Balfour, Arthur, 187
Baroda, Gaekwar of, 2
Barratt, Reginald, 90, 129–30
Beadon, Major H. C., 115, 169–70
Bengal
 anti-colonial agitation, 1, 23–7,
 34–6, 47, 136

Muslim response to end of
 partition, 22, 28–43, 67
partition of, 1–4, 13, 18, 21–38,
 43–9, 57, 61, 67, 74, 119
permanent settlement of land, 9,
 162–3
reunification of, 18, 27–8, 43, 45,
 46–9, 67
 see also the 'Bengal problem';
 communalism as colonial strategy
the Bengal problem, 22–4
Bhaiacharya, 167–8
Bharatpur
 stone quarries, 146–7
Bhola (dispossessed Delhi farmer), 175
Bhownaggree, Sir Mancherjee
 Merwanjee, 100
Bihar, 28–36, 67
Birdwood, George, 124–7
Bombay, 70, 87–91, 108, 113, 129
boycotts as anti-colonial strategy, 5,
 23–4, 185
British School at Rome, 90, 122
 see also Lutyens, Edwin
Brodie, John, 88–96, 139
Butler, Harcourt, Member for Education,
 Government of India, 29–39
Buxton, Noel, 13

Cain, Peter J., 12, 76, 98
Calcutta
 anti-colonial activities, 22–4, 46,
 55, 107
 capital of British-India, 2–4, 22, 25,
 27, 31–2, 36–40, 50, 67
 Chamber of Commerce, 69–72
 commercial community, 8, 12,
 32–5, 68–72, 99, 156
 canal colonies, 76–8, 103, 161–5, 178–81
 see also Lower Bari Doab (Punjab)
Carlyle, Sir Robert, Member for Public
 Works, Government of India,
 29–35

Printed and bound in Great Britain by
CPI Group (UK) Ltd, Croydon, CR0 4YY